LIFE AND LABOUR
IN THE
NINETEENTH CENTURY

CAMBRIDGE
UNIVERSITY PRESS
LONDON: BENTLEY HOUSE
NEW YORK,   TORONTO,   BOMBAY
CALCUTTA, MADRAS: MACMILLAN

LIFE AND LABOUR

IN THE

NINETEENTH CENTURY

BEING THE SUBSTANCE OF LECTURES DELIVERED
AT CAMBRIDGE UNIVERSITY IN THE YEAR 1919 TO
STUDENTS OF ECONOMICS, AMONG WHOM WERE
OFFICERS OF THE ROYAL NAVY AND STUDENTS
FROM THE ARMY OF THE UNITED STATES

BY

C. R. FAY, M.A.

Late Fellow and Lecturer of Christ's College, and Reader
in Economic History at the University of Cambridge

CAMBRIDGE
AT THE UNIVERSITY PRESS
1943

First Edition 1920
Second Edition 1933
Third Edition 1943

PRINTED IN GREAT BRITAIN

PREFACE

My thanks are due to Mr F. W. Lawe of St John's College for the Map and explanatory Appendix at the end of the volume; also to a number of friends for assistance in making the index and preparing the book for the press.

The highest hope that can be entertained of such a book as this is that it will direct the student to other and better books. For this reason full references are given in footnotes to all authorities, secondary as well as primary.

The big secondary authorities may be grouped under the following heads:

(1) *Biographies:*
> *Dictionary of National Biography.*
> F. Podmore: *Robert Owen.*
> E. I. Carlyle: *William Cobbett.*
> Graham Wallas: *Francis Place.*
> John Morley: *Richard Cobden.*
> G. M. Trevelyan: *John Bright.*

(2) *Social studies:*
> J. L. and B. Hammond: *The Village Labourer* (1760–1832); *The Town Labourer* (1760–1832); *The Skilled Labourer* (1760–1832).

(3) *Special Problems:*
> A. V. Dicey: *Law and Opinion in England.*
> T. Mackay: *History of the English Poor Law* (1834–1908).
> B. L. Hutchins and A. Harrison: *A History of Factory Legislation.*
> A. E. Dobbs: *Education and Social Movements* (1700–1850).

(4) *Popular Movements:*
> J. R. M. Butler: *The Passing of the Great Reform Bill.*
> M. Hovell: *The Chartist Movement.*
> M. Beer: *A History of British Socialism*, Vol. I. to 1835. (Vol. II. announced.)
> S. and B. Webb: *The History of Trade Unionism.* (New Edition, 1920, deals with developments from 1890 to 1919.)
> Catherine Webb: *Industrial Cooperation.*
> J. M. Baernreither: *English Associations of Working Men* (Friendly Societies).

The primary authorities fall into two groups.

(1) OFFICIAL PUBLICATIONS. These may be divided as follows:

   (a) The Statutes of the Realm,

   (b) Hansard's *Parliamentary Debates*,

   (c) Parliamentary Papers "Blue Books"—in particular the Reports of Parliamentary Committees and of Commissions.

It may seem somewhat naïve to indicate the way to use these, but I believe that the initial slight difficulty in finding the volume required is a reason why many undergraduate students do not consult them. I also believe that an early familiarity with such books not only enhances the interest of the subject, but arouses a desire to do original work. The following brief aids to their use in the Cambridge University Library are, therefore, given:

Notes for Readers, price 2d., sold at the door of the Library, furnishes the plan and classification of the Library.

The Statutes are in the Law Room. The simplest way to run down an Act of Parliament is to consult the *Chronological Table of All the Statutes* (1918)—the last book on the shelf of Statutes.

Thus: the Poor Law Amendment Act of 1834 is shewn as 4 & 5 Will. 4 (1834) c. 76 (Poor Law Amendment), i.e. the 76th chapter, or Statute, passed in the Parliamentary year 1834, written as "the fourth-and-fifth" year of the reign of King William IV.

Hansard is in Cockerell's Building. It is arranged chronologically in 3 series. Thus, Hansard 3rd S. LXXXVII. 1054, means the 87th volume of the 3rd Series (which begins at 1830), p. 1054. The year (in this case 1846) is shown on the back of every volume.

The *Parliamentary Papers* are mostly in the old Divinity School and Law Room (see *Notes for Readers*, p. 15); but to find a particular Committee or Commission it is necessary to go first to the Catalogue Room and consult the indices (B.9.45—). The simplest way is to begin on the subject index of **Parliamentary Papers** by P. S. King & Son; and from this (when you have got the year of the Paper) to turn to the Parliamentary indices adjacent to it.

But there is one difficulty. The General Parliamentary Index for 1801–52 gives I. Bills, II. Reports of Select Committees, but omits Commissions. The last are the most important documents of the period. It is therefore necessary either to refer to the separate annual index, the last Parliamentary Paper of the year (which is placed among the Parliamentary Papers), or to use the intermediate indices. For the convenience of students the two following intermediate indices have now been placed in the Catalogue Room, along with the other general indices:

> 1845, Vol. xliv.: containing an index for 1832–44,
> 1850, Vol. xlvii.:   ,,   ,,   1844–50.

These and the later indices in the Catalogue Room give the Commissions; and they are arranged very conveniently by subjects, with subheadings as follows:

> I. Bills,
> II. Reports:
> > 1. Committees,
> > 2. Commissioners,
> III. Accounts and Papers.

Some further slight trouble may arise in spotting the title under which the Paper is classed. For example, in P. S. King's *Catalogue* the famous Mines Report of 1842 is indexed under W, Women and Children's Employment; in the Parliamentary Index under C, Children's Employment. Again, Lord Durham's Report on the Affairs of British North America (1839) is catalogued by P. S. King under C, Canada; in the Parliamentary Index under D. Earl of Durham. In order to render such assistance as I may, I have compiled a special index (p. 313) of references to Acts of Parliament and Parliamentary Papers. I also append here the year and official number of a few famous Commissions:

> Factory Commission, 1833, XX and XXI.
> Poor Law Commission, 1834, XXVII.
> Durham's Report on the Affairs of British North America, 1839, XVII.
> Hand-loom Weavers' Commission, 1841, X.
> Children's Employment Commission:
> > First Report (Mines), 1842, XV.
> > Second Report (Trades and Manufactures), 1843, XIII.
> Midland Mining (South Staffs.) Commission (Commissioner, Mr Tancred), 1843, XIII.
> Commission on Condition of Framework Knitters (Commissioner, Mr R. M. Muggeridge), 1845, XV.
> Trades Unions Commission: Final Report, 1868–9, XXXI.
> Truck Commission, 1871, XXXVI.

The general student will not do more than dip into one or two of the above, but it may be explained that these references are to the Reports only. Each big inquiry has additional volumes containing evidence, supplementary reports, diagrams, maps, *précis*, etc.; and hidden away among these may be found much fascinating matter on topics allied to the subject of the inquiry.

(2) MANUSCRIPTS, PUBLIC RECORDS, ETC. Among these the following are of special importance in this period:

Place MSS. in the British Museum, catalogued under "Additional Manuscripts". Home Office Papers at the Record Office. The Collection compiled by Professor H. S. Foxwell and now in the Goldsmiths' Library, Imperial Institute, South Kensington.

I am so much indebted to Professor Foxwell's Collection that I give an extract from the notice written by him for the *Dictionary of Political Economy* (1909 Edition, Appendix to Vol. III. "Economic Libraries," pp. 720–722):

The Goldsmiths' Company's Library of Economic Literature. This is a collection of books and tracts intended to serve as a basis for the study of the industrial, commercial, monetary, and financial history of the United Kingdom.... After thirty years of labour the catalogue contains over 30,000 distinct entries, without taking account of a mass of political literature acquired incidentally, and a large collection of original Acts of Parliament of special economic interest.... In economics, more perhaps than in any other subject, its historical sources are largely of an occasional, non-formal character; and the brief contributions of practical men are often of much greater value than the more systematic disquisitions of professed writers. Hence there is an exceptionally large proportion of pamphlets and tracts in the library, not much less in number than 20,000....

Here then is a great harvest. Who will help to reap it?

C. R. F.

March, 1920.

It may be that some readers of this book are business men or working men. Such readers are invited to turn at once to Chapter XIV and the Chapters following. They will there find what the author conceives to be—from an industrial standpoint—the heart of the matter; and they will be able to correct or confirm the picture, there presented, from their own working experience and their own local traditions.

PREFACE TO SECOND EDITION

FOR the sake of economy the map and explanatory appendix on the Localisation of Industry are omitted, and the index (which contains a few references to the appendix) has not been disturbed. Apart from the rewriting of page 274, the changes are only verbal.

C. R. F.

Cambridge
May, 1933

THIRD EDITION

AGAIN the changes are only verbal.

C. R. F.

Cambridge,
December, 1942

CONTENTS

PART I

PART II

PART I

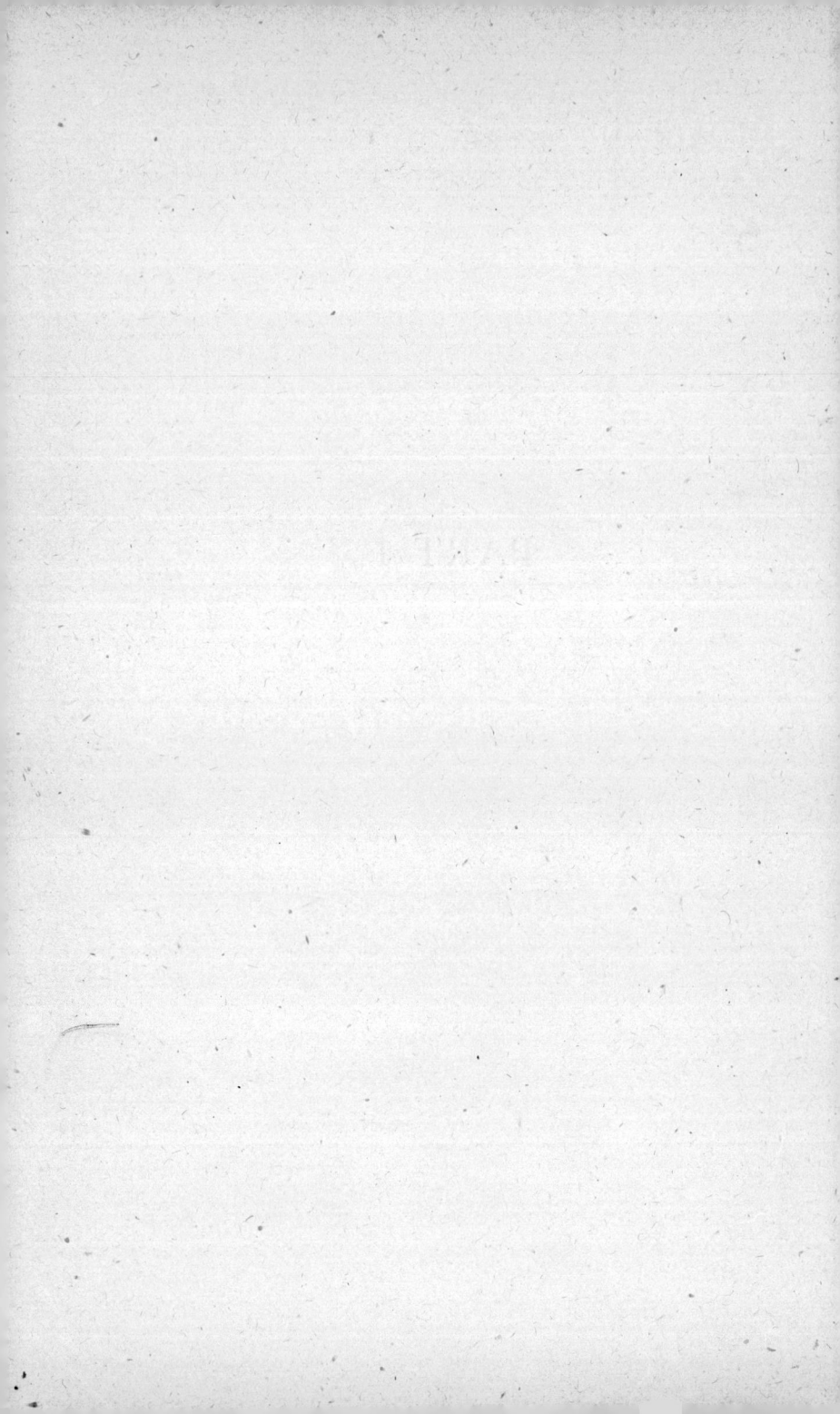

PART I

CHAPTER I

THE INTERNATIONAL BACKGROUND (1815–1830)

1. Castlereagh, Canning and Wellington

From 1815 to 1830 three statesmen controlled the foreign policy of England: Castlereagh, 1815–1822; Canning, 1822–1827; Wellington[1], 1827–1830.

Castlereagh was Pitt's right-hand man during the negotiation of the Irish Union in 1800; and in 1805, the year of Austerlitz and Trafalgar, the dying statesman made him Secretary of State for War and the Colonies. In 1812 Castlereagh became Foreign Secretary, and at the Congress of Vienna (1814) he was England's senior plenipotentiary. This was the hey-day of his fame. After 1815 his unpopularity in domestic affairs obscured his services as Foreign Minister. He was not the originator of the Government's domestic policy, but, as leader of the House of Commons (the Home Secretary, Lord Sidmouth, being in the House of Lords), he was its mouthpiece; and whether he had to defend the unpopular[2] Income Tax, as in 1816, against the nation's "ignorant impatience of taxation"[3], or to move the suspension of Habeas Corpus, he was impervious at all times to criticism and threats. But the strain of office told upon him and in August 1822 he committed suicide, even as had Whitbread, the brewer, in 1815, and Romilly, the lawyer, in 1818.

On hearing of his death Byron gloated and delivered himself of epigrams:

> So Castlereagh has cut his throat!—the worst
> Of this is—that his own was not the first.

Byron also wrote an epitaph—but we must pass on.

[1] In the reconstructed Tory Ministry of 1828, Wellington was Prime Minister and Aberdeen Foreign Secretary.

[2] An Irishman (in England—the tax was not imposed in Ireland till 1853) wrote on his assessment paper: "Take notice, I have cut the throats of all my horses, I have shot all my dogs, I have burnt all my carriages, I have dismissed all my servants except my wife, and therefore I conceive I cannot be liable to any assessment whatever"—William Smart, *Economic Annals* (1801–20), p. 469.

[3] This was the expression which the Opposition accused him of using. See *Hansard*, 3rd S. XXXIII. 228 and 458.

George Canning was a man of brilliant parts, brilliant as a scholar at Eton and Christ Church, brilliant as an orator, brilliant as a wit. "He saw everything in a flash, he divined the weak point of an opponent or a policy in a second"[1], but he was sensitive and ambitious and a mocker of men. Quarrels (including a duel with Castlereagh), resignations, refusals loomed large in his life; and the greater part of his work was crowded into the last five years. Like Huskisson, he was a liberally-minded Tory. The two represented in turn the port of Liverpool (which perpetuates their memory in the streets and docks named after them), and acquired an insight—in Huskisson's case an unrivalled insight—into the mind of commercial England. Huskisson, Shipping and Navigation are inseparable associations; but the figure of Canning is more elusive. His jests we know full well.

> Pitt is to Addington
> As London is to Paddington.

So Canning wrote, and covered the "Doctor" (for Addington's father was physician to the Earl of Chatham) with immortal ridicule. His rhyming despatch of 31 January, 1826, is the one cheery item in the dull complexities of the Navigation Laws and the fungus-like growth of tariff discriminations which had overspread that once massive code. It ran:

Separate Secret and Confidential.   (In Cypher.)

FOREIGN OFFICE,
January 31*st*, 1826.
SIR,

In matters of Commerce the fault of the Dutch is offering too little and asking too much. The French are with equal advantage content—so we clap on Dutch bottoms just 20 per cent. Chorus, 20 per cent., 20 per cent. Chorus of English Custom House Officers and French Douaniers. English, "We clap on Dutch bottoms just 20 per cent."; French, "Vous frapperez Falk avec 20 per cent."

I have no other Command from His Majesty to convey to your Excellency to-day.

I am, with great truth and respect,
Sir,
Your Excellency's
Most obedient humble servant
GEORGE CANNING[2].
H. E.
The Rᵗ Honᵇˡᵉ Sir Charles Bagot, G.C.B., Hague.

---

[1] H. W. V. Temperley, *Life of Canning*, p. 263.
[2] Version in *Notes and Queries*, 4th Series, I. p. 438.

Canning died in 1827 after being Premier for only four months, and he was buried, as he would have desired, at the foot of the grave of Pitt.

The Duke of Wellington needs no introduction, but a machine gunner returning to economics may perhaps be allowed this thought—Wellington in the end outmatched his opponents, as decisively as Foch outmatched Ludendorff. To resist the *tirailleurs* he created outpost troops of Light Infantry, who excelled the French sharp-shooters at their own tactics. He evaded the weight of Napoleon's artillery bombardments (and Napoleon was the greatest artillery general of all time) by skilful concealment of his troops behind the crest, and with his battalions deployed in a firing line of two ranks he mowed down Napoleon's advancing columns. He was able to do all these things because he had mastered, even better than its author, the meaning of Napoleon's maxim that "in war fire power is everything, the rest is of small account". Therefore Wellington's infantry was trained to fire straighter and faster than any infantry in Europe.

The year of Waterloo was the zenith of Wellington's career, as it was of Castlereagh's, and his conservative opposition to domestic change brought on him some of the odium which worried Castlereagh into suicide; but he weathered this, as he weathered every difficulty of his life, and, when he died in honour in 1852, it could be said of him that he had never deserted his Sovereign in a difficulty, and that in three great constitutional crises—Catholic Emancipation 1829, the Reform Bill 1832, and the Repeal of the Corn Laws 1846—he had saved his country from disaster and his fellow Peers from making fools of themselves.

> Foremost captain of his time,
> Rich in saving common-sense[1].

---

[1] Tennyson: *Ode on the Death of the Duke of Wellington.*

2. THE HOLY ALLIANCE AND THE QUADRUPLE ALLIANCE

The Congress of Vienna rearranged the map of Europe and prescribed the terms of peace. But how was this peace to be kept? Two solutions were propounded, the one ideal, the other practical.

The ideal was enunciated by the Czar of Russia in the Holy Alliance, whereby the Sovereigns of Russia, Prussia and Austria bound themselves "agreeably to the words of Holy Scripture which commends all men to love as brothers, to remain united in the bonds of truth and indissoluble brotherly love; always to assist one another; to govern their subjects as parents; to maintain religion, peace and justice. They consider themselves but as members of one and the same Christian family commissioned by Providence to govern the branches of one family. They call on all Powers who acknowledge similar principles to join this Holy Alliance".

To England's representative this was a "piece of mysticism and nonsense"; and in the event the Holy Alliance proved a loud-sounding nothing.

The practical solution was the one followed. It was a European Concert based on the alliance of the four great Powers on the winning side. Into this concert France was admitted three years after Waterloo; for by 1818 the Army of Occupation had been withdrawn, and France, aided by English financiers, had given guarantees for her remaining debts to the Allies.

The professed object of the Quadruple Alliance was to keep the peace, but under Metternich, the Austrian Chancellor, and notwithstanding the opposition of England, it became the champion of reaction, maintaining the peace of Europe by stifling the efforts of the peoples of Europe to secure constitutional reform.

Thus in 1820 it sanctioned the intervention of Austria in Italy for the purpose of restoring the autocracy of Naples. "States", it ordained, "which have undergone a change of government due to revolution, the result of which threatens other States, *ipso facto* cease to be members of the European Alliance". In which case "the Powers bind themselves...if need be by arms to bring back the guilty State into the bosom of the Great Alliance"[1]. In 1822 it authorised France to suppress the liberal revolt in Spain, and in 1826 it favoured France's design of extending its repressive activity to Portugal. The Greek War of Independence was repellent to Austria, but Phil-Hellenic sentiment in England and France made intervention against Greece impossible, with the result that in 1827 England and France, joined by Russia, pledged themselves to secure the autonomy of Greece, and in 1831 the terms of her independence, boundaries and constitution, were agreed upon and guaranteed by them.

3. THE POLICY OF ENGLAND

On the main issue England's policy was consistent throughout these years. She worked for peace, favouring the rôle of conciliator, but she would not allow herself to be dragged into intervention on the side of reaction, and she was prepared to oppose intervention by other Powers up to the point of intervening on the other side.

Thus Castlereagh pronounced the domestic revolution in Spain (1822), "a matter with which, in the opinion of the English Cabinet, no Foreign Power has the smallest right to interfere". Canning continued Castlereagh's policy in more assertive fashion. Whereas Castlereagh tried to use the Alliance as an instrument for maintaining peace between the Powers, Canning advertised England's opposition to continental reaction by flouting the Alliance and taking a line of his own. Metternich described him as "the malevolent meteor hurled by an angry Providence upon Europe". His rejoinder to the intervention in Spain was the recognition of the independence of the revolted Spanish Colonies in South America. As he said in Parliament on December 12, 1826, "I called the New World into

---

[1] Castlereagh protested against this doctrine, arguing that the guarantees of Vienna (1814) were territorial and did not extend to internal questions. The guarantees given by the Covenant of the League of Nations are similarly confined.

existence to redress the balance of the Old"[1]. The next year he defied the alliance of the Great Powers even more openly by sending a British force to Lisbon to protect the Constitutional party in Portugal against the intrigue of the Powers[2].

Wellington, the soldier, was less bellicose than Canning. In 1822, in the Spanish broil, he laid down, as our representative at the Congress of Verona, that "while there was no sympathy and would be none between England and Revolutionists and Jacobins", England must insist on "the right of nations to set up over themselves whatever form of government they thought best". In 1828 he insisted on the withdrawal of the English troops from Portugal; and he based his action on the profound experience which he had obtained of Spanish and Portuguese affairs during the Peninsular War. He objected to the British Army being used as a cat's paw in Peninsular quarrels, and he objected equally to England being turned by Portuguese refugees into an insurgents' den.

The support given to the cause of Greek independence led to friction with Turkey, from whom Greece had revolted. England unexpectedly found herself in a state of war with Turkey, when in the October of 1827 the allied fleets destroyed the Turkish fleet in Navarino Bay. But in the Russo-Turkish War, which developed out of this, when the Turk proclaimed a Holy War and Russia accepted the challenge, England resumed her traditional rôle of friendship with Turkey and assisted in securing the final independence of Greece, less from enthusiasm for the cause of Greece than from the desire to have at the gate to the East a genuinely independent kingdom, and not one which, while nominally a part of the Turkish Empire, might be an outpost of Russia. Therefore friendship with the "sick man", infidel and tyrant though he was, was deemed preferable to concerted action against him, which might end by killing him.

[1] *Hansard*, 3rd S. XVI. 397.
[2] Canning's intervention was in accordance with an old treaty obligation, and official records show that Castlereagh was prepared to intervene in the same sense in 1821.

4. THE U.S.A. AND THE MONROE DOCTRINE

In the Western Hemisphere there was fortunately no longer any conflict of interest between England and her revolted daughter, the United States of America. In 1823 it was rumoured that France was anxious to extend her intervention from the Old World to the New. England bluntly said "no", and was backed by the United States. On December 2, 1823, President Monroe, with Secretary Adams behind him, sent to Congress the famous message, which is the origin of the Monroe Doctrine. The message declared:

> With the existing colonies or dependencies of any European Power we have not interfered, and shall not interfere. But with the governments who have declared their independence and maintained it— [the reference is to South America]—and whose independence we have on great consideration and on just principles acknowledged, we could not view any interposition for the purpose of oppressing them, or controlling in any other manner their destiny, by any European Power, *in any other light than as the manifestation of an unfriendly disposition towards the United States*[1].

America's duty was summed up by Jefferson thus: "Our first and fundamental maxim should be, never to entangle ourselves in the broils of Europe. Our second, never to suffer Europe to intermeddle with cis-Atlantic affairs....Great Britain is the nation which can do us the most harm of anyone, or all on earth; and with her on our side we need not fear the whole world"[2].

To this policy America was faithful in the decades that followed, departing from it only when Germany's methods of warfare and the threat which Germany's methods implied to all free Governments on both sides of the Atlantic made it impossible to separate the affairs of Europe from the affairs of

---

[1] *Cambridge Modern History*, VII. p. 369.

[2] J. B. Henderson, *American Diplomatic Questions*, p. 321. The Monroe Doctrine, as enunciated in 1823 went further than Canning liked in the assertion of America's separateness from Europe. Its scope was greatly extended in the course of the century; and now by Article 21 of the Covenant of the League of Nations it has been officially recognised in international law.

America. Only then was it realised that "there is no limited liability in humanity's affairs"[1].

The steady insistence on "hands off America" was an unalloyed benefit to all the peoples of the New World, and the United States were ready to admit that it demanded from them a *quid pro quo*. Indirectly, indeed, the Monroe Doctrine did interfere with the policy of Europe in Europe; for the cooperation of Great Britain and the United States in the liberation of South America weakened the Holy Alliance in Europe, and making the New World safe for democracy made the Old World less secure in its legitimism[2]. But in the matter of direct action America recognised that she was pledged to non-intervention in Europe. This standpoint, and the length of time it was consistently upheld, throw light on America's policy during the recent War. At first a few of us thought, and thought wrongly, that America, though she knew she ought to enter the War, was holding back from considerations of profit and the fear of unfavourable reactions on her internal peace. Then later, not merely a few, but many of us thought that when she was clearly moving towards war she moved too slowly, encumbered by a democratic publicity which made decisive action impossible. We learnt our mistake in this matter too, when we saw how, once war had been declared by her, she adopted instantly the system of national service at which we had shied for two acrimonious years. But what we can also see now, as students of history, is that America was restrained, for a time, by an unwillingness to go back on the instinctive policy to which she had definitely committed herself in 1823 and which since 1823 she had faithfully observed.

5. To-day and One Hundred Years Ago

To-day, as a hundred years ago, we have before us an ideal and a fact: the Covenant of the League of Nations and Peace. But the two are not divorced. The working out of the ideal is

[1] A. F. Pollard, "The Monroe Doctrine", *History, The Quarterly Journal of the Historical Association.* April, 1919, p. 12.

[2] A. F. Pollard, *op. cit.* p. 9.

embodied in, and takes first place in. the terms of peace which have been signed.

Between 1815 and 1832 the ideal was lost in the actual, and the actual was unlovely. For the head was the head of Metternich, even though the restraining hand was England's. What of to-day? The history of a century ago must not be repeated. After 1815 the alliance of the Great Powers, which crushed at birth the Holy Alliance, degenerated into a league for the suppression of domestic revolution. Neither the League of Nations nor the Big Three must be a machine for the suppression of Bolshevism. Bolshevism may mean anarchy. Nevertheless, it is not the function of a league or alliance to concert campaigns against Bolshevism; rather must it provide the frame-work within which the nations of the world may effect national change without a Bolshevist aftermath.

The shadow that lay across England's path and made her policy tortuous a century ago was Russia—not because Russia was East of Italy, or of Austria, or of the Baltic, but because she was West of Asia, in which lay British India. Since those days inventions have abolished the geographical significance of East and West. The shadow therefore can be cast from any quarter. Between Russia and the United States there is no manner of parallel, racial, political or economic. But in the future the established sea power of the British Commonwealth and the growing sea power of the United States will meet in neutral areas, it may be in the waters of China and Japan, it may be in those of South America. They will not meet as rivals for territory, but as rivals in commerce. If this rivalry is allowed to produce what diplomatists call "situations", it will signify for both nations the bankruptcy of statesmanship and for the world an end to the possibilities of peace. At present such a catastrophe is so alien to the wishes of both countries that the mention of it seems like the stirring up of trouble. But its appearance in reality would be a disaster so unspeakable that we must lock it up in our minds as that thing above all others which must not even begin to follow from our increased contact by land, sea or air.

CHAPTER II

THE OLD COLONIAL SYSTEM

1. THE EFFECT OF THE LOSS OF THE AMERICAN COLONIES ON COLONIAL POLICY

THE old Colonial System was like an attempt to base family life on an arrangement from which everything is eliminated but the marriage settlement. The tie of profit and loss was supposed to replace the sense of common citizenship. Although the rule of England was mild as compared with that of other countries, and although on the contractual basis England expended at least as much as she received, the inevitable result among high-spirited colonists was revolt. The American Colonies revolted in 1775, and the independence of the U.S.A. was recognised in 1783. The war left the combatants estranged. The Americans, like the Boers, remembered their smoking homesteads. To England the war was an unpleasant episode, to them their national epic; and they met the supercilious contempt of aristocratic England with a democratic bounce alien to their deeper instincts. The commercial friction set up by the Napoleonic War led to hostilities between England and the U.S.A. in 1812. In August 1914 when the Great War broke out the two great nations had just celebrated a century of peace.

England forgot the tragedy across the Atlantic in the conquest of the world's markets. To the desire for Empire, which fascinated the sensational project-hunting spirit of the 18th century, there succeeded another mood of commercialism, a narrow *laissez-faire* optimism, which looked on Colonies as useless encumbrances and on the United States as a good riddance to bad rubbish. The wealth of a man who lived in Nova Scotia, it was argued, enriched us no more than that of one who lived in Massachusetts. When Bentham, as a citizen of France, addressed

the National Convention in January 1793, the title of his address
was, "Emancipate your Colonies", and his foremost argument
an appeal to business interest:

> Trade is the child of Capital....It is quantity of capital, not extent
> of market, that determines the quantity of trade....
>   Are you attacked at home? Not a man can you ever get from
> them; not a sixpence. Are they attacked? they draw upon you for
> fleets and armies[1].

If the loss of America had aroused the Home Government to a
more enlightened policy towards the Colonies which remained,
some good would have issued out of evil, but it had no such
result. In 1778, when it was too late to avert disaster, Lord
North, in an Act popularly termed the Magna Charta of the
British Colonies, surrendered England's claim to tax the
colonies[2]. The surrender made, England's colonial policy became feeble. In 1783 she abandoned Minorca, Tobago and
Florida, and all but abandoned Gibraltar. Territorial expansion
in India was offset by narrow-minded and negligent treatment of
colonies peopled by men of white blood. For fifty years British
North America was decried as a field for emigration, and in the
boundary disputes between Canada and the States Canadian
interests received scant consideration. The friction with France
and the United States over their rights in the Newfoundland
Fisheries was carelessly perpetuated. Australia was deemed to
be suitable only for convicts, New Zealand all but fell into the
hands of France, and South Africa (which passed formally into
our possession in 1814) was treated with weakness and incon-
sistency. The House of Commons took more interest in an Enclosure or Turnpike Bill than in any measure affecting the most
vital interests of the Colonies, and the extensive powers,
nominally wielded by the Secretary of State under the control
of the imperial legislature and public opinion, devolved on permanent officials, who dwelt "in the large house which forms the

---

[1] Bentham, *Works*, IV. 411, 414.
[2] The Act reserved to the Imperial Government the power to impose
duties "for the regulation of commerce", but the net proceeds of these
were to go to the colony in which they were levied.

end of that *cul de sac* so well-known by the name of Downing Street"[1].

2. HUSKISSON AND IMPERIAL PREFERENCE

Between 1815 and 1832 there was only one man who displayed in any large degree the qualities of imperial statesmanship. He was William Huskisson, President of the Board of Trade 1823–27 and Secretary for War and the Colonies 1827–8. The range of Huskisson's services to British industry and commerce—his writings on currency and his work for the return to a gold standard (he was a member of the Bullion Committee of 1810), the codification of the Customs with the aid of his subordinate, J. Deacon Hume, the reform of the tariff in all its branches, the removal of prohibitions, the reduction of duties on raw materials to nominal amounts and of duties on imported manufactures to levels low enough to discourage smuggling, the straightening out of the tangle of the Navigation Laws, the abolition of shipping and tariff discriminations in return for reciprocal treatment from other countries—the range of these services, and the fact that the purely national side of them was the foundation of the financial policy completed by Peel and Gladstone, have caused the imperial aspect of Huskisson's policy to receive less attention than it deserves.

Huskisson himself did not consider it subordinate. Although in his later days he struggled against the agricultural protectionism of his own party, and although Ebenezer Elliott, the Corn Law rhymer, lamented his death in 1830 with "a nation's tears", Huskisson, be it remembered, was a member of the Committee which promoted the notorious Corn Law of 1815. With the Napoleonic blockade fresh in his mind, he believed that the law of 1815 was needed to keep England independent of Europe and to prevent the new areas of supply in England, Ireland and the Colonies from falling out of cultivation. Particularly did he support the measure of preference which the Act of 1815, like earlier Acts, gave to colonial corn.

[1] Wakefield (quoting Charles Buller), *View of the Art of Colonization*, Oxford Edition (1914), p. 284.

When he revised the Navigation Laws, he retained two restrictions, one intended to give us the advantage of the "long
haul" in the ocean-going shipping which was "the nursery of
seamen and the foundation of naval power"[1], and the other
confining inter-imperial trade to British and colonial ships.
Even in the old days the Navigation Laws had been interpreted
so as to allow the Colonies their own commercial marine. But
the revolt of the United States, by creating an independent
country in what had been the hemisphere of our own or other
nations' plantations, upset the scheme of the Navigation Laws.
Huskisson therefore was concerned to see that any concession
made by us to the United States, now our most formidable rival,
should be immediately extended to other countries, and also
that restrictions removed from our own trade should be removed
instantly from colonial trade as well. "It is", he said of Canada
in 1827, "by liberal treatment and by admitting the inhabitants
of this extensive territory, as much as possible, into a participa-
tion of all the benefits of our own navigation and commerce...
that we may expect to ensure their attachment and to maintain
them in a state of colonial connection alike beneficial to us and
to themselves"[2].

When reducing to nominal level the duties on raw materials,
he exempted timber. Objectors, he said, "must recollect that
Canadian timber, considering that it grew in one of our own
colonies, and was transferred in our own ships, was a most
valuable trade to Great Britain"[3].

Finally, when the United States in 1825 retaliated against the
preferences which England enjoyed in her own Colonies on the
ground that they revived the recently abolished shipping discriminations, Huskisson pronounced this "a pretension unheard
of in the commercial relations of independent States"[4]; and
when in 1830 the mutual retaliations to which this dispute led
were removed, the preferences survived.

After Huskisson's death the cause of imperial preference fell

[1] Speech on the British Commercial Shipping Interest, May 7, 1827—perhaps the greatest of Huskisson's speeches. (*Speeches*, III. 108.)
[2] *Speeches*, III. 110, May 7, 1827.   [3] *Ibid.* II. 362, March 25, 1825.
[4] *Ibid.* II. 315, March 21, 1825.

into disrepute. Sufficiency in war time was becoming an old man's nightmare. The policy of preference degenerated into a squabble between the Manchester merchant and the country gentleman, each thinking solely of immediate national ends. With the adoption of Free Trade the colonial preferences automatically disappeared. They dropped out one by one, like tired horses who cannot finish the course. Corn fell out in 1846: and then sugar took up the running, flogged into a last effort by the tireless energy of Lord George Bentinck. Timber for a while struggled on alone, to collapse dead beat in 1860.

The voluminous debates on colonial preference are among the most depressing things in Hansard. The most generous voice came from the member for Gateshead. William Hutt (later a Commissioner for the foundation of South Australia and a leading member of the New Zealand Company), released for a moment the spirit of Huskisson. Huskisson, on the eve of retirement, had said of English policy in Canada, "England cannot afford to be little. She must be what she is, or nothing"[1]. Hutt, in the same strain seventeen years later (1845), exclaimed:

"Oh, the incurable perversity of human folly! When shall we begin to make a rational use of the mighty means which Providence has placed within our reach? When we shall have a Colonial Minister worthy of the name, a statesman sagacious and capable enough to turn the direction of our over-flowing capital towards the Dependencies of the British Crown, and to raise up —as he may raise up in rapid progression—new Anglo-Saxon nations in Southern Africa, Australia and New Zealand....I ask the House to concede to them the right of importing their grain into this country free....To the colonies it opens out a new avenue of prosperity and power, to this country it offers extension to commerce, a stimulus to manufactures and relief to the suffering rural population; and while its tendency will be to spread British colonization over the most distant regions of the globe, it will also unite and knit together the various Dominions of our wide-spread Empire in the bonds of mutual interest and mutual goodwill"[2].

[1] *Speeches*, III. 287, May 2, 1828.   [2] Hansard, 3rd S. LXXX. 302.

The concession for which Hutt appealed was refused. Had it been granted it would have made little difference. For by this time England was in a Free Trade frenzy, and the Colonies were receiving free government which, contrary to expectation, they employed to discard free trade. In Huskisson imperialism and liberalism went hand in hand. After his death imperialism was picked up by protection, and for some years the two kept house together in uneasy and ambiguous companionship. Then came the Irish famine, and when Sir Robert Peel raided the premises, he found the couple nursing a sickling in the last stages of fiscal consumption. So perished Imperial Preference.

3. THE SYSTEM CONDEMNED BY THE THEORISTS OF 1830

It is from the reformers that we derive our pictures of the un-reformed system which roused them to their effort. The writings of Owen, the investigations of Oastler, Fielden and Sadler, the reports and evidence of Committees and Commissions tell us what life was like in the factories and mines in the old days. Similarly, the band of reformers known as the "theorists of 1830"—Edward Gibbon Wakefield, Charles Buller, Sir William Molesworth and, greatest of all, John George Lambton, Earl of Durham—gave the death blow to the old colonial system by describing in vivid and often humorous language exactly what that system was. Lord Durham's Report of 1839 on the Affairs of British North America, perhaps the ablest official document ever penned, preceded the institution of responsible government there, just as at home the Commissions of 1833 and 1842 preceded the legislation regulating factories and mines.

Durham was brought up to the Army. He was a fiery tempered man, the "Radical Jack" of the Reform Bill days and the "King Jog" of the *Creevey Papers*[1]. Wakefield was trained as a Land Surveyor, but eloping at the age of 20 with a Ward of Court, and ten years later abducting an heiress, he was visited

---

[1] So nick-named because he "considered £40,000 a year a moderate income—such a one as a man might jog on with". He was a coal-owner. *Creevey Papers*, p. 374.

with a term of imprisonment, from which he came to study the penal system of England and the effect of the convict settlements on Australia. Buller and Molesworth were at Trinity College, Cambridge, whence Molesworth was expelled for offering to fight a duel with his tutor. They were a high-spirited quartette, and Buller was the leader in wit.

Mr C. H. Currey in his survey of British Colonial Policy (1783–1915) writes of them: " They maintained, with radiant enthusiasm, that ample opportunity should be given for the development of political and personal individuality, that the diversity of human nature and of human personality should be afforded the fullest scope. Their public careers were inspired by this fundamental and life-giving principle, and it is because they succeeded in making it the basic principle of England's colonial policy that the British Empire is to-day a fact of such cardinal importance in the world "[1].

The specific blots in the old colonial system were:

(i)   **The ignorance of the Colonial Governors,** who fell into the hands of a clique on their arrival.

Durham showed what happened in Canada:

A Governor, arriving in a colony, in which he almost invariably has had no previous acquaintance with the state of parties or the character of individuals, is compelled to throw himself almost entirely upon those whom he finds placed in the position of his official advisers.... Every successive year consolidated and enlarged the strength of the ruling party. Fortified by family connexion, and the common interest felt by all who hold, and all who desired, subordinate offices, that party was thus erected into a solid and permanent power, controlled by no responsibility, subject to no serious change, exercising over the whole government of the Province an authority utterly independent of the people and its representatives, and possessing the only means of influencing either the Government at home, or the Colonial representative of the Crown[2].

(ii) **The reckless disposal of unimproved lands.**

In Canada the outstanding grievance was the Government's reservation of one-seventh of all new land for the clergy of the Established Church. As Durham pointed out:

[1] Currey, *British Colonial Policy*, p. 71.
[2] *Report on the Affairs of British North America from the Earl of Durham* (1839), p. 29.

The great objection to reserves for the clergy is, that those for whom the land is set apart never have attempted, and never could successfully attempt, to cultivate and settle the property, and that, by that special appropriation, so much land is withheld from settlers, and kept in a state of waste, to the serious injury of all settlers in its neighbourhood[1].

Wakefield exposed the mistaken land policy in Australia. Thus of West Australia he observes:

> In disposing of the waste land the Government began by granting 500,000 acres (nearly half-as-much as the great county of Norfolk) to one person....At length, though by a very brief process, an immense territory was appropriated by a few settlers, who were so effectively dispersed, that, as there were no roads or maps, scarcely one of them knew where he was[2].

(iii) The horrors of the emigration ships[3].

The vessels were ill-ventilated, ill-provisioned, over-crowded and almost unseaworthy. They were frequently so old that it was dangerous to crowd on much sail, with the result that the voyage was unduly prolonged. The ship's food, which was coarse and unwholesome, could only be supplemented at exorbitant prices by the needy travellers. The men who sailed in the capacity of medical superintendents were often ignorant of the rudiments of their profession[4]. Many of the passengers died on the outward voyage, and fever was usually so prevalent among them that emigrant vessels bound for Quebec always proceeded immediately and as a matter of course into quarantine. Along with its surplus population the Mother-country sent its surplus disease.

Durham proved this out of the mouths of doctors::

> As to those who were not sick on arriving, I have to say that they were generally forcibly landed by the masters of vessels, without a shilling in their pockets to procure them a night's lodging, and very few of them with the means of subsistence for more than a very short period. They commonly established themselves along the wharfs and at the different landing-places, crowding into any place of shelter they could obtain, where they subsisted principally upon the charity

---

[1] *Report on the Affairs of British North America from the Earl of Durham* (1839), p. 78.

[2] Wakefield, *Art of Colonization*, p. 433.

[3] Cf. Currey, *British Colonial Policy*, p. 31.

[4] *Report on the Affairs of British North America* (1839)—quoting the evidence of Dr Poole, p. 91.

of the inhabitants. For six weeks at a time from the commencement of the emigration-ship season, I have known the shores of the river along Quebec, for about a mile and a half, crowded with these unfortunate people, the places of those who might have moved off being constantly supplied by fresh arrivals, and there being daily drafts of from 10 to 30 taken to the hospitals with infectious disease. The consequence was its spread among the inhabitants of the city, especially in the districts in which the unfortunate creatures had established themselves. Those who were not absolutely without money got into low taverns and boarding-houses and cellars, where they congregated in immense numbers, and where their state was not any better than it had been on board ship. This state of things existed within my knowledge from 1826 to 1832, and probably for some years previously[1].

(iv) **The abuse of Colonial Patronage.** At one time a deaf and dumb Peer governed Barbadoes; and a public official in England drew a salary for being Secretary to the Council of Jamaica, in which island he had never set foot[2]. "The patronage of the Colonial Office", said Charles Buller, "is the prey of every hungry department of our government. On it the Horse Guards quarters its worn-out general officers as governors: the Admiralty cribs its share, and jobs which even parliamentary rapacity would blush to ask from the Treasury are perpetrated with impunity in the silent realm of 'Mr Mother Country'"[3].

(v) **The centralisation of Colonial policy in the hands of the permanent officials in Downing Street, and the absence of local self-government, comparable with that enjoyed by American townships.**

Appeals by the colonies to "Mr Mother Country" were futile.

"There are rooms in the Colonial Office", wrote Buller, "with old and meagre furniture, book cases crammed with colonial gazettes and newspapers, tables covered with baize, and some old and crazy chairs scattered about, in which those who have personal applications to make are doomed to wait until the interview can be obtained. Here, if perchance you should some day be forced to tarry, you will find strange anxious-looking

---

[1] *Report on the Affairs of British North America* (1839). Evidence of Dr Morrin, p. 87.

[2] Temperley, *Cambridge Modern History*, XI. p. 757.

[3] Quoted in Wakefield, *Art of Colonization*, p. 292.

beings, who pace to and fro in feverish impatience, or sit dejected at the table, unable, in the agitation of their thoughts, to find any occupation to while away their hours, and starting every time that the door opens, in hopes that the messenger is come to announce that their turn has arrived. These are men with colonial grievances. The very messengers know them, their business and its hopelessness, and eye them with pity, as they bid them wait their long and habitual period of attendance. No experienced eye can mistake their faces, once expressive of health, and confidence, and energy, now worn by hopes deferred, and the listlessness of prolonged dependence.... Some are silent; some utter aloud their hopes or fears, and pour out their tale on their fellow-sufferers; some endeavour to conciliate by their meekness; some give vent to their rage, when, after hours of attendance, the messenger summons in their stead some sleek contented-looking visitor, who has sent up his name only a moment before, but whose importance as a Member of Parliament, or of some powerful interest or Society, obtains him an instant interview. And if by chance you should see one of them at last receive the long-desired summons, you will be struck at the nervous reluctance with which he avails himself of the permission. After a short conference you will generally see him return with disappointment stamped on his brow, and, quitting the Office, wend his lonely way home to despair, or perhaps to return to his Colony and rebel. These chambers of woe are called the *Sighing Rooms*; and those who recoil from the sight of human suffering should shun the ill-omened precincts "[1].

[1] Buller, *Responsible Government for Colonies*, London (1820): quoted in Wakefield's *Art of Colonization*, pp. 295–6.

CHAPTER III

REPRESSION AND REFORM AT HOME

1. THE EFFECTS OF WAR AND THE INDUSTRIAL REVOLUTION

Towards the end of the long war with France (1793–1815) food prices mounted rapidly. The course of events in 1810–11 showed that the state of English industry was highly unstable. Commercial friction with the United States, the stringency of the Continental blockade and reckless trading in the new markets of South America precipitated a commercial crisis, which broadened into a general depression. But between 1812 and 1814 there was a partial revival, and, when peace drew near, the whole nation, with a gasp of relief, looked forward to an era of plenty. Peace came, but not plenty; and, bewildered by the paradox, the conscious minority among the working classes and their champions in higher stations of life demanded the reason. Some said it was the new Corn Law, others attributed it to excessive taxation, governmental extravagance and sinecures, but the explanation which found most favour, because it was thought to comprehend the whole, was the imperfection of our "Matchless" Constitution. The agitation for parliamentary reform, which during the war savoured of disloyalty, revived, and with relapses and recrudescences continued till the passing of the Reform Act in 1832.

During all these years the nation felt that economic distress and political ferment somehow went hand in hand. But there was very slight appreciation of the economic side of the problem, of the revolution which had occurred in the economic structure of the country and of its economic consequences—the increased division of processes and classes, and the increased inter-dependence of trade upon trade and country upon country. It was realised, indeed, as the years went on, that there was a certain rhythm in the ups and downs of industry, but the problem of cyclical fluctuation, which is studied so closely to-day[1], was obscured by the narrower issue of the apparent conflict of interest between industry and agriculture. If agriculture prospered when industry was distressed, the manufacturers attributed it to the landlords' Monopoly. If agriculture was depressed when trade flourished, the country gentlemen declared that the Lancashire cottons which flooded Poland brought in return the Polish corn which threw British farms out of cultivation. Both parties were agreed that something must be done to pacify the working classes. But instead of setting their own house in order they expended themselves in recrimination. The manufacturers organised the campaign for free food, the agriculturists took up the cause of the factory worker.

2. 1815–1819: The Six Acts

The unrest of 1815–16 is vividly described by Samuel Bamford, a Lancashire weaver, in the opening pages of his *Life of a Radical*.

It is a matter of history, that whilst the laurels were yet cool on the brows of our victorious soldiers on their second occupation of Paris, the elements of convulsion were at work amongst the masses of our labouring population; and that a series of disturbances commenced with the introduction of the Corn Bill in 1815, and continued, with short intervals, until the close of the year 1816. In London and Westminster riots ensued, and were continued for several days, whilst the Bill was discussed; at Bridport there were riots on account of the high price of bread; at Bideford, there were similar disturbances to prevent the exportation of grain; at Bury, by the unemployed, to destroy machinery; at Ely, not suppressed without bloodshed; at Newcastle-on-Tyne, by colliers and others; at Glasgow, where blood was shed, on account of the soup kitchens; at Preston, by unemployed weavers; at Nottingham, by Luddites, who destroyed 30 frames; at Merthyr Tydvil, on a reduction of wages; at Birmingham, by the unemployed; at Walsall, by the distressed; and December 7th, 1816, at Dundee, where owing to the high price of meal, upwards of 100 shops were plundered[2].

These disorders were simultaneous reactions to economic distress. Luddism was no new thing in the Midlands. The Luddite

---

[1] A modern work is D. H. Robertson's *Study of Industrial Fluctuation* (1915).
[2] *Life of a Radical*, p. 6.

riots date back to 1779, when a crazy lad, Ned Ludd, broke stocking frames. War distress increased the army of General Ludd, and the condition of the hosiery trade in 1815 supplied a fresh incentive. The master hosiers cut prices and pushed cheap goods, which depreciated skilled work. In the lace trade, an adjunct of hosiery, improved machinery was believed to be a cause of unemployment, and the workers wrecked lace frames in Loughborough and Nottingham. For a similar reason the cloth-workers of the West Riding attacked mills and smashed shearing machines. In South Staffordshire, the colliers harnessed themselves, sometimes eighty to a team, to wagons filled with coal, and dragged them (would that they did so to-day!) to London, Leicester and Liverpool, displaying a placard, "Willing to work, but none of us will beg". In the Eastern Counties there were "Bread or Blood" riots, accompanied by destruction of threshing machines and the burning of ricks and barns.

The victims of economic distress lent a ready ear to the Radical Reformers. Bamford goes on:

At this time the writings of William Cobbett suddenly became of great authority; they were read on nearly every cottage hearth in the manufacturing districts of South Lancashire, in those of Leicester, Derby and Nottingham; also in many of the Scottish manufacturing towns. Their influence was speedily visible; he directed his readers to the true cause of their sufferings—misgovernment, and to its proper corrective—parliamentary reform. Riots soon became scarce, and from that time they have never obtained their ancient vogue with the labourers of this country.

Cobbett set the whole country talking and speech-making. "Hampden[1] Clubs were now established in many of our large towns and the villages and districts around them"[2]. The followers of Spence[3] were their rivals in volubility. Major Cartwright[4] toured the Provinces, reiterating his life-long plea for universal suffrage, and those who found the Major too re-

---

[1] John Hampden, who led the Parliamentary opposition to the illegal taxation of Charles I, was venerated as the champion of popular liberties.
[2] *Life of a Radical*, p. 6.   [3] See below, p. 68.
[4] John Cartwright, "the Father of Reform", began agitation in 1780. In 1813 he was arrested in the course of a political tour, but soon released, and in 1820 he was tried for sedition and fined £100.

spectable revelled in the extravagances of Thistlewood and Henry Hunt. The Radical Reformers became an institution in London, and the Provinces offered their moors to the itinerant demagogue.

In December 1816 there was an uproar in Spa Fields, London, the sequel to a Spencean Meeting of "distressed manufacturers, artisans and others"[1]. The mob broke into a gunsmith's shop, began shooting and were in possession of the district until the military arrived. Of the six people arrested five, when they came up for trial in 1817, were unaccountably acquitted, but the sixth, a drunken sailor on furlough, was publicly hanged with military pomp.

On top of the Spa Fields riot came the outrage on the Prince Regent, February 1817, when the windows of his coach were smashed as he returned from the opening of Parliament; and the general situation looked so serious that Parliament appointed a Committee of Enquiry, which reported that the various agitations in the country, the Hampden Reform Clubs and the Spencean Land Clubs, gave proof of a traitorous conspiracy for the overthrow of established government and the division of property!

Government descended with a hand so severe that it was likened to the White Terror of 1815 in the restored monarchy of France.

In February 1817 it suspended the Habeas Corpus Act, and took power to secure and detain persons suspected of conspiracy. It passed the Seditious Meetings and Assemblies' Act (known as the "Gagging Bill"), which stiffened the legislation passed in the 1790's against revolutionary propaganda. In this act the Spencean Land Clubs were suppressed by name (Section 24). Finally, it urged magistrates to apprehend persons guilty of publishing blasphemous and seditious pamphlets and writings. This, however, was resented as an attack on the liberty of the press; and in a celebrated test case (December 1817) a bookseller named Hone, who had published profane parodies such as "the Sinecurists Creed", was acquitted by a jury against the efforts

[1] Smart, *Economic Annals* (1801–20), p. 493.

of the Attorney-General and Lord Chief Justice to obtain a conviction[1].

Confirmatory proofs of conspiracy came from the Midlands and North, where excitement was created by the March of the Blanketeers. On March 10, 1817, 10,000 to 12,000 persons assembled in Manchester in order that half of their number should march to London with a petition against the suspension of Habeas Corpus. Some of the leaders were arrested on the spot, but parties set off equipped with blankets (hence the name of the march), shoes, knapsacks and food. A considerable body was stopped at Stockport, twenty reached Ashbourne in Derbyshire, and there the march ended. This episode and the reports of a projected insurrection in Manchester caused the suspension of Habeas Corpus to be continued till March 1, 1818.

1818 witnessed a sudden return of industrial prosperity, and the Government felt that the quiet in the country permitted the raising of the suspension.

1819 began in optimism and ended in gloom. By March it was seen that early hopes were being falsified. Manufacturing stagnated. There was a notable decline in the output of cloth, and every market for our goods was reported glutted, while large cargoes of raw cotton continued to arrive. Emigrants poured out to the United States from England and Scotland. In July there were strikes. "If trade does not increase", wrote Sydney Smith on the day of Peterloo (August 16, 1819), "there will be a war of the rich against the poor"[2].

All June the reformers were holding great meetings in the Provinces, feeding on the industrial discontent. The Birmingham meeting appointed their own mock M.P., and the Manchester Radicals, under Orator Hunt, when warned that they would not be allowed to imitate Birmingham, organised a demonstration, which took place in St Peter's Fields on August 16.

In rude imitation of military formation in fours, they collected to the number of 50,000–80,000, carrying flags and emblems

---

[1] A vivid account of the trial is given by Harriet Martineau, *History of the Peace* (1816–1846), chap. X.

[2] Smart, *Economic Annals* (1801–20), p. 690.

marked "No Corn Laws", "Vote by ballot", "Equal representation or death". There was no violence till the Manchester Yeomanry, upon receipt of orders to assist the Deputy-constable in arresting the leaders, rode for the hustings. In the confusion which ensued the Yeomanry got into difficulties, and the chief magistrate, fearing for their safety, ordered the officer commanding the troops in reserve to charge. The ground was soon piled high with the stricken mob. Eight were killed and some 400 taken to hospital, most of the injuries being caused by the stampeding of the crowd to avoid the horses' hoofs.

In ten minutes from the commencement of the havoc, the field was an open and almost deserted space. The sun looked down through a sultry and motionless air. The curtains and blinds of the windows within view were all closed. A gentleman or two might occasionally be seen looking out from one of the new houses before mentioned, near the door of which, a group of persons (special constables) were collected, and apparently in conversation; others were assisting the wounded, or carrying off the dead. The hustings remained, with a few broken and hewed flag staves erect, and a torn and gashed banner or two drooping; whilst over the whole field were strewed caps, bonnets, hats, shawls, and shoes, and other parts of male and female dress: trampled, torn and bloody. The yeomanry had dismounted,— some were easing their horses' girths, others adjusting their accoutrements; and some were wiping their sabres. Several mounds of human beings still remained where they had fallen, crushed down and smothered. Some of these still groaning,—others with staring eyes, were gasping for breath, and others would never breathe more. All was silent save those low sounds, and the occasional snorting and pawing of steeds[1].

The incident of St Peter's Fields was called "Peterloo" (a parody on the battle of Waterloo)[2]. Carlyle, writing in 1843, saw in the Chartism of his day the bitter heritage of Peterloo: "The number of the slain and maimed is very countable, but the treasury of rage, burning hidden or visible in all hearts ever since,...is of unknown extent"[3].

---

[1] Bamford, *Life of a Radical*, p. 168.
[2] A week after "Peterloo" J. E. Taylor, later the founder and first editor of the *Manchester Guardian*, published the first fourteen weekly tracts, entitled *The Peterloo Massacre* (F. A. Bruton, *The Story of Peterloo*, p. 7).
[3] *Past and Present*, vol. I. chap. 3.

Hunt, Bamford and other leaders were arrested, and at the York Assizes in the spring of 1820 they were found guilty of conspiracy, Hunt receiving two years' imprisonment and the rest one.

In November 1819 the Regent confronted Parliament with an alarmist speech on sedition, and despite the protest of leading Whigs, the legislation known as the "Six Acts" was hurried through before the end of the year:

1. **Training Prevention.** No military training was permitted except under the order of the Lord Lieutenant of the county. The Act is still in force.

2. **Seizure of Arms.** The magistrates were empowered to search for arms in private houses and to arrest persons carrying them in public. The Act applied to specified counties in the Midlands, the North of England and South Scotland; at the request of the Justices in Session it might be extended to other counties. The members for the county of Durham and the city of Nottingham unsuccessfully opposed the inclusion of their constituencies in the list. The Act was of two years' duration and was not renewed.

3. **Misdemeanours.** This was an Act to prevent delay in the administration of justice. Introduced originally by the Lord Chancellor as a permanent law reform, it suited the temper of the remaining Acts, because it gave the judiciary the power, which the many previous statutes of repression failed to give, of making an immediate example of political agitators.

4. **Seditious Meetings.** Meetings of more than fifty persons to discuss affairs of Church or State or industry must be notified by a requisition from seven householders. The Justice of the Peace had power to alter time and place, and only residents within the particular township or parish might attend.

The Act was of five years' duration and was not renewed. It was aimed at the huge open air gatherings of itinerant orators like Hunt. It stiffened the Acts of 1799 (Corresponding Societies) and of 1817 (Seditious Meetings); and it attached special penalties to banners, music and any kind of military array. The

Acts of 1799 and 1817 are still in force; and it was under these Acts and the common law, and not under the Act of 1819, that the Chartists were liable at a later date to be prosecuted.

5. **Blasphemous and Seditious libels.** Publishers found guilty under this heading were liable to fine, imprisonment and transportation.

The Act, with small amendments, is still in force. It was drafted with a view to prevent any circumventions of earlier legislation directed to this end.

6. **Newspaper stamp duties.** All papers which did not exceed two sheets or which were sold at a less sum than 6d., exclusive of the duty to be charged thereon, were deemed to be newspapers and subject to a stamp duty of 4d.

The Act was aimed especially at cheap pamphlets issued in large numbers, which tended "to excite hatred and contempt of the Government and Constitution". The Act was finally repealed in 1869, but in 1836 the 4d. duty had been reduced to 1d., after a campaign by William Lovett and his publishing friends[1].

The Six Acts, said Mackintosh, the Whig lawyer, amounted "to an almost complete suspension of the Constitution".

February 1820 was marked by a final act of disorder in the Metropolis—the Cato Street Conspiracy. The design was to murder the members of the Cabinet, while dining with the Prime Minister, Lord Liverpool; but one of the confederates was an informer and the conspiracy was nipped in the bud, Thistlewood, the head of it, and four others being executed for high treason. In April an insurrectionary movement in the neighbourhood of Glasgow came to a head at Bonnymuir, but was suppressed without difficulty. The *Annual Register* of 1820 declared that "to the Acts of 1819 we must in no small degree ascribe the quiet state of the country in 1820".

1820 brought a partial revival of trade, swelling into a trade boom in 1826. Prosperity then declined gradually, and conditions were bad in the two years preceding the passing of the

[1] See below, p. 261.

Reform Bill. Throughout the period from 1815 to 1832 the coincidence of industrial depression and popular unrest is marked.

3. THE POLICY OF REPRESSION

What must be our judgment on the policy of repression?

The executive action of the Government is defensible. The country was in the process of transformation from war to peace, and in a highly inflammable condition. If the Government had not suppressed the wearing of arms and unauthorised military training, its civil authority would have broken down. Order was maintained at this time with less injury to person and property than in 1830–32, when the economic situation was easier and the political excitement greater.

Peterloo was the price paid for the lack of an efficient police force. The half-trained Yeomanry, recruited from shopkeepers and manufacturers, knew little about the management of horses and less about the management of a crowd. By contrast the regular troops who were present behaved with coolness and moderation. In 1839, during the Chartist turmoils, more threatening situations were surmounted by the tact of Major-General Sir Charles Napier, the regular soldier in command of the Northern District.

Government, Parliament and the upper classes generally showed a remarkable inability to distinguish between violent reactions to economic distress and the legitimate expression of political unrest. They had no conception that the Hampden Political Clubs, the Spencean Land Clubs and the various reform gatherings were necessary safety-valves of popular emotion. They stupidly dismissed the programme of political reform as an assault on the sacred Constitution, and the agrarian programme of the Spenceans as a war against the still more sacred rights of property. Their suspicion of cheap literature was their greatest folly, for they advertised the opinions which they wished to suppress and convinced the people that the Government dreaded the utterance of the truth.

4. Francis Place and the Reformers

During the events which led up to the Reform Bill of 1832, the central figure in the Metropolis outside Parliament was the Westminster tailor, Francis Place. Cobbett, the farmer-politician, by his writings and speeches fired the towns and the countryside. Sydney Smith, the clergyman, by his inimitable humour (we have not forgotten to this day "Dame Partington and her Mop"[1]) made the Tories look ridiculous. James Mill in the first number of the *Westminster Review* laid bare the facts of the Constitution. Brougham and Macaulay voiced the desire of the middle classes for moderate reform, "those hundreds of thousands of respectable persons", whose praises Brougham sang in the House of Lords[2]. But it was Francis Place who held in his hands the threads of popular organisation, and made it possible during the crucial months for Whigs, Radicals and business men to pull together, and for London and the Provinces to speak with a single voice. He had begun in 1807 with the organisation of the Westminster electorate, when they sent Sir Francis Burdett to the House to champion popular liberties. Through Place's influence John Cam Hobhouse became Burdett's colleague in 1820. In 1824–25, with the assistance in

[1] "As for the possibility of the House of Lords preventing ere long a reform of Parliament, I hold it to be the most absurd notion that ever entered into human imagination. I do not mean to be disrespectful, but the attempt of the Lords to stop the progress of Reform reminds me very forcibly of the great storm of Sidmouth, and of the conduct of the excellent Mrs Partington on that occasion. In the winter of 1824 there set in a great flood upon that town—the tide rose to an incredible height—the waves rushed in upon the houses, and everything was threatened with destruction. In the midst of this sublime and terrible storm, Dame Partington, who lived upon the beach, was seen at the door of her house with mop and pattens, trundling her mop, squeezing out the sea-water, and vigorously pushing away the Atlantic Ocean. The Atlantic was roused. Mrs Partington's spirit was up; but I need not tell you that the contest was unequal. The Atlantic Ocean beat Mrs Partington. She was excellent at a slop or a puddle, but she should not have meddled with a tempest. Gentlemen, be at your ease—be quiet and steady—you will beat—Mrs Partington". (Stuart J. Reid, *Life and Times of Sydney Smith*, pp. 274–5.)

[2] "The genuine depositaries of sober, rational, intelligent and honest English wisdom. Unable though they be to round a period or point an epigram, they are solid, right-judging men, and above all, not given to change", etc., etc. (Hansard, 3rd S. VIII. 251, Oct. 7, 1831.)

Parliament of Joseph Hume, once an Indian Army doctor and now the generalissimo of retrenchment, Place organised the case of the Trades Unions with such cleverness and moderation that Parliament was persuaded into the very liberal Act of 1824 and dissuaded from a *complete* repudiation of it the year following[1].

During the Reform Bill struggle Place presided over the National Political Union in the Metropolis, and although his moderation was suspect to the extreme Radicals, who founded opposition unions, he prevented the radical cause from nullifying itself by internal dissension.

What Place did in London, Thomas Attwood, the banker of currency fame, did for the Provinces. The Birmingham Political Union for the Protection of Public Rights, which he founded in January 1830, became the model of the political unions in the rest of the country. Place and Attwood and the organisations which they controlled convinced reasonable men in Parliament that the reform agitation was something better than "a horde of ragamuffins howling for the ballot and the blood of the aristocracy"[2]. Ministers were not ashamed to allude to their meetings. Lord John Russell, adverting to the resolution carried by 100,000 Birmingham men on Newhall Hill, said: "It is impossible that the voice of a faction should prevail against the voice of a nation"[3]. The Government grew anxious about its popular allies when the demonstrations culminated in riots as at the end of 1831, but Attwood urged that its suspicions were groundless and pointed out that in places where there were strong Unions no outrages occurred[4].

[1] Place's version is given in Place, British Museum Add. MSS. 27,798, "Narrative of Proceedings for Repeal of Combination Laws"—quoted in Chap. VIII of Graham Wallas' *Life of Francis Place*.

[2] J. R. M. Butler, *The Passing of the Great Reform Bill*, p. 241.

[3] Oct. 3, 1831. See *Dictionary of National Biography* (Supplement), Thomas Attwood.

[4] Butler, *op. cit.* p. 299.

5. The Passing of the Reform Bill

The Whigs came into office in 1830, pledged to reform by tradition and necessity, by tradition because reform was their heritage from Fox, by necessity because the possible alternatives —fiscal reform and catholic emancipation—had been filched from them by the Tories. Earl Grey, who had been in opposition since 1807, was Premier. His lieutenants in the coming fray included Henry Brougham, his brilliant but erratic Lord Chancellor, "Old Wickedshifts" of the *Creevey Papers*; Lord John Russell, the "finality Jack"[1] of a later day, but now distinguished by his youthful ardour for reform; Lord Durham, the Premier's fiery son-in-law; and the even-tempered indispensable Althorpe, who desired above all things to escape from the burdens of office. Durham and Russell were members of the Committee of Four which drafted the Reform Bill (the other two being Lord Duncannon and the "Radical baronet", Sir James Graham). Russell introduced it in Parliament. Althorpe, as leader of the Lower House, steered it through the Commons, and the Premier himself assumed the heavier burden of persuading the Lords and the Crown.

The struggle lasted from March 1, 1831, when the first Reform Bill was introduced in the House of Commons, to June 4, 1832, when the third Reform Bill passed the third reading in the House of Lords.

On March 2, 1831, in the debate on the motion to bring in the Bill, Macaulay made the speech which is among the greatest things in English rhetoric:

Turn where we may, within, around, the voice of great events is proclaiming to us, Reform, that you may preserve....Renew the youth of the State. Save property divided against itself. Save the multitude, endangered by its own ungovernable passions. Save the aristocracy, endangered by its own unpopular power. Save the greatest, and fairest, and most highly civilised community that ever existed, from calamities which may in a few days sweep away all the rich heritage of so many ages of wisdom and glory. The danger is

---

[1] On June 23, 1837, he referred to the Reform Bill as a "final measure"— Hansard, 3rd S. XXXVIII. 1502.

terrible. The time is short. If this Bill should be rejected, I pray to
God that none of those who concur in rejecting it may ever remember
their votes with unavailing remorse, amidst the wreck of laws, the
confusion of ranks, the spoliation of property, and the dissolution of
social order[1].

The second, the critical reading, passed by one vote. Macaulay
has described the scene:

"You might have heard a pin drop as Duncannon read the
numbers. Then again the shouts broke out and many of us shed
tears. I could scarcely refrain. And the jaw of Peel fell; and the
face of Twiss was as the face of a damned soul; and Herries
looked like Judas taking his necktie off for the last operation.
We shook hands, and clapped each other on the back and went
out laughing, crying and huzzaing into the lobby"[2].

On April 19 the Government was defeated in Committee.
Parliament was dissolved, and a pro-Reform Parliament was
returned. The second Reform Bill was introduced forthwith,
passed through the Commons in September 1831, and sent up
to the Lords. It was calculated that out of the 112 holders of
peerages created before 1790 no less than 108 voted for the
Bill, but the creations of the war and the bishops were almost
solidly Tory, and they were led by the Duke of Wellington, who
had solemnly declared in 1830 that he had never read or heard
of any measure which could in any way satisfy his mind that the
state of the representation could be improved[3].

On October 8, the Lords threw out the Bill by a majority
of forty-one. The country, now roused to the highest pitch of
excitement, broke into tumultuous protest. The papers appeared with black borders, the Provinces rained petitions, and
there were grave riots at Derby, Nottingham and Bristol. At
Bristol[4] (October 30) the Mansion House was sacked and many of

[1] *Miscellaneous Writings and Speeches* (Popular Edition, p. 492).

[2] Macaulay in a letter to Ellis, March 30, 1831.

[3] Butler, *op. cit.* pp. 97 and 286 n.

[4] The *Bristol Gazette and Public Advertiser* of Nov. 3, 1831 gives a good
account of the riots.

The following is taken from Home Office papers—28. 1831:

"Oct. 31, 1831: Major Mackworth to General Fitzroy Somerset.

"Since I wrote yesterday to Colonel Egerton, several very painful incidents
have taken place in this City. In two sides of Queen Square, every house is

the central buildings were burnt down. Political Unions sprang up like mushrooms in every part of the country.

In December 1831, amid the distractions of a cholera outbreak, the third Reform Bill was introduced. By the end of March 1832 it had reached the Lords, and on April 13, after an all-night debate, the second reading was carried by nine.

The popular rejoicing was vast, but premature; for on May 7 the Government met with a defeat in Committee and on May 9 resigned. For eleven days the ordinary business of the nation was suspended. On May 18, after the Duke of Wellington had failed to form a Ministry, the King, who on the 15th had returned to his old Ministers, consented to create sufficient peers to carry the Bill. The threat sufficed; on June 4 the third reading was carried, on June 7 the measure became law.

Under the Act many of the ancient boroughs in the South of England were totally or partially disfranchised, and their seats were given to new centres of population in the Midlands and North. For the boroughs a uniform £10 household franchise was established. In the counties the old 40s. freeholders were reinforced by copyholders, long lease holders and tenants at will paying a rent of £50 a year.

"The final and total result was the addition of some 455,000 electors to the roll—an addition which more than trebled the electorate. In the towns political power was vested mainly in the merchants, manufacturers, and shopkeepers; in the counties in the landowners and the farmers"[1].

Since 1832 the franchise has been three times extended. Furthermore, in 1872 vote by ballot was substituted for open voting, and since 1911 members of Parliament have been paid.

---

burnt to the ground including the Mansion and Custom House (23 in number)—the three gaols are burnt, two toll houses and the Bishop's Palace—our small number of Cavalry (about 100)...were nearly knocked out.

"I have observed too that the great mass of the people excepting some of the principal inhabitants were very averse to military interference; at least they hooted and pelted us, and as I mentioned yesterday compelled some of the 100 [sc. cavalry] to fire. The events of the night effected a complete change in this respect, and our men have since been received with shouts of joy".

[1] J. A. R. Marriott, *England since Waterloo*, p. 99.

Disraeli's Act of 1867 gave the franchise to householders and lodgers paying £10 rent, and thus reached the bulk of the working class population in the towns. Gladstone in 1885, by making the franchise uniform for counties and boroughs, brought in the agricultural labourer. Finally, the Reform Act of 1918 gave a vote to the adult male population and to women over 30.

6. ECONOMIC *VERSUS* POLITICAL POWER

"The crowning discovery of the nineteenth century", say the spokesmen of Guild Socialism, "was that democratic government made no difference to the life of the ordinary man. Nominally self-governing he remained in bondage". And again: "economic power is the key to political power. Political democracy has been unmeaning because it has reflected the power of an economic aristocracy"[1].

Is this sound history? It is obviously not, if we think of the British Dominions and what the grant of responsible self-government has meant to them. But if the generalisation is confined to 19th century England, it expresses a half-truth.

No one would have suspected that the Tory Government of 1820, fresh from Peterloo and the Six Acts, had ten years of life before it, during which it would pass through an unreformed House of Commons a sweeping series of commercial reforms, repeal the laws against Combinations, remove disabilities on Nonconformists and settle the burning issue of catholic emancipation. No one, at any rate no enthusiast for reform in 1832, would have suspected that the achievements of the Whigs (1832–41) would have been as meagre and sometimes as unpopular (e.g. the new Poor Law) as they were. It is true that in the 30's Parnell reformed the Excise, that Rowland Hill introduced the Penny Postage, that the cheap newspaper was established in power and that people began to move about the country in trains, but these things were not showy from a party standpoint and they were obscured by the greater events of the 40's, when

[1] G. H. D. Cole and W. Mellor, *The Meaning of Industrial Freedom*, pp. 2 and 40.

the Tories were again in office—Free Trade, Corn Law Repeal,
Factory and Mines Legislation, and the Bank Act of 1844.

But on a deeper view of history the generalisation will not
stand, even for England. In England, as contrasted with
France, economic stress and political ferment have never precipitated political catastrophe, for English instincts are utterly
in favour of what is called "reformism" or "successiveness".
The Reform Bill of 1832, which enfranchised the middle classes,
brought the working classes, with whose support it was carried,
to the threshold of the franchise. This threshold they crossed
without excitement thirty-five years later, and the course of
legislation from the Trade Union Act of 1871 to the Trade
Disputes Act of 1906, together with the more recent legislation
establishing an eight hours' day and a minimum wage in coal
mining, is evidence that the working classes by political action
have gained economic advantages which, without a vote, they
most certainly would not have obtained. It may be that but
for this they would have forced on civil war, but that is another
question.

We are ever apt to disparage a prize as soon as we have won it.
If we wish to imagine what the lack of a vote meant to the
working classes in 1832, let us remember the feelings of women
only a few years ago. The supporters of Women's Suffrage will
no doubt be disappointed if they expect the vote to produce an
immediate economic millennium. But this they will not expect
if they have reflected on history, for it is the lesson of history
that political power strengthens economic status by a process of
infiltration which is at once gradual and certain.

CHAPTER IV

THE INFLUENCE OF JEREMY BENTHAM

1. JEREMY BENTHAM

JEREMY BENTHAM, the son of a lawyer, was a legal genius, possessed of comfortable private means, and socially a benevolent recluse. When the celebrated French lady, Madame de Staël, came to London, she sent a message through his friend and editor, Dumont: "Tell Bentham I will see nobody, till I have seen him". "Sorry for it", said Bentham, "for then she will never see anybody"[1].

He was born in 1748, three years after the last attempt to restore the Stuarts to the throne of England, and he died in 1832 on the eve of the passing of the Reform Bill. Regarded in his youth as extravagantly subversive, he ended his life a venerated leader of English thought, and numbered among his disciples conservative statesmen, radical philosophers, legal luminaries and the earliest school of English socialists.

2. LAW REFORMS

His profound knowledge of law made him a formidable critic of legal abuses. To every custom, every law and every judicial process, he applied the test, "what is the use of it?" He pinned it down as a barrister pins a witness in cross-examination. If it failed under the test, he condemned it root and branch, regardless of its historical prestige or of appeals to abstract right.

He entered Oxford at the precocious age of 13, but in this home of intellectual conservatism he found nothing save restraints. At the outset of his University career he was made to subscribe to the Thirty-nine Articles of the Church of

---

[1] Bentham, *Collected Works* (edited by John Bowring, 1843), x. 467.

England, and henceforth to him the road to Oxford was paved with perjury[1]. "Universal perjury in Oxford men, and indifference to perjury in Cambridge men"—such was the distinction he drew between the sister Universities[2]. Of the College Lecture Room (he was a member of Queen's College) he writes: "We just went to the foolish lectures of our tutors, to be taught something of logical jargon"[3]. Passing from Oxford to the Bar, he took no greater pleasure in his profession than he had taken in Blackstone's lectures at Oxford. He soon abandoned it, and seemed for a time, to his father's distress, to be passing into the obscurity of failure. But at 28 he began to find himself, and, when he followed up his *Fragment on Government* with the *Principles of Morals and Legislation,* his reputation as a legal critic and political philosopher was assured.

The shortcomings of lawyers and the law haunted him all his life. In the index to his *Works* the entries under "Lawyer" include the following:

Lawyers—The only persons in whom ignorance of the Law is not punished.

> Least of all men exposed to the operations of humanity.
> Their interest in technical jargon.
> Incidentally, animadverted on. (156 citations.)

No writer has been borrowed from more than Bentham, but, as Talleyrand said, "pillé de tout le monde, il est toujours riche"[4]. The legal historian, Sir Henry Maine, Professor of Law and Master of Trinity Hall, Cambridge, wrote, "I do not know a single law reform effected since Bentham's day which cannot be traced to his influence"[5].

How then in the sphere of law was Bentham's influence exerted?

He set out to make law simple, comprehensible and pure. Legal fictions, so dear to the hearts of lawyers, aroused in a special degree his wrath. Why do judges invent fictions? For one of two purposes—"either that of doing in a roundabout way

---

[1] "It is thus that the first lesson the young man learns, and the only lesson he is sure to learn, is perjury". *Works,* II. 210.
[2] *Works,* X. 571.   [3] *Ibid.* X. 41.
[4] *Works,* XI. 75.   [5] *Early History of Institutions,* p. 397.

what they might do in a direct way, or that of doing in a roundabout way what they had no right to do in any way at all "[1].
His writings produced results over the whole field of English
law.

It was he who supplied the intellectual stimulus to the reform
of the Criminal Law, which is associated more particularly with
the names of Romilly and Mackintosh. Sir Samuel Romilly
began the crusade in 1808 with an attack on the laws against
stealing, then so severe that the juries would not convict on
them. For example, there was a law of Elizabeth still in force
which made a capital offence of stealing privately from the
person, but Romilly could only find one single instance where
an offender convicted under it had suffered death[2]. The old
school maintained with characteristic optimism that we had
lived happily and securely under these laws. Private stealing
from shops, it was said in Parliament in 1810, was on the
increase, and nothing but the terror of death would keep retail
shops from unavoidable loss, bankruptcy and ruin[3]. The
reformers insisted that certainty was a greater preventive than
severity; and Elizabeth Fry, the prison reformer, reinforced
this unanswerable argument by evidence of the mental conditions of prisoners and of their responsiveness to kindly
treatment. They felt, she told Romilly, that they had only
been thieves, but that their governors were murderers[4].

Sir James Mackintosh carried on Romilly's work. In 1819
upwards of two thousand crimes, very different in their degrees
of enormity, were still punishable with death. The prisons and
hulks were notorious nurseries of crime, and Australia, our
youngest Colony, was being populated by gaolers and gaol-birds.
Mackintosh obtained and presided over a Committee of Enquiry,
and the knowledge thereby elicited was the foundation of the
long series of laws which between 1823 and 1861 reduced the
number of capital crimes until murder and high treason alone
were left.

---

[1] *Works*, x. 75 (Extracts from Bentham's Common Place Book).
[2] Smart, *Economic Annals* (1801–20), p. 174.
[3] *Ibid.* p. 229.   [4] *Ibid.* p. 635.

Laws less directly affecting the life of the people, but not less directly issuing from the Benthamite fountain, were those, passed during the middle of the 19th century, which introduced greater simplicity and freedom in dealing with land and property in general. It was Benthamism, too, which inspired the legislation establishing religious liberty: the Nonconformist Relief Act (1812), the Test and Corporation Act (1828), the Roman Catholic Relief Act (1829), the Nonconformists' Chapel Act (1844), and the Marriage Acts from 1835 onwards. Lastly, the long series of Oaths Acts had the two-fold effect of opening Parliament to persons not otherwise eligible and of enabling even atheists to give evidence and enforce their rights in a Court of Justice[1].

Similarly, in the political and industrial sphere, the Reform Act of 1832, the Municipal Reform Act of 1835, and the new Poor Law of 1834[2] aimed at the removal of corruption and waste. Old England needed a tonic, and Benthamism prescribed a double dose of freedom. Just as the object of the authors of the Reform Bill was to give the vote to the greatest number of politically free men, so the object of the Poor Law Commissioners was to force the state-aided pauper into economic independence.

3. PHILOSOPHY OF GREATEST HAPPINESS

Bentham's great maxim and the source from which he derived it may be described in his own words: "Priestley was the first (unless it was Beccaria) who taught my lips to pronounce this sacred truth: that the greatest happiness of the greatest number is the foundation of morals and legislation"[3].

With this maxim Bentham identified what he called "the Principle of Utility". On the touch-stone of utility evil was synonymous with pain, good with pleasure; and poetry was no better than push-pin[4]. In this way Bentham's maxim of

---

[1] See Dicey, *Law and Opinion*, pp. 201 sqq.
[2] See below, p. 94.   [3] *Works*, X. 142.
[4] "Prejudice apart, the game of push-pin is of equal value with the arts and sciences of music and poetry. If the game of push-pin furnish more pleasure, it is more valuable than either". *Works*, II. 253.

"greatest happiness" has come down in history as the badge of the English Utilitarians[1].

Bentham, with his passion for simplicity, tried to apply his maxim and its accompanying principle of utility to moral philosophy as well as to practical politics. As a moral philosophy, happiness and utility are very inadequate explanations of what human motive ought to be or is. The pig in his pig-sty is supremely happy, and so is the drunkard, but both are ignoble. Men court the pain of wounds and death, not because they have mistaken the content of happiness, or because they imagine these pains to be the means of reaching another world where they will sing in the angelic chorus for evermore, but because they are prepared to make sacrifices in order that the right may triumph. But in the sphere of practical politics Bentham's maxim supplied a sound working rule. Law is of necessity concerned with external and general things, and here happiness and utility have their place.

4. POLITICAL PHILOSOPHY

On the political side Bentham interpreted his maxim in a democratic sense, so that it meant "every man is to count for one, and no man for more than one". With the logic of this we may quarrel. We may ask, "Is the happiness of a savage or an apple-woman to count for as much as the happiness of a Shakespeare?" But once again the rule is a sound working rule. What society needs to-day, as it needed then, is the reduction of social inequalities and the elimination of placemen and profiteers. Democracy may not appeal to us in theory, utility may not be the lines on which we justify it, but we know full well that the

[1] "It was in the winter of 1822–23 that I formed the plan of a little society, to be composed of young men agreeing in fundamental principles— acknowledging Utility as their standard in ethics and politics....The name I gave to the society was the Utilitarian Society. It was the first time that any one had taken the title of Utilitarian; and the term made its way into the language from this humble source. I did not invent the word, but found it in one of Galt's novels [*vide D.N.B.*: Galt, John], the *Annals of the Parish*, in which the Scotch clergyman, of whom the book is a supposed autobiography, is represented as warning his parishioners not to leave the Gospel and become utilitarians". John Stuart Mill, *Autobiography*, p. 79. For an account of the school see Leslie Stephen, *The English Utilitarians*.

practical alternatives to democracy are Kaiserism on the one hand and Bolshevism on the other.

Bentham knew it too. Equality without security, he argued, is useless. When the two are in conflict, equality must yield. Of the levelling apparatus of communism he wrote: "This pretended remedy, seemingly so pleasant, would be a mortal poison, a burning cautery, which would consume till it destroyed the last fibre of life. The hostile sword in its greatest furies is a thousand times less dreadful"[1]. We can guess what Bentham will say to Lenin, when they meet in Hades!

5. Self-interest and "Laissez-faire"

Bentham's belief in security was a justifiable belief, but it was coupled with a further belief which was not, and which may be summed up in the phrase, "trust to self-interest". Or, as Bentham puts it in the opening chapter of his *Manual on Political Economy*: "Generally speaking, there is no one who knows what is for your interest, so well as yourself—no one who is disposed with so much ardour and constancy to pursue it"[2].

This belief, which Adam Smith before him based on natural law, Bentham drew from his notion of utility. If men are allowed to pursue their own interest, the public good will be achieved. For each man knows what will be useful to him, and what is useful to each and every will be useful to all.

The lack of a thorough ethical psychology left Bentham hazy on the subject of motive. How a legislature, which is composed of people who cannot help acting from self-interest, is to legislate for the general good is a conundrum which he never solved. Indeed, in almost the last lines he ever wrote he confessed, "I am a selfish man, as selfish as any man can be. But in me somehow or other selfishness has taken the form of benevolence!"[3]   *See pelus.*

The belief in the virtues of enlightened self-interest had results both good and bad.

---

[1] Bentham, *Theory of Legislation* (Paternoster Library, 1896 ed.), p. 121.
[2] *Works*, III. 33.   [3] *Ibid.* XI. 95.

One good result of the belief in *enlightened* self-interest was the zest which it aroused for education. With this zest Bentham inspired his disciples, among whom none was more ardent than Francis Place. It remained for John Stuart Mill, on whom the mantle of Bentham fell, to reconcile compulsory education with individual liberty[1].

Again, to the disciples of Bentham, *laissez-faire* did not mean, as it did to titled loungers like Lord Melbourne, "let things be, don't worry". It was a war-cry, sounding the attack on every law or social convention which hindered freedom of development. It was a campaign for the overthrow of long-established abuses.

On the other hand the belief contributed to the distrust of working class association. A philosophy which envisaged society as a collection of independent units, seeking individual expression, was necessarily blind to the most fundamental human instinct, the instinct for self-help through association. The practical outcome of this exaggerated individualism was hostility towards any form of positive social policy. Individualism was inspiring only so long as the battle against old-established abuses was being fought. When these had been removed or greatly mitigated, and new legislation was needed of a positive order for the improvement of health and housing, the upholders of *laissez-faire* became the fretful opponents of social reform[2]. "The opponents of factory regulation made many efforts to drown the cry of '10 Hours a day' with the popular shouts

---

[1] See Mill, *On Liberty*, Chapter v.

[2] Thus Cobden writes in 1836: "No child ought to be put in a cotton mill at all so early as the age of 13 years", but he proceeds to argue against the 10 Hours Bill, deprecating "that spurious humanity, which would indulge in an unreasoning kind of philanthropy at the expense of the independence of the great bulk of the community". Cobden to W. C. Hunt, Morley's *Life of Cobden*, Popular Edn. Appendix, p. 954.

Examined before the Health of Towns Committee (1840) he says nothing but "yes", "yes", "yes", when confronted with facts of housing conditions taken from the *Reports of the Manchester Statistical Society*.

Edmund Ashworth, the Bolton manufacturer and brother of Henry Ashworth, an original member of the Anti-Corn Law League, told this Committee that: "Young men brought up in a cottage have no feeling of the inconveniences arising from it and consequently do not desire an enlarged one" (Q. 1834). The Committee with difficulty extracted the admission that factory owners frequently compelled their workpeople to live in factory owners' houses.

of 'Reform', 'No Corn Laws'"—so writes 'Alfred' in his *History
of the Factory Movement*[1]. This negative attitude, which did so
much harm in domestic affairs, had equally baneful results on
imperial policy. It encouraged both in Englishmen and in the
inhabitants of the self-governing Dominions the idea that any
measure of imperial construction was an attack on national
liberties.

6. BENTHAM AS AN ECONOMIST

Bentham was a lawyer first and an economist second, but as
was the fashion of his day, he compiled a *Manual of Political
Economy*. The tone is set by the introduction:

"With the view of causing an increase to take place in the
mass of national wealth, or with a view to increase of the means
either of subsistence or enjoyment, without some special reason,
the general rule is, that nothing ought to be done or attempted
by government. The motto, or watchword of government, on
these occasions, ought to be—*Be quiet*"[2].

The *Non-Agenda* are the main items in the book; and his
illiberal tirade against Colonies makes paltry reading beside the
large-minded statesmanship of Adam Smith. The *Manual*, however, was a bye-product. He wrote much more to the point when
he was tackling a specific evil, such as the uselessness of the laws
limiting the rate of interest (*Defence of Usury*, 1787), or when he
was recommending improvements in the methods of pauper
management. Here he tried to construct, and his notions,
though fantastic, were humane.

Bentham's *Manual* had this much in common with the political
economy of the classical economists. Its phraseology was technical and invited misinterpretation. It is true that the classical
chain of reasoning was highly abstract, but it was set in motion
by the topics of the day, and suggested conclusions which
accorded with its disciples' bias. Out of the high price of corn
during the War came the classical Law of Diminishing Returns;
out of the Currency troubles of the suspension period came

[1] "Alfred" [Samuel Kydd], *History of the Factory Movement* (1857), I. 214.
[2] *Works*, III. 33.

Ricardo's Theory of Money and Foreign Trade; out of the
Poor Law and Ireland came Malthus' Law of Population. And
the disciples of the Classical Economy obtained the solutions
they desired. Cash payments were resumed, the new Poor Law
was a Malthusian Poor Law, the Corn Laws were repealed, and
in 1854 the last of the laws against usury was swept from the
Statute Book.

Another bond of union was Bentham's hatred of legal
monopoly. The economic counterpart of this was an unbounded
faith in the virtues of competition. Finally, the whole doctrine
of utility, with its exaggeration of self-interest, permeated at
every point the assumptions of those who claimed to be following
the laws of Political Economy. How closely the two were
associated in the popular mind may be seen from the early
writings of Thomas Carlyle, by whom the monster "Utilitaria"
and the "dismal science" are constantly presented as different
phases of the same error.

But it may be doubted if any of the classical economists or of
their critics in the world of letters realised how Bentham could
be used against them. Bentham started people thinking about
a calculus of pain and pleasure. In modern economic theory this
plays an important part in connection with Marginal Utility
and Consumer's Surplus of Satisfaction. But before it was
introduced into current economics by Stanley Jevons, the
notion had been seized upon out of the pages of Bentham by
the little group of rebellious thinkers, known as the Early
English Socialists.

Minter Morgan, the versifier of the band, contemptuously
dismisses:

> McCulloch, Malthus, Mill[1], a triad famed
> For bold assertions which are soon disclaimed.

But Bentham he hails:

> Bentham that veteran in the cause of Truth,
> Holds on his course with all the fire of youth,
> Unmasks hypocrisy, detects device
> And with surpassing skill exposes vice[2].

---

[1] James Mill (1773–1836), not his son John Stuart Mill (1806–1873).
[2] J. Minter Morgan, *Reproof of Brutus* (1830), pp. 53 and 54.

The early socialists admired Bentham because he was sweeping away the tangle from the ground on which they hoped to build. Bentham saw no beauty in the old muddles. They failed by the calculus of pleasure and pain, and they must go.

Bentham's influence is visible in Charles Hall, the earliest of the socialist writers. Hall was a doctor who had studied infantile mortality and found that the deaths of the poor "are to those of the rich in proportion as two to one". The reason was the disproportion in the material of happiness at the disposal of rich and poor. To redress this balance he advocated progressive taxation in what must surely be one of the earliest expositions of the theory. With reference to the Income Tax he writes:

We have observed that the present mode is—if a person of £100 a year pays £10, a man of £1,000 pays £100 a year. In this case the former gives up something highly useful if not necessary to his family, whilst the latter gives up nothing but what is in a much less degree useful, and bordering on such as are superfluous. What a man of £10,000 a year gives up is in a still less degree useful, and approaching still nearer to what is superfluous. It would be desirable that the part each rich man should pay towards the taxes should be regulated by some gradually increasing series[1].

To the disciples of John Stuart Mill this would have seemed confiscation, a piece of "Finchley Common morality"[2]. And yet who read Bentham the more correctly? Hall did, and so did another member of the band, William Thompson, a professed disciple of Bentham. It was on the test of happiness that Thompson condemned the existing system of distribution. He headed his *magnum opus*: "An enquiry into the principles of the distribution of wealth most conducive to human happiness; applied to the newly proposed system of voluntary equality of wealth".

[1] Hall, *Effects of Civilisation* (1805), p. 206.
[2] Cf. *Commons Committee on Income and Property Tax* (1861). Evidence of Wm Newmarch, F.R.S. (for many years secretary of the Political Economy Club, and the author of the two additional volumes of Tooke's *History of Prices*)—

Q. 328. You disapprove, with Mr Mill, of taxation upon any principle of graduation? Entirely and emphatically.
Q. 736. ...That is what I call Finchley Common morality, when savings are taxed. [Finchley Common was a disorderly spot at this time.]
Q. 747. You are against a graduated income tax, are you not...? Yes.
Q. 748. Why? Because it is confiscation.

7. The Reformer and the Man

To sum up, Bentham was greatest as a legal critic. From him came the impetus to reform in criminal and civil law. His spirit is breathed in the greater part of the social, industrial and political legislation enacted between 1815 and 1870. As a philosopher he was the leading exponent of utilitarianism, with its ambiguous maxim, "the greatest happiness of the greatest number"; and he interpreted this in a sense which made it the central plank of radical democracy. Under his influence *laissez-faire* held the field in English industry and commerce for the greater part of a century. Lawyer first and economist second, he nevertheless influenced profoundly the classical economists, and his calculus of happiness linked him with the early English socialists, who led the assault on the classical stronghold.

But in interpreting Benthamism, let us not lose sight of Bentham, the man. He was a recluse and a dreamer, not of romance, but of model codes and mechanical perfections. If we could ask him what he considered his greatest creation, we should hear perhaps no word of Law Reform, but an outburst of praise for his darling *Panopticon*—the model prison, so planned that from one point in the building the inspector could see all that was going on in every portion of it. The father of utilitarianism expected more from a dome of glass than from the most perfect code of law. If Bentham had married, his wife would have adored him and corrected his proofs; and he in return would have been playfully amorous without prejudice to his book-shelves, his sacred tea-pot (Dicky by name), and all the little whims of the intellectual hermit.

CHAPTER V

THE SPIRIT OF ASSOCIATION

1. Voluntary Association

THE student of Dicey's *Law and Opinion in England*—a classic which all should read—is invited to distinguish three periods:

I. The period of old Toryism or Legislative Quiescence (1800–1830).

II. The period of Benthamism or Individualism (1825–1870).

III. The period of Collectivism (1865–1900).

Bentham lived during the first period. His name is given to the second period, and a chapter (Lecture 9) expounds the debt of Collectivism to Benthamism.

The student, therefore, comes to wonder if there is anything which is not Benthamism. Benthamism, he says to himself, stands for individualism. How then can the period of Benthamism include the humanitarian legislation which begins with the first Factory Act of 1802 and broadens out during the middle of the century into the elaborate code regulating the conditions of employment in workshops, factories and mines? How can a monster beget an angel?

We may perhaps throw light on this difficulty by suggesting that the *social* trend from 1825–1870 cannot be compressed into a single process. "Individualism" may suffice to define the dominant *legal* trend, but it conceals the influence exerted on the legislature from without and from below by the action of voluntary associations. The period of voluntary association coincides with the period of individualism, and bridges the transition to the period of collectivism.

2. ROBERT OWEN AND SOCIAL RESPONSIBILITY

What Bentham was to individualism, Robert Owen was to
voluntary association. Bentham himself was an admirer of
Owen and supported his business philanthropy, but, as expressions of a social attitude, Benthamism and Owenism were
poles asunder. The contrast between the two is admirably displayed in the evidence given before the Factory Committee of
1816 by two representatives of the employing class, Josiah
Wedgwood of pottery fame and Robert Owen himself.

"In the state of society", said Wedgwood, "in which there is
evidently a progressive movement, it is much better to leave things
as they are than to attempt to amend the general state of things in
detail. The only safe way of securing the comfort of any people is to
leave them at liberty to make the best use of their time, and to allow
them to appropriate their earnings in such way as they think fit"[1].

Robert Owen thought otherwise. In a couple of answers he
exposed the fallacy of enlightened self-interest. The answers
seem obvious enough to-day, but in 1816 they were as the voice
of one crying in the wilderness. He was asked whether he believed that "there is that want of affection and feeling on the
part of parents, that would induce them to exact from their
children more labour than they could perform without injury to
their health"; and he replied:

I do not imagine that there is the smallest difference between the
general affection of the lower order of the people, except with regard
to that which may be produced by the different circumstances in
which they are placed[2].

The second question was: "Do you conceive that it is not
injurious to the manufacturer to hazard, by overwork, the health
of the people so employed?"

Answer. If those persons were purchased by the manufacturers
I should say decisively, yes; but as they are not purchased by the
manufacturer and the country must bear all the loss of their strength
and their energy, it does not appear, at first sight, to be the interest
of the manufacturer to do so[3].

[1] *Commons' Committee of* 1816, pp. 64 and 73.
[2] *Ibid.* p. 38.   [3] *Ibid.* p. 28.

Owen had grasped the meaning of social responsibility, and his life was devoted to social service. But he was too wayward to observe the conventions of society and passed beyond the accepted social pale. The factory reformer became the socialist. Whether his disciples comprehended his philosophy we may doubt, but he understood better than anyone else their instinct for association and he gratified it.

It is not contended that Owen was responsible for all the associative effort of his generation; for with political and religious associations he had no sympathy. But the spirit which infected him infected others after him, rousing them to associate now for this, and now for that, social or religious or political purpose.

3. Types of Association

We may divide associations for social purposes into two classes.

To the first class belong associations formed to secure the abolition of some abuse. These naturally disappear when their object is attained. For example, there was the Anti-slavery Campaign in which Joseph Sturge and his Quaker brethren, following in the footsteps of William Wilberforce, played so prominent a part. By an organised crusade of political education the Abolitionists induced an originally hostile Parliament to emancipate the West Indian negroes in 1833, and to shorten the period of semi-servile apprenticeship in 1838. Yorkshire was the home of the Short Time Committees, which organised the campaign against White Slavery in England; and the Ten Hours Movement caused the Ten Hours Bill in 1847 to become the law of the land. From Lancashire came the Anti-Corn Law League, whose story is told in chapter XII.

The second class of association was the association for economic betterment—the Friendly Society, the Co-operative Society, the Trade Union. Conceived in enthusiasm and self-inspired, these Associations asked only of the State a legal framework in which to develop, but they did not win it without struggle and delay.

4—2

The Government was anxious to encourage thrift, but the development of the Friendly Societies was impeded for a time by legislation aimed at political conspiracy. The Corresponding Societies Act of 1799 prevented the Friendly Societies from forming a central organisation with branches, and the Dorchester Labourers in 1834[1] discovered the peril into which the ritual of oaths might lead innocent men.

These deterrents were removed by enabling legislation. In 1829 a central authority, the Registrar of Friendly Societies, was appointed to certify the rules of Friendly Societies desirous of registration, and to receive from these five-yearly returns, which were to be laid before Parliament. The Act of 1834 authorised the formation of societies for any "purpose which is not illegal". By subsequent legislation, which was rounded off in the comprehensive Act of 1875, further privileges and safeguards were conferred. But the Friendly Society Movement throughout the 19th century was wholly voluntary. In 1911 the trend was reversed by the passing of the National Insurance Act.

The Co-operative Societies were more suspect. They crept into legal recognition as the children of the Friendly Society, under the "frugal investments" clause of the Act of 1846, being compelled by the legal prejudice against association in restraint of trade to adopt this unnatural method. The dual element of trading and thrift was recognised when they were brought under the Industrial and Provident Societies Act of 1852; and in 1862 they received the boon of limited liability conferred on Trading Companies by the Companies Act of the same year. The accident of their legal origin survives; for in the United Kingdom all co-operative stores are still in the eyes of our law Industrial and Provident Societies, being registered under the Industrial and Provident Societies Act of 1893. To-day the Co-operative Movement is drawing closer to politics, following the lead of most of the continental countries, notably Belgium and Germany. Though we cannot say that there is any indication of the nationalisation of the movement, we may note that the growth of municipal trading in the 90's was, in principle, an application

[1] See below, p. 200.

of the consumers' association to monopolies of distribution such as tramways, water, electricity and gas.

The State was hostile to the growth of the Trade Union. The Act of 1799, with the amending Act of 1800, prohibited all Combinations of Workmen. The Act of 1824 legalised combinations in generous terms; but the Act of 1825 went back on this, curtailing the things which they might legally do and subjecting them once again to the common law of conspiracy[1]. Huskisson in justifying this change of face expatiated on the tyranny of a militant trades unionism, "representing a systematic union of the workmen of many different trades"[2]. It was a "kind of federal republic", whose mischievous operations, if not checked, would keep the commercial classes "in constant anxiety and fear about their interests and property". Arnold of Rugby a decade later wrote of them in the same strain: "You have heard I doubt not, of the trades unions; a fearful engine of mischief, ready to riot or assassinate; and I see no counteracting power"[3].

The counteracting power was their own weakness. The early militancy burnt itself out, and was succeeded at the turn of the century by a "New Spirit and a New Model". The new spirit was anti-militant, and the new model was a trade union representing a single craft. The Amalgamated Society of Engineers was founded in 1850 and served as a model to the Carpenters, Tailors, Compositors, Iron-founders, Bricklayers and others. The Trade Unions were now respectable, and in 1871 the State recognised the fact.

The transition to collectivism is marked by the growth of collective bargaining in the last thirty years of the 19th century. Socialism revived, and the new Socialism was State-Socialism. A Labour Party appeared in Parliament, and the State was called upon to play an increasing part in the settlement of industrial disputes and the determination of wages and hours. Then came the War, with its abnormal extension of Governmental activity

[1] For an analysis of the Acts of 1824 and 1825 see Dicey, *Law and Opinion*, pp. 189–195.

[2] March 29, 1825. *Speeches*, II. 369 sqq.

[3] Letter to the Chevalier Bunsen (1834), quoted in Lytton Strachey, *Eminent Victorians*, p. 197.

(rationing of materials, controlled establishments, dilution of labour, etc.). With the return of peace the prime issue is seen to be the relation of the State to the industrial corporations within the State, the Trade Union on the one hand and the Combine on the other—what shall it leave to them? how shall it control them?

4. THE STATE AND SOCIAL REFORM

In all the movements we have mentioned the spiritual stimulus, the initial drive and the solid successes have been provided by voluntary association. The State has not been the pioneer of social reform. Such a notion is the mirage of politicians. It has merely registered the insistent demands of organised voluntary effort or given legal recognition to accomplished facts. This is the distinctive note of English social development in the 19th century.

CHAPTER VI

ROBERT OWEN

1. New Lanark To-day

NEXT time you are in Scotland, go to the Falls of Clyde. Below Cora Linn, and a few paces from the cave into which Wallace sprang for safety, a part of the torrent is diverted on to a waterwheel, which supplies power to a machine shop. The wheel, like the shed in which it works, is old and much repaired. It is the wheel which used to drive the New Lanark Cotton Mills in the days of Robert Owen.

In 1913, when the writer visited New Lanark, the mills were the property of the Gourock Rope Co. Ltd. The original mill buildings have disappeared through fire or demolition, but traces of Owen's day survive. On the south side of the present mills some grass-grown steps lead towards an old building called the Dancing House. The basement in Owen's time was used as a kitchen. On the top floor are the Dancing Halls, with plain narrow galleries, from which a hundred years ago princes, statesmen and visitors from all the world over looked down with curious wonder at factory workers engaged in dance and drill. The galleries now are empty and dirty. The old School House, to the north of the Dancing House, also survives, and with its front of Grecian columns has some pretensions to architectural beauty. The author espied on a shelf in the Dancing House a dusty model which, so the worker showing him round had been assured by his father, was the original model of the Owenite Orbiston Community. Another workman, an old man of 84, remembered seeing Owen's wooden "Monitors" (see p. 58) lying about. He described them as square pieces of wood, like a two pound weight with four colours, white, black, blue and yellow—"white was the best and black the worst".

2. Owenite Literature

Go next to a library containing a collection of Owenite literature, such as that in Professor Foxwell's collection at the Goldsmiths' Library, Imperial Institute, South Kensington. Do not attempt to read it all, for if you do it will take you a twelvemonth, but arm yourself with Frank Podmore's excellent biography of Robert Owen (1906), and with the *Bibliography of Robert Owen, the Socialist, 1771–1858*, compiled by the National Library of Wales (1914), and make your own selection. You will do well to read the following:

1. *A New View of Society: or Essays on the Principles of the Formation of the Human Character, etc.* 1813–14.

2. *Observations on the Effect of the Manufacturing System.* 1815.

3. *Commons' Committee on the State of Children employed in the Manufactories of the United Kingdom.* 1816. Evidence by Robert Owen.

4. *Mr Owen's report to the Committee of the Association for the Relief of the manufacturing and labouring poor.* 1817. (Laid before the Commons' Committee on the Poor Laws 1816–19.)

5. *Report to the County of Lanark of a plan for relieving public distress and relieving discontent.* 1821.

Turn, too, over the files of Owen's periodicals—*The Crisis* (1832–1834), *The New Moral World* (1834–1846), Robert Owen's *Journal* (1851–1852), *The Millennial Gazette* (1856–1858)—all of them edited and mainly written by Robert Owen. And finally, read more closely *The Economist*, an Owenite periodical edited by George Mudie (1821–1822): the *Co-operative Magazine and Monthly Herald*, published with several changes of title by the London Co-operative Society (1826–1830): and the *British Co-operator* (April–Oct. 1830). The last three give the origins of Co-operation in this country[1].

---

[1] For a full list of early co-operative periodicals see H. S. Foxwell, Appendix to Anton Menger's *The Right to the Whole Produce of Labour*, pp. 253, 254.

3. NEW LANARK (1799–1824)

Owen's career divides into two periods: the New Lanark period (1799–1824), and the period subsequent to this (1824–1858).

From 1799 to 1809 Owen was manager of the New Lanark Mills and partner with some Manchester merchants. In 1809 he bought out his Manchester partners for £84,000, and found other partners in Scotland. The latter, however, objected to his expenditure on education and social betterment, so he resigned the managership and bought the business over their heads for £114,100 (the odd £100 secured it), and took a third set of partners, which included four Quakers and Jeremy Bentham. But Owen went too far even for them. In 1824, after serious friction, he resigned the management, which he had not actively exercised for several years, and in 1829 he ceased to be a shareholder.

At New Lanark Owen achieved great things. Successful in an age when many were making fortunes, chivalrous in an age when calculation ruled supreme, Owen set up an industrial edifice which was a source of amazement to his workpeople and the world at large. He reduced the hours of work, paid full wages and abstained from dismissals during a period of business stagnation, established a sick fund, a savings-bank, and a store which supplied the necessaries of life at wholesale prices, and built for the children of his workpeople a school in which he taught them by object-lesson, nature study, song, and dance. The workers responded quickly. Drunkenness and illegitimacy, prevalent vices in the old days, disappeared, and all the while the business prospered. Owen's philosophy was a simple one. Environment is the cause of differences in character, and environment is under human control. If the care of inanimate machines yields such high profits, how much more will be yielded by the care of animate men and women? But the adult cannot profit by this care unless as a child he is educated aright. Unfortunately, Owen's views on education brought him into conflict with the Church and the world of respectability, so that the benevolent, quixotic employer of New Lanark, admired of princes and con-

sulted by Parliament, became the arch-heretic, the outcast, the
father of Socialism. But outlawry only increased his following
by rallying to his side that great section of the working class
which was alive to existing evils and passionately eager for
emancipation. When he retired in disgust from the world of
Capitalism, he carried his disciples with him whither he pleased.

Even at New Lanark Owen showed the fantastic side which in
later life became so pronounced. The zeal with which he in-
spected the workpeople's dwellings, hunting for specks of dirt
or dust, enraged the women folk, who called the Inspecting
Committee "Bug Hunters". Still more fantastic was the device
which he introduced for the maintenance of discipline. Each
worker had, suspended above his or her head, a block of wood,
called a "Silent Monitor", and the colour at the front told the
conduct of the individual during the preceding day. Bad was
denoted by black, indifferent by blue, good by yellow and
excellent by white. Workers who objected to the colour
awarded to them had the right of complaint to Owen himself.
But he says: "Such complaints very rarely occurred. The act
of setting down the number in the book of character, never to
be blotted out, might be likened to the supposed recording angel
marking the good and bad deeds of poor human nature"[1]. In
his school the minimum age of admission was one, and in order
that no harsh words or actions might hurt the children's character, he selected as schoolmaster a certain James Buchanan, who
had been "previously trained by his wife to perfect submission
to her will"[2].

These things, however, are only trifles. They do not alter the
fact that his work as a model employer and pioneer of education
brought him world-wide celebrity, and caused him to be consulted by Parliament and Public Bodies on matters connected
not only with education but also with schemes of social ameliora-
tion, to which from 1815 onwards his time and writings were
devoted. Owen was a dreamer, but he looked forward. He believed in machinery and understood the possibilities of large
scale industrial production. He was, therefore, heard with re-

---

[1] Owen's *Autobiography*, I. 81.   [2] *Ibid.* I. 140.

spect by historical and statistical writers like Malthus, who rejected impatiently the doctrines of perfectibility propounded by William Godwin.

4. COMMUNITY EXPERIMENTS

In 1821 a "Co-operative and Economical Society" was formed in London, its ultimate object being—to quote the constitution—"to establish a village of unity and mutual co-operation, combining agriculture, manufactures, and trades upon the plan projected by Robert Owen". This opened the era of Community experiments[1], Orbiston in Scotland and a cluster of others in England, ending with the Harmony Community, of which Owen was for sometime the president, at Queenwood, Hampshire. Their makers dreamed of a brotherhood of freely associating individuals, rid of the oppressions of Government and the frauds of competition; working for the joy of work, and playing with orderly zeal; pursuing agriculture where they would see the whole process from the sowing of the seed to the eating of the grain, and manufacturing with the aid of triumphant machinery the simple and useful products that would suffice for their maintenance. But the altruistic ardour of the townsmen was not equal to the successful conduct of rural economy, and bad cooking brought on indigestion, the parent of egoism.

However, it was in this rare atmosphere that the eminently solid Co-operative Movement was born.

> Our Cargo is Labour, our goal is the Land,
> And Owen, our Captain, bids all heave a hand.

5. THE LEADER OF WORKING-CLASS MOVEMENTS

Between 1824 and 1829 Owen had been absent in America, founding a community there, and losing money over it. In 1829 he returned, and from 1830 to 1834 he was the central figure in the wave of associative enthusiasm which swept over the

---

[1] See G. J. Holyoake, *History of Co-operation*, c. x. "The Lost Communities". *The Co-operative Magazine* (1826) vol. I. supplies details about Orbiston, Exeter, Cork, and Newhome (Jersey).

English working classes at this time. He was President of the
first Co-operative Congresses (Congress was a word which he
brought from America), President of the National Equitable
Labour Exchange in London, and President of the Grand
National Consolidated Trades Union of Great Britain and
Ireland. Political Associations, however, had no attraction for
him, and he viewed with disdain the excitement over the Reform
Bill of 1832. Reform meetings were too noisy and petty. He
liked great sweeping schemes which he, Robert Owen, could
direct. So too, although his evidence before the Factory Committee of 1816 was the evidence of an enlightened reformer, he
took no part in the Ten Hours Movement in the 'thirties and
'forties. At this stage of his career factory reform seemed to him
a paltry thing, a compromise with the Demon of Competition.

6. CO-OPERATION

While Owen was in America, the London Co-operators were
busy with propaganda. Their journals give evidence of discussion
and intention rather than of performance, but they record:

1824. London Co-operative Society (Barton Street).

1825. London Co-operative Society (Red Lion Square).

1826. April. Project of a big community within fifty miles
of London.

1826. June. Co-operative Community Fund Association (1st
London Co-operative Community—a small scale venture).

1827. Union Exchange Society (Red Lion Square): a store
projected by the L.C.S. to raise funds for a community.

1830. 1st London Co-operative Society: store-keeper, William
Lovett.

1830. 1st London Manufacturing Community.

With Owen's return, the Co-operative Movement spread to the
Provinces. The *Birmingham Co-operative Herald* (1st number
April 1, 1829) was followed by the *Lancashire* later *Lancashire
and Yorkshire Co-operator* (1831). Between 1831 and 1834 seven
Co-operative Congresses were held—Manchester, 1831; Birming-
ham, 1831; London, Gray's Inn Road, 1832; Liverpool, 1832;

Huddersfield, 1833; London, Charlotte Street, 1833; Barnsley, 1834. Owen presided at four of these, and his journal *The Crisis* supplies the information for the proceedings at the last three.

The exact nature of these early co-operative societies is not always clear. The Brighton society was advertised as the model. "They purchased at wholesale prices such articles as they were in the daily habit of consuming...adding the difference or profit to the common stock (for it is a fundamental rule of these societies never to divide any portion of the funds, but to suffer it to accumulate till it becomes sufficient to employ all the members thereon...)"[1]. The societies were a combination of retail store and productive society, and they were ready to sell their goods to outsiders or exchange them with those of other societies. The store element predominated at first, when co-operation was regarded as a means of raising funds for the establishment of a land community. At the time of the Trades Union boom the productive side took first place. Work in a co-operative society was advocated as an alternative to employment by capitalist employers.

It would seem that some hundreds of these societies were in existence for a time, but they were as short-lived as the early trades unions. Barely a dozen of the co-operative stores now in existence date back to this early period. It was not till 1844 that the Rochdale Pioneers opened their store, and set the Co-operative Movement on the lines since followed by the rest of England and most other countries of Europe. These lines are, sale of goods at market prices, cash payment, and distribution of surplus profit among members proportionately to the amount of their purchases[2]. But the connection between the old and the new Co-operation is visible in the first rules of the Rochdale

---

[1] *Birmingham Co-operative Herald*, April 1829, No. 1.

[2] Rochdale's claim to have been the first society to pay a dividend on purchases has been challenged. A notice in the *Co-operative News* of 1870 runs: "To all whom it may concern:—this is to certify that when the Meltham Mills (Yorkshire) Cooperative Society was established in 1827, it commenced paying profits on the amount of each member's purchases at the store—witness my hand, this 30th day of September, 1871, as one of the founders of the said store—John Broadbent." The examination of old dividend books supports the claim.

Pioneers. The Society's objects embraced the establishment of a store for the sale of provisions, clothing, etc., the building of houses for its members, the manufacture of such articles as would give employment to those of its members who were out of work or under-paid, a "self-supporting Colony of united interests", and a Temperance Hotel.

7. THE EQUITABLE LABOUR EXCHANGES

The small productive societies above-mentioned at first disposed of their goods to neighbours or, by barter, to other societies. To organise the exchange, a Co-operative Bazaar was opened at 19 Greville Street by the First London Co-operative Society in 1830. Owen took up the idea, and on September 3, 1832, started the National Equitable Labour Exchange in Gray's Inn Road. The idea was that goods should be brought to the Bazaar and exchanged on the basis of the time spent in their production. Time notes were to take the place of coin. In fact this principle was never followed. The storekeeper valued the goods brought to him in base coin, and reckoning one hour as equal to sixpence, priced an article which he judged worth 10s. at "20 hours".

The Exchange opened with a boom, and the court-yard was blocked with goods. The Labour Notes went to a premium, and it was fondly believed that the millennium had arrived. Some of the neighbouring shop-keepers, some of the theatres, and even the toll-keeper at Waterloo Bridge took Labour Notes instead of sixpences. But this did not last long. The cunning ones took from the store the goods that were under-valued and resold them at a profit, while the bad bargains remained as unsaleable stock. Quarrels ensued. The owner of the premises turned out Owen and set up in opposition, whereupon Owen moved to other premises and tried once again.

The chief customers of the Exchanges were small societies of carpenters, shoemakers, painters, hatters and tailors, who tried in this way to sell articles made by their unemployed members. For a little while their efforts prospered. The cloth-makers re-

ported that they had exchanged cloth for leather, the carpenters
fitted up a shop for the shoemakers who had promised shoes in
exchange. But they could not eat shoes or clothes, so they took
their goods to the Bazaar, received Labour Notes and went with
these to the bread shop. There they found that there was no
mysterious virtue in a Labour Note. The shop-keeper would give
no more for the notes than he could get in value from a pick at
the Bazaar, and often he gave considerably less, because the
workers were starving and ready to take anything. By 1834 the
Labour Exchanges had perished, and they would not have
lasted as long as this, had not Owen paid in large sums out of
his own pocket, including the profits on his Sunday lectures.

As we trace the unhappy careers of the Land Communities and
Labour Exchanges, we naturally ask how one who had been a
successful manufacturer could expect such ventures to succeed.
The answer is, that Owen and his disciples were uncompromising
idealists, who soared above mundane things. When, for the fulfil-
ment of their ideal, they were forced to descend to the world of
reality, in which alone things can be done, they descended with
a bump which surprised them and smashed their ventures. They
failed, not because their ideals were wrong, but because they
were incapable of accommodating themselves to facts so prosaic
as the processes of agriculture and the technique of £. s. d.

8. TRADES UNIONS

Owen next moved on to Trades Unions.

In 1825 Place had written to Sir Francis Burdett: "He knows
nothing of the working people who can suppose that, when left
at liberty to act for themselves, without being driven into
permanent associations by the oppression of the laws, they will
continue to contribute money for distant and doubtful experiments, for uncertain and precarious benefits"[1]. The outburst
of militant unionism (1830–1834) gave the lie to this confident
pronouncement; and Place watched its rise and fall, regretting
that the working classes had been drawn away from politics by

---

[1] Graham Wallas, *Francis Place*, p. 217.

the "nonsensical doctrines preached by Robert Owen and others respecting communities and goods in common"[1].

The Trades Union Movement, however, was wider than Owenism, and Owen did not see eye to eye with its militancy. It was to him a second best. It is surely a perversion of history to say, as do the exponents of Guild Socialism, that at the present day "the world is returning to the ideas of Owen", that Owen "saw that Labour, in order to control its own life, must create an instrument capable of carrying on production", and that Owen "aimed at one big union to include all the workers, fashioned according to a definite design"[2]. The designer of "villages of unity and mutual co-operation" would have shrunk from the remorseless aggression of class-conscious warfare. Whatever Owen's faults were, he was never a blackmailer of Society. If he was fascinated by the idea of one big union, it was not because he saw in it a weapon for delivering a simultaneous stroke, but because he hoped to make thereby wholesale conversions to the gospel of Owen. In any case his connection with the movement was brief, briefer even than the movement itself, for he resigned his presidency of the "Grand National Consolidated Trades Union of Great Britain and Ireland", when they appointed as an official someone who in Owen's opinion was intemperate and untrustworthy.

9. LATER YEARS

From 1834 to 1858, the year of his death, Owen was a visionary pure and simple. The period down to 1834 he declared had been "an awful crisis" in human affairs, now happily terminated; and therefore his paper, *The Crisis*, was to be replaced by *The New Moral World, in which Truth, Industry and Knowledge will reign for ever triumphant*. In 1835 he founded "The Association of all Classes of all Nations". Applicants had to attend his Lectures for three months, and were examined in his philosophy before being elected members. In 1836 he claimed to have 100,000 members. A writer has called this phase of his work

[1] Quoted in Webb, *History of Trade Unionism*, p. 141.
[2] Cole and Mellor, *The Meaning of Industrial Freedom*, p. 14.

"a forestalling of University extension tacked on to the co-operative and trade unionist movement"[1]. It was certainly this, but it was also at every turn a resounding advertisement of Owen himself. So great was his hold on his disciples that they listened to him week after week expounding with little variation his New View of Society and the details of his own career. But this Association too, after a brief life, passed away, degenerating in its last days into a meeting-place for the denunciation of marriage and religion; and in 1839 Owen went off to Queenwood in Hampshire to become the Governor of the Harmony Community. This, the last of the Community experiments, perished through mismanagement and lack of funds in 1845.

In the last ten years of his life the visionary became the spiritualist, absorbed in table rapping and the issue of rhapsodic journals, such as the *Journal Explanatory of the Means to well-place the Population of the World* (1851–52), and the *Millennial Gazette* (1856–58). In 1858 he died at his birthplace in Newtown, Montgomeryshire, at the age of 87.

Owen was at once an autocrat and a lover of the people: an egoist with an intense belief in himself, and yet uniformly benevolent and overflowing with kindness. His life was one long protest against the unnecessary misery which he saw around him. It was a protest, too, against the narrow orthodoxy of the religious teachers of the day, who complacently assured their flocks that the divisions of poor and rich, the sorrows of the one and the luxuries of the other, were the work of a divine providence. Owen was the arch-heretic of the 19th century. He rejected the gospel of Manchester and preached in its place the gospel of socialism. With him it was a dream. Later and less presuming men have made it a reality.

---

[1] *Dictionary of Political Economy*. Robert Owen.

CHAPTER VII

THE ORIGINS OF BRITISH SOCIALISM

1. DEFINITION OF SOCIALISM

"ALL theoretical attempts to show the proletariat the goal of its efforts, to call upon it to take up the struggle, to organise the struggle, to show it the way along which it must march if it is to succeed—all that is what we understand by modern Socialism and all practical attempts actually to carry out these ideas we call the Social Movement. Socialism and the Social Movement, therefore, are but two sides of the same phenomenon. Their relation to each other is that of thought and deed, of soul and body"[1].

This is an attempt to define Socialism according to its historical content, and it is an attempt along the right lines. The verbal antithesis of Socialism is individualism, but this antithesis has little significance. The socialists of the early 19th century were strong individualists, when judged by the standards of to-day. The historical antithesis to Socialism is not individualism but capitalism, an -ism, however, which no one officially professes. Both terms derive their significance from the economic changes which date from the middle of the 18th century and bear the name of the Industrial Revolution. These changes divided the population much more sharply than before into rival camps of employers and employed, on the one side the capitalist employer, on the other side the proletariat of employees, whose protest was Socialism. Socialism is thus the product of recent industrial history, and inasmuch as England was the country in which the industrial revolution was first accomplished, England was also the country in which Socialism had its birth.

[1] Sombart, *Socialism and the Socialist Movement*, p. 14.

2. ANTECEDENTS

Socialism had historical antecedents in this country, as in others, but, if a word is desired by which to express them, "communism" is to be preferred. Communism takes us back to the days of Plato's *Republic* and the first Christian communities, whose members were "of one heart and of one soul: neither said any of them that ought of the things which he possessed was his own; but they had all things common"—as is written in the Acts of the Apostles, chapter iv, verse 32.

In English history the spirit of communism breaks out in times of national stress. In the days of Wycliffe John Ball raised the standard of social revolt. He called upon the people to fell the great ones of the earth and deliver themselves from bondage. "Things cannot go well in England nor ever will, until all goods are held in common, and until there will be neither serfs nor gentlemen, and we shall all be equal"[1].

The next call to social reconstruction comes at the time of the Reformation. Sir Thomas More's *Utopia* (1516) is Plato's community in Christian form.

The years of the Commonwealth (1649–60) witnessed the decline and fall of the Diggers or True Levellers, whose leader was Gerrard Winstanley. Like Spence at a later day, Winstanley was engrossed by the idea that the great crime of Society was land robbery. The earth was a common treasury, and this treasury had been filched from the people. He therefore summoned his followers to dig up commons, parks and other untilled lands. But the Diggers' efforts were not popular with the peasantry. Of two of their settlements we are told that the people "pulled down the few huts, cut the spades and hoes to pieces and maltreated the diggers"[2].

The inspiration of communism is the same throughout the ages. It is the cry of the poor and oppressed, the appeal to unselfishness, the demand for equality of persons and sharing of

---

[1] Froissart, *Collection des Chroniques*, VIII. c. 106: quoted in Beer, *History of British Socialism*, p. 28.
[2] Beer, *op. cit.* p. 62.

things, and it is always on the land, never in the town, that the new state of society is to be planted. For the land is the symbol of the simple, the natural, the perfect life. These beliefs and yearnings are at times dormant, but at other times, amid the stress of national and religious excitement, they burst forth in word and deed, in Utopian dreams and the ugly reality of Peasants' Wars.

In England the 18th century opened sluggishly, and ended in a raging torrent. The spirit of religion was quickened by Methodism, which made its strongest appeal to the new industrial mass, the human product of the new industrial revolution. Christianity itself was challenged by the generation which came after Wesley. Paine in his *Rights of Man* (1790) proclaimed the age of reason, Godwin in his *Political Justice* (1793) enunciated the philosophy of anarchy. An old cry was raised in new form, when Thomas Spence in 1775 proposed that the rent of all lands should be divided among the people, even as the rent of the enclosed moor outside his native town of Newcastle had been divided among the freemen of the town[1].

But these were small voices beside the reverberating crash of the French Revolution. All the elements of discontent in England responded to its echo. Organisations sprang up to applaud and extend the triumph of liberty. Thomas Hardy, a Scottish shoemaker, founded the London Corresponding Society (1792), and the left wing of the Whigs formed themselves into the Friends of the People. The Government, confronted by war abroad and the threat of revolution at home, adopted a policy of repression. The Corresponding Societies Act of 1799 scotched the revolutionary societies, though not before they had roused the industrial districts of Lancashire and Yorkshire to a knowledge of the French Revolution. For the first five years of peace the policy of repression was continued and stiffened, but the very stiffening is a proof that the measures by which order had been maintained in war-time would not be tolerated in peace. The laws against association and the expression of opinion were notori-

---

[1] *On the Mode of Administering the Landed Estate of the Nation as a Joint-Stock Property, in Parochial Partnerships by Dividing the Rent* (1775).

ously evaded, and therefore, as soon as the Government dared,
the pressure was relaxed and a vent was allowed to the forces of
discontent. Hence the political unions, hence trades unions and
co-operation, hence also the first clear voice of Socialism.

3. ORIGIN OF THE WORD

None of the early English socialists used the word "socialism"
or called themselves "socialists", but the appellation is justified.
The bulk of their writings appeared in the same decade as the
word. Their critique was of the same order as that which was
prevalent in the meetings and debates at which the word first
made its appearance. When they came to construct, they
accepted in whole or part a gospel of Owenism, and Owenism
was synonymous with Socialism.

Beer[1], in his notice of the *Co-operative Magazine* (1826–30)
(which was mainly a résumé of the proceedings of the London
Co-operative Society) says:

"In these debates the term 'socialist' must have been coined.
It is found for the first time in *The Co-operative Magazine* of
November, 1827—in the same year in which Robert Owen published, in *The New Harmony Gazette*, a series of articles under the
head 'Social System'". And he goes on:

"In a footnote to a communication of the Brighton Co-
operators the editor of the *Co-operative Magazine* observes that
the value of a commodity consisted both of present and past
labour (capital or stock), and the main question was 'whether
it is more beneficial that this capital should be individual or
common'. Those who argued that it should be in the hands of
individual employers were the modern political economists of
the type of James Mill and Malthus, while those who thought it
should be common were 'the Communionists and Socialists'".

But we can point to an earlier use; for in the Diary of William,
second son of Robert Owen, published in 1906 by the In-
diana Historical Society, U.S.A., there occurs under the date
"November 21, 1824", the following entry: "Mr Lloyd, after

---

[1] *History of British Socialism*, I. 187.

dinner...returned with us (i.e., W. and R. Owen), and we read to him the proposals for a socialist community".

"Socialist" is here interchangeable with "Owenite" or "Co-operative". And the early English socialists, who have been styled Ricardian Socialists because of the extent to which they drew on Ricardo's theory of labour value, may with equal propriety be styled Co-operative Socialists, when we wish to particularise them by their constructive proposals.

G. J. Holyoake, in his *History of Co-operation*, carries us over the succeeding decade. "For 13 years now (1831 44) co-operation has to be traced through Socialism. Store-keeping had in many cases failed, and, where successful, its profits were insufficient to pave the way to the new world, much less defray the costs of that rather extensive erection. Grand schemes were revived, in which idleness and vice, silliness and poverty were to cease by mutual arrangement. This state of things came to bear the name of Socialism"[1]. And again: "The members of the Grand Society of All Classes of All Nations wisely refused to be called Owenites, although they persisted in their affection for Mr Owen, whom they designated at the same time their 'social and right reverend father'. At the Manchester Congress of All Classes of All Nations...they determined to call themselves 'Socialists'"[2]. After 1838 the socialist movement was swallowed up in Chartism. The official mind diagnosed Socialism as a new edition of communism, distinguished by irreligion and immorality. This is a reflex of Owen's revolt against orthodox religion and the suspected community of sex in the Owenite Communities. It was also believed that Owen and his leading supporters advocated the artificial restriction of population[3]. The bundle of Home Office papers marked "1840—Socialists" is mainly a collection of correspondence with incensed prelates, who had complained of irreligion and blasphemies at Queenwood (the Harmony Community) and elsewhere.

The movement died down in England, but the word stuck.

[1] Holyoake, *History of Co-operation*, I. 115.
[2] *Ibid.* I. 144.
[3] See G. J. Holyoake, *Sixty years of an Agitator's Life*, part I, chap. 25— "The mysterious parcel left at the *Manchester Guardian* Office".

From England it was taken to France. Louis Reybaud, in the preface to his *Socialistes Modernes*, bearing the date of April, 1856, says: "Voici vingt ans bientôt qu'au début de cette suite d'études, j'eus le triste honneur d'introduire dans notre langue le mot de *socialiste*, sans prévoir quel bruit ni quelles luttes s'y rattacheraient". His studies include Saint Simon, Fourier and Owen, but he does not deal with the writers whom we know as the early English socialists.

After the publication in 1848 of John Stuart Mill's *Principles of Political Economy*, English economists, as Professor Foxwell says[1], were men of one book, and though Mill frequented the meetings of the early co-operators[2], he does not seem to have counted them as socialists. Socialism for him meant the romantic Utopias of Fourier and Owen, or the academic industrialism of Saint Simon and Comte. It is to the influence of Mill and to the absorption of the co-operative socialists in Chartism that we must ascribe the curious neglect under which the early English socialists for many years suffered.

4. THE EARLY ENGLISH SOCIALISTS

Among the Ricardian Socialists five stand out:

Charles Hall, M.D.   1805. The Effects of Civilisation on the People of the European States.

1805. Observations on the principal Conclusion in Mr Malthus's *Essay on Population*.

William Thompson.   1824. An Inquiry into the Principles of the Distribution of Wealth most conducive to Human Happiness, etc.

[1] Introduction to Anton Menger, *Right to the whole Produce of Labour*, p. 78.

[2] Holyoake, *History of Co-operation*, I. 92.

Cf. "When this debate (sc. on population) was ended, another was commenced on the general merits of Mr Owen's system....The principal champion on their side was a very estimable man, with whom I was well acquainted, Mr William Thompson, of Cork".—J. S. Mill, *Autobiography*, p. 124.

William Thompson.	1827.	Labour rewarded. The claims of Labour and Capital conciliated.
John Gray.	1825.	A Lecture on Human Happiness.
	1831.	The Social System.
Thomas Hodgskin.	1825.	Labour defended against the claims of Capital.
	1832.	The Natural and Artificial Right of Property contrasted.
John Francis Bray.	1839.	Labour's Wrongs and Labour's Remedy.

We have spoken already of Hall and Thompson (p. 47 above). Thompson was at once the disciple of Bentham and Owen. In imitation of Bentham, he left his body to science. In admiration of Owen he left his property to found Co-operative Communities and his books to the Library of the first community thus founded. But this part of his Will was successfully disputed on the ground that it was a bequest for immoral purposes. A good example of the horror which Owenism aroused among the respectable classes is furnished by this trial. In all solemnity the Counsel opposing the Will declared: "It is very unfair that we married men should be debating this topic, it ought really to be tried by a jury of matrons"[1].

John Gray, an old schoolboy of Repton and a prosperous man of business, spent his later life in London and Scotland brooding upon the ills of society and expressing in print his wrath and remedies. Thomas Hodgskin was a Radical journalist, who lectured at the newly established Mechanics Institute in London and afterwards joined the staff of *The Economist* at the time that Herbert Spencer was writing for it. John Francis Bray was a journeyman printer, but of his life we know very little.

The theme of all these writers was the Right of the Labourer to the Whole Produce of his Labour. Cobbett had preached the Right to Subsistence, which he based on a curious glorification of the Elizabethan Poor Law, but with Cobbett's desire for the revival of an agricultural past the early socialists had no sym-

---

[1] Quoted in *The Crisis*, 1833, IV. 55.

pathy. Twenty years later Louis Blanc was to proclaim in Paris the Right to Work, but this Right also would have left them cold. For, if some people in England had too little work, many more had far too much. The Right to Work elevated the State into a great giver out of livelihood, and they hated the State. The Right which accorded with their environment was the Right to the Whole Produce of Labour, and in their hands it was a theme of hope. They saw that England was a country of immense productive capacity, and they believed that this capacity could be made to yield happiness to the working classes, if it were accompanied by a more equitable system of distribution. The classical economists, the gloomy and mechanical speculators of the Ricardian School, had, in their opinion, committed the fatal blunder of confining their attention to production and neglecting distribution altogether. They were angered by the ugly paradox of Englishmen starving in the richest and most progressive country in Europe, and they denounced in scathing terms the pessimisms of the Ricardian economists, who threw their rigid laws of wages, population and diminishing returns, like a wet blanket, over the passionate demands of the workers for a better state of things.

The Ricardian Socialists were fairly unanimous on their critical side. They appealed with confidence to the economists themselves for the vindication of their main contention. They could find in the writings of Locke, Adam Smith and Ricardo passages which seemed to justify their claim that labour was the source of all value. They fastened on the classical distinctions between productive and unproductive labour, between the natural and artificial systems of society, between fixed and circulating capital, and they elaborated these into an argument to the effect that there was a great pool of surplus value, which by the chicanery of the exchanges the merchants and capitalists seized for themselves, but which belonged by right to the labourers who created it. They fortified their arguments with statistics drawn from Patrick Colquhoun's Treatise on *The Wealth, Power and Resources of the British Empire* (1815). Again and again they quoted figures from his famous Table Four, which sets forth the distribution of the national income among the various ranks, degrees and descriptions in the realm, from the Royal Family with £146,000 a year down to the labouring people employed in agriculture and mines with a family income of £45 a year. After reading their arguments and illustrations, we feel that they anticipated Marx's theory of surplus value, without wrapping themselves in Marx's gloomy fatalism or supporting their theory by the argument from history, which Marx extracted from his researches into English Parliamentary Papers. It is to be noted that the contact between Bray and Marx is direct, for the latter, in his *Misère de la Philosophie* (1847), quotes nine pages from Bray's book, *Labour's Wrongs and Labour's Remedies*, though in his greater work, *Das Kapital*, he does not even mention Bray's name. It was fortunate for Marx that Bray was so little remembered.

On their constructive side the socialists were not in complete agreement. Hodgskin was an out-and-out individualist; Bray drew near to modern Socialism by advocating State ownership of the means of production. But the position of both was exceptional. The standpoint of Thompson and Gray was more characteristic of the early socialist thought. These two swallowed Owenism and Land Utopias entire. In Owen they forgot Ricardo, and in one respect this was a pity. A closer study of Ricardo might have led them to avoid some of the nonsense about currency and credit with which their Utopias are disfigured.

CHAPTER VIII

COBBETT AND COBBETT'S ENGLAND

1. LIFE

WILLIAM COBBETT was born at Farnham in Surrey in 1762. He died in June 1835, member of Parliament for the town of Oldham in Lancashire. In this same period of years England grew from a country mainly agricultural with its centre of gravity in the South into a country mainly industrial with its centre of gravity in the North.

In 1784 Cobbett, in a second attempt to join the Navy, was enlisted by mistake in the 54th of the Line[1], and between 1785 and 1791 was with his regiment in Nova Scotia. He rose with exceptional speed to the rank of Sergeant-Major; and, if we may believe his own account, he was a terror to his C.O., his Adjutant and his Quartermaster. His officers he considered "supreme Jackasses". "They in fact resigned all the discipline of the Regiment to me, and I very freely left them to swagger about and to get roaring drunk out of the profits of their pillage"[2]. He had to instruct his Adjutant in punctuation and spelling, and when the station was visited by Government Commissioners, it was Cobbett who had to draw up the report. He soon fell foul of the thing that is as old as war itself, the peculation of the Quartermaster. "The Quartermaster, who had the issuing of the men's provisions to them, kept about a fourth part of it to himself. This the old Sergeants told me had been the case for many years"[3]. He therefore collected evidence, bent on exposing the abuse as soon as he was out of the Army, but when his chance came in 1792, he declined to appear before the Court Martial and hid himself.

[1] The 54th West Norfolk—since amalgamated with the 39th Dorsetshire Regiment.
[2] *Political Register*, December 6, 1817.
[3] *Ibid*. June 17, 1809 (column 902).

In 1792 he married, and after a tour in France went out to the United States. In 1800 he returned to England, and in 1801 set up with a partner as bookseller and stationer at the Crown and Mitre in Pall Mall Street, London. He opened his English venture with the issue of *Porcupine's Works*, a reprint of his American writings in twelve volumes. (His literary activities in America had included a daily newspaper named *Porcupine's Gazette*.) On January 16, 1802, he issued the first number of the famous *Political Register*, which, with varying fortunes and at various prices, was continued to the year of his death.

At first the *Register* was ultra-Tory, and the mob broke his windows in Pall Mall when he declined to join in the rejoicings over the peace of Amiens in 1802. Cobbett wrote:

The alliterative words, peace and plenty, sound well in a song, or make a pretty transparency in the window of an idiot; but the things which these harmonious words represent are not always in unison[1].

The idiots in reply made a pretty transparency in the windows of his shop. But about the time of Pitt's death (1806), Cobbett changed his politics[2], passing from ultra-Toryism towards ultra-Radicalism. The soldier life, which explains his early Toryism, left memories of abuses, which turned him into the eager champion of soldiers' wrongs. In 1810 he came into conflict with the law by his denunciation of the savage way in which the revolt of the militia at Ely was quelled by the German Legion in English service. The men's grievance was stoppage of pay for knap-sacks, and Cobbett in his *Register* scoffed at the Government's severity. "O, yes; they merit a double-tailed cat. Base dogs! What, mutiny for the sake of the price of a knap-sack! Lash them! Flog them! Base rascals!"[3] But Cobbett incautiously concluded the article with remarks about loyalty and French methods (or Prussian methods as we should call them now); and for this he was punished with two years' imprisonment, a fine of £1000 and heavy bail as a security for good behaviour in the future.

[1] Quoted in E. I. Carlyle, *William Cobbett*, p. 86.
[2] Cf. *Edinburgh Review*, July 1807.
[3] *Political Register*, July 1, 1809 (column 993).

Just at this time (1810) the Report of the Bullion Committee provoked a national controversy, and Cobbett in gaol became a student of the currency. His opinions were issued in a series of letters in the *Political Register* (1810–11), which were afterwards issued as a pamphlet, *Paper against Gold*. To the end of his life he was bitten with the currency mania, and although between 1812 (when he came out of prison) and 1819 currency topics were over-shadowed by other issues, Cobbett never let them rest, and he got his chance for a second campaign during the period of the resumption of cash payments (1819–23) and the depression of agriculture with which it was popularly associated.

Cobbett regarded the paper currency as one of the three great burdens left by the Napoleonic war, the other two being taxation and the national debt. He argued that to permit the holders of debt stock created during the period of depreciation to reap the full benefit of the resumption of cash payments in the enhanced value of their holdings, would be an act of injustice to the general body of taxpayers; and he frightened the Government by spreading abroad the idea that the only remedy was something which in plain language meant the repudiation of the national debt. "The public debt", he said once, "may be compared to a barrel of Wiltshire ale which when once tasted is sure to be drunk out"[1].

In the social disturbances of 1815–19 Cobbett, warned by two years of gaol, played a cautious part. In 1816 when, as Bamford testified, Cobbett was read on every cottage hearth (see above, p. 24), he took the greatest care to avoid the incitement of disorder. On November 30 he published in his *Letter to the Luddites* a defence of machinery, which, in the opinion of Harriet Martineau, "must have been far more effectual than a regiment of dragoons"[2]. But he knew that Government had no intention of allowing him to remain at large, whatever he actually wrote; and when Habeas Corpus was suspended, he left for America, where he stayed till 1819.

The price of his *Register* had been 1s. 0½d., a price too high for individual working men to afford. Accordingly on November 2,

---

[1] *Manchester Lectures* (1832), III. 7.
[2] Harriet Martineau, *History of the Peace* (1816–1846), **p. 29.**

1816, while continuing to issue the stamped edition of the
Register at 1s. 0½d., he also published an unstamped edition at
2d.[1], at the same time reprinting several back numbers in the
cheaper form. He avoided the stamp duty of sixpence a copy
on newspapers by omitting all items of news[2]. It was to stop
this in particular that the Government passed the Newspaper
Stamp Duties' Act of 1819 (p. 29, above).

The Government succeeded in its purpose. It destroyed for a
time the bulk of his sales; and the consequent loss of income,
added to the expense of an unsuccessful election (for in 1820, on
his return from America, he stood for Coventry), landed Cobbett
in bankruptcy in June 1820.

Between 1820 and 1830 Cobbett was the leading popular force
in the agitation for political reform. In addition to these
activities, he found time to write the works which entitle him to
an enduring place in English literature. In this decade were
published the *Monthly Sermons*, 1821–22, *Cottage Economy*[3],
1821–22, *The History of the Protestant Reformation*, 1824–25,
The Poor Man's Friend, 1826 ("This is my favourite work.
I bestowed more labour upon it than upon any large volume
that I ever wrote"), *Advice to Young Men*, 1829, and, greatest
of all, the *Rural Rides*, published in 1830 and consisting of letters
written on his tours between 1820 and 1826.

When Cobbett reduced the price of his *Register* in November
1816, his enemies called it "Twopenny Trash". Accordingly in
1830 he took the name which his enemies had presented to him
for some papers he was issuing in the course of the Reform Bill

---

[1] This circumstance and the advertisement given to Cobbett in the often
quoted passage by Bamford are liable to leave the impression that about
1816 Cobbett for the first time became a factor of national importance.
The following quotations will correct this:

Jan. 1810. The *Edinburgh Review* (vol. 15) points, in proof of the growth
of the "democrats", to the "prodigious sale and still more prodigious circulation" of Cobbett's *Register*.

Feb. 1813. Wellington (*Dispatches*, x. 101) writes from the Peninsula:
"Our newspapers have already got hold of it (a squabble upon the Cortes),
and if Cobbett takes it up, it is not unlikely to get into Parliament".

[2] E. I. Carlyle, *William Cobbett*, p. 189.

[3] The *Edinburgh Review*, vol. 38, contains a sympathetic review of this
work.

controversy. *Twopenny Trash, or Politics for the Poor* ran from July 1830 to July 1832. These years saw his last fight with the law, and Cobbett gained a brilliant victory. He was prosecuted by Government for abetting by his articles in the *Political Register* the disorders which accompanied the revolt of the agricultural labourers in 1830. The trial took place at the Guildhall in July 1831, and Cobbett undertook his own defence with astonishing vigour and ability. The jury could not agree, and Cobbett was acquitted. "The prosecution of Cobbett", says his biographer, "was almost the last occasion on which an English Ministry endeavoured to restrain the political utterances of the press by legal proceedings"[1].

In 1832 he entered the House of Commons as member of Parliament for Oldham, and here he was less successful than when he had the country for his audience and was bound by no rules save those set by the perils of the law. His last three works were the *Legacy to Labourers*, 1834, the *Legacy to Parsons*, 1835, and the *Legacy to Peel*, 1836 (published posthumously). In June of 1835 he died, after a short illness, surrounded by his family in the quiet of his farm.

2. Character and Place in History

The fight which Cobbett so gamely waged with pen and voice against the bludgeons of authority extorted from his contemporaries a reluctant admiration, even while they professed disgust at his character and style.

"We once tried", said the *Edinburgh Review*, May 1823 (Vol. 38), "to cast this Antaeus to the ground, but the earthborn rose again and still staggers on.... It is best to say little about him and keep out of his way: for he crushes, by his ponderous weight, whomsoever he falls upon; and what is worse, drags to cureless ruin whatever cause he lays his hands upon to support". Hazlitt in his *Table Talk* (1821) says: "He is a kind of fourth estate in the politics of the country. A very honest man with a total want of principle. Whatever he finds out is his own, and

---

[1] E. I. Carlyle, *William Cobbett*, p. 273.

he only knows what he finds out. Every new *Register* is a kind of new Prospectus"[1]. Bentham, whilst owning the celebrity of Cobbett's pen[2], formed from hearsay a poor account of his oratory. "As a speaker, Cobbett, they say, is nothing: Hunt very great"[3]. A character so mild as Bentham's was offended by Cobbett's virulence. "Cobbett is a man filled with *odium humani generis*, his malevolence and lying are beyond anything"[4].

"To the modern reader", writes the late Professor Smart, "at least to one who considers personalities, strong language and vulgarity always a weakness and generally a mistake—the *Register* is very wearisome reading"[5]. But this is hardly fair. Party politics usually make tedious reading for a later age, and Cobbett wrote party politics for the people. Without the spice of personal abuse his writings would have fallen as flat as the rantings of a Methodist preacher or the dissertations of a Moral Force Chartist. It is Cobbett's distinction that in addition to ephemeral journalism he wrote enduring literature, and it is by this that he has a right to be judged at the bar of posterity.

A living critic more generously appraises him thus—"a typical example of a combination of feudal sentiment with socialistic sympathies..., the father of the Conservative socialism which we more often connect with the names of Kingsley and Disraeli"[6]. But this perhaps is to put him too near to the angels. For he was no angel, but rather a very human creature, a bundle of emotions and prejudices. He was a typical John Bull, a stout fellow in homespun well over six feet high, who watched over England, gun in hand and bulldog beside him, like the *John Bull* on our book-stalls to-day. He had his spiteful side, as who would not who made his living by trouncing others? He involved himself in tangles with literary and political friends, which his kindliest biographer cannot explain away. He was not

---

[1] Essay 6, "Character of Cobbett".

[2] *Collected Works,* x. 459. Letter from Bentham to Cobbett.

[3] *Ibid.* x. 601.   [4] *Ibid.* x. 570.

[5] Smart, *Economic Annals* (1821–1830), p. 93.

[6] H. S. Foxwell, Introduction to Menger, *The Right to the whole Produce of Labour*, p. 99.

a man you would choose for your attorney or trustee, but he was just the man to speak up for you in a crowd. And to speak up for *his* people—the poor and the labourers of England—whatever the hurt to others or to himself, Cobbett never failed.

Do you like to see people jolly and contented? Cobbett did. "National prosperity shows itself in very different ways; in the plentiful meal, the comfortable dwelling, the healthy and happy countenances, and the good morals of the labouring classes of the people"[1]. He would have "good wages to the labourer, paid him by the farmer at the fireside, over a familiar mug of ale, as in former times; and not half wages, handed to him by a bailiff from one of the outhouse windows of Daddy Coke's agricultural villas"[2].

Do you hate tea-drinkers and prohibitionists? Cobbett will sing you a hymn of hate. "I view the tea-drinking as a destroyer of health, an enfeebler of the frame, an engenderer of effeminacy and laziness, a debaucher of youth, and a maker of misery for old age"[3]. Out upon the "canting lousy Methodists, who inveigle the pennies even from the servant girls; while all these are pouring out their pamphlets by millions, and all of them preaching up the doctrine that bacon, bread and beer, corrupt the soul of man, and that potatoes, salt and water, are sure to lead to eternal salvation"[4]. The jovial, beer-drinking parsons chuckled with glee, but when Cobbett came to Tithes and the Establishment, it was the dissenters' turn to smile. Open the January number (1831) of *Twopenny Trash*, and mark him arguing that it is legal, just and necessary to take away all tithes and pay off the national debt. For tithes were given to the Clergy for the succouring of the poor, and the poor had a right to them. "They know that YOU pay a large part of these taxes (he is referring to sums voted for the relief of poor clergy), and yet they would refuse you relief in cases even of the extremest distress!"[5]

And, as he suspected parsons, so also he suspected the place where parsons were bred. "Upon beholding the masses of

---

[1] *Paper against Gold*, Letter 3, p. 49.   [2] *Twopenny Trash*, II. 167.
[3] *Cottage Economy*, p. 18.   [4] *Twopenny Trash*, I. 173.
[5] *Twopenny Trash*, I. 165.

buildings, at Oxford, devoted to what they call 'learning', I could not help reflecting on the drones that they contain and the wasps they send forth!"..."One half of the fellows who are what they call *educated* here, are unfit to be clerks in a grocer's or mercer's shop"[1]. Hatred of Oxford was the only bond of sympathy between William Cobbett and Jeremy Bentham.

Perhaps then you fancy Cobbett was a bit of a bolshevik. Perish the thought! Cobbett loathed towns and the great Wen of London most of all. Nothing but the scents of the country could restore his temper. Well, if not a bolshevik, surely an atheist. For did he not, when he returned from America, in 1819, bring with him the bones of the atheist, Tom Paine? He did, and he toured England with them and the spectacle fell flat, but it gave Byron his chance—

> In digging up your bones, Tom Paine,
>   Will. Cobbett has done well:
> You visit him on earth again,
>   He'll visit you in hell.

And yet this showman of atheistic bones was the writer of *Cobbett's Monthly Sermons*. These sermons were hailed with delight by the poor and admired by the educated. They were read from many pulpits, with the omission, one must suppose, of the paragraphs which denounced parsons and tithes. Listen to a sentence from the *Sermon on the Rights of the Poor*:

To profit by deceits practised on the community at large; to cheat our neighbours and countrymen by means of short measures, false balances and extortions; this bespeaks a heart odiously wicked; this bespeaks greediness, dishonesty and cruelty; what, then, must the man be, who can deliberately and systematically act in the same way towards those, who, in his field, or under his very roof, exert their strength and exhaust their ingenuity for his benefit: and who are content if they obtain a mere sufficiency of food and of raiment out of the fruits of that labour, which gives him all the means of indulgence in luxurious enjoyments? What must the man be, who can see his table spread with dainties, with all that nature aided by art can set before him to pamper his appetite; who knows, that he owes no part of this to his own labour; and yet, who can, while he affects to thank God for the blessing, studiously defraud and degrade those whose

---

[1] *Rural Rides* (Edn by Pitt Cobbett, 1893), I. 42.

labour has created all that he possesses, all that fills his heart with pride?[1]

Was the real Cobbett just an ardent teacher driven by persecution into politics?

Certainly he had a passion for knowledge and the gift of imparting it to others. He tells us how, when a truant lad on the road to Kew, he spent his last 3d. on the *Tale of a Tub* and in consequence slept supperless under a haystack. "I learnt grammar when I was a private soldier on the pay of 6d. a day.... To buy a pen or a sheet of paper I was compelled to forego some portion of food, though in a state of semi-starvation"[2].

As a father—and there were few better fathers—he wrote for his third son, James Paul, an English grammar. Would that there were such English grammars to-day! In Letter 19 he was explaining the use of singular and plural, and he says, "We may say, 'The gang of borough tyrants *is* cruel': or that 'The gang of borough tyrants *are* cruel'; but if we go on to speak of their notoriously brutal ignorance we must not say: 'The gang of borough tyrants *is* cruel and *are* also notoriously as ignorant as brutes'. We must use *is* in both places or *are* in both places". Jimmy surely never went wrong after this.

But as a teacher Cobbett had a curious idea of historical evidence. Facts, if they were not supported by his own observations, were to him no facts at all. The census returns of 1821 were "the biggest lie ever put in print, even in romance". They showed a huge increase in the population, whereas, according to Cobbett, "the size of the churches alone was sufficient to convince any man of sound judgment that there had been a prodigious decrease!" He also dabbled in Church History. But how he was able to prove from a Government Report on the Labouring Poor of Ireland for 1823 that half our national debt had been contracted "to get the means of compelling the Catholic National Church of Ireland to submit to the Protestant Church", and that, "to effect this purpose, the English people

---

[1] *Monthly Sermons* (Sermon on the Rights of the Poor), p. 94.
[2] *Advice to Young Men*, Letter I, para. 44.

had been reduced to beggary", passes, as Professor Smart says[1], the human comprehension.

But even if we could pardon his cavalier attitude to historical evidence, we should still find him hard to follow as a teacher. For he teaches only when he is in the mood; and if it pleases him he abandons teaching for a political skirmish, or for a hue and cry after Malthusian criminals. The contents of his *Cottage Economy* promise admirably—"information relative to the brewing of beer, making of bread, keeping of cows", etc., etc. Ideal information for cottagers and Waterloo veterans proposing to settle on the land! But when the cottager or ex-soldier opened it with a view to instruction in the art of brewing, as likely as not he would find a tirade against taxation or a denunciation of excise-men.

No! Cobbett will not do as a teacher, he travels too far from the beaten track. Travel, in fact, was his passion. The man who above all things loved to ride on horseback through the fields and lanes of England loved also to range with his pen over the problems of England. He did not follow a settled plan, he roamed at leisure up and down the social field. Agriculture and the Agricultural Labourer, the Poor Law, Ireland, Population, Emigration—these were the themes of many a discourse, and if the historian to-day were to set himself the task of tracing the transition from agriculture to industry in the England of Cobbett's day, he would find in Cobbett's writings apt illustrations for every section of his theme.

The Agricultural Labourer

There is no finer account of the degradation of the labourer than the following:

All of you who are 60 years of age can recollect that bread and meat, and not wretched potatoes, were the food of the labouring people; you can recollect that every industrious labouring man brewed his own beer and drank it by his own fireside; you can recollect that, at every wedding and every christening, such labouring man had a barrel of ale in the house provided for the occasion; you can recollect when the young people were able to provide money before they were

[1] Cf. Smart, *Economic Annals* (1821–30), p. 173.

married, to purchase decent furniture for a house, and had no need to go to the parish to furnish them with a miserable nest to creep into; you can recollect when a bastard child was a rarity in a village, and when husbands and wives came together without the disgrace of being forced together by parish officers and magistrates; you can recollect when every sober and industrious labourer that was a married man had his Sunday coat, and took his wife and children to Church, all in decent apparel; you can recollect when the young men did not shirk about on a Sunday in ragged smock-frocks with un-shaven faces, with a shirt not washed for a month, and with their toes peeping out of their shoes, and when a young man was pointed at if he had not, on a Sunday, a decent coat upon his back, a good hat on his head, a clean shirt, with silk handkerchief round his neck, leather breeches without a spot, whole worsted stockings tied under the knee with a red garter, a pair of handsome Sunday shoes, which it was deemed almost a disgrace not to have fastened on his feet by silver buckles. There were always some exceptions to this; some lazy, some drunken, some improvident young men; but I appeal to all those of you who are 60 years of age, whether this be not a true description of the state of the labourers of England when they were boys[1].

And in 1831 he closed his last great fight for the agricultural labourer with these words:

If, however, your verdict should be—which I do not anticipate— one that will consign me to death by sending me to a loathsome dungeon, I will with my last breath pray to God to bless my country and curse the Whigs, and I bequeath my revenge to my children and the labourers of England[2].

The Poor Law

When England lay under the shadow of the old Poor Law and wages were being subsidized out of the Poor Rates, the reformers tried to call a halt. Cobbett was instantly up in arms. Poor relief, he said, was not a charity, but a legal right, a right to subsistence; and the repudiation of this right by Malthus and his School enraged him as a soldier and an Englishman.

How can Malthus and his nasty and silly disciples, how can those who want to abolish the Poor Rates, to prevent the poor from marry-ing; how can this at once stupid and conceited tribe look the labouring

---

[1] *Twopenny Trash* (1831), I. 195.
[2] *A Full and Accurate Report of the Trial of Wm Cobbett, Esq.*, 1831.

man in the face, while they call on him to take up arms, to risk his life in defence of the land?[1]

Population

The Malthusians lamented the growth of population. The parsons preached continence to the poor. So Cobbett wrote *A Surplus Population Comedy*.

Squire Thimble.   Pray, young friends, of procreation
                                Of breeding children, shun the woes.
                                Check the surplus population
                                Restraint that's moral interpose.

The dialogue continues:

But, young woman, cannot you impose on yourself a "moral restraint", for 10 or a dozen years?

Betsy.   Pray what is that, Sir?

Squire Thimble.   Cannot you keep single till you are about 30 years old?

Betsy.   Thirty years old, Sir!! (Stifling a laugh.)

Whereupon worthy Farmer Stiles chimes in:

God never sends mouths without sending meat.

Ireland

Then as now the eternal problem. Then even more so because any check to the population of England would be nullified, it was believed, if the "vacuum" were immediately filled by low grade prolific Irish.

Cobbett plunges into the eternal problem, and in a few words tells us how Ireland's unhappiness has made England unhappy too.

Go and read this (he is referring to a work describing England's greatness in the happy days of old) to the poor souls who are now eating sea-weed in Ireland; who are detected in robbing the pig troughs in Ireland; who are eating horse flesh and grains in Lancashire and Cheshire; who are harnessed like horses and drawing in gravel in Hampshire and Sussex...who are, all over England worse than the felons in the jails[2].

Emigration

Emigration, not for the emigrant's good or for the good of the country to which he emigrated, but emigration for the relief of

---

[1] *Poor Man's Friend*, Number 2.   [2] *Ibid*. Number 3.

over-populated England was the panacea of the 1820's. Cobbett, like Richard Oastler[1] ten years later, loathed the very word. He fell upon "those who are hatching schemes of emigration". "The bare thought of forced emigration to a Foreign State is enough to make an Englishman mad"[2].

So Cobbett ranged over England's problems. But he also toured through England. Let us travel with him on one or two of his rural rides, setting off from the great Wen of London. We are at Ipswich, it may be, on the Eastern Tour:

There is no doubt, but that this was a much greater place than it is now. It is the great outlet for the immense quantities of corn grown in this most productive county, and by farmers the most clever that ever lived. I am told that wheat is worth six shillings a quarter more, at some times, at Ipswich than at Norwich, the navigation to London being so much more speedy and safe. Immense quantities of flour are sent from this town. The windmills on the hills in the vicinage are so numerous that I counted, whilst standing in one place, no less than seventeen. They are all painted or washed white; the sails are black; it was a fine morning, the wind was brisk, and their twirling altogether, added greatly to the beauty of the scene, which, having the broad and beautiful arm of the sea on the one hand, and the fields and meadows, studded with farmhouses, on the other, appeared to me the most beautiful sight of the kind that I had ever beheld[3].

Or we are riding down the Valley of the Avon in Wiltshire. The exquisite beauty of the scene, a startling contrast to the human misery which he knew it to contain, rouses him to an angry outburst.

It seemed to me, that one way, and that not, perhaps, the least striking, of exposing the folly, the stupidity, the inanity, the presumption, the insufferable emptiness and insolence and barbarity, of those numerous wretches, who have now the audacity, to propose to *transport* the people of England, upon the principle of the monster Malthus, who has furnished the unfeeling oligarchs, and their toad-eaters, with the pretence, that *man has a natural propensity to breed faster than food can be raised for the increase*; it seemed to me, that one way of exposing this mixture of madness and of blasphemy was, to take a look, now that the harvest is in, at the produce, the mouths,

---

[1] *Commons Committee on Hand-Loom Weavers* (1834): Q. 291 "I do hate emigration".

[2] *Poor Man's Friend*, Number 2.

[3] *Rural Rides*, II. 296.

the condition, and the changes that have taken place, in a spot like this, which God has favoured with every good, that he has had to bestow upon man[1].

And yet this traveller in thought and deed would not have mankind constantly on the move. He once met a woman, thirty years old, who had never been more than two and a half miles from home:

Let no one laugh at her, and, above all others let not me, who am convinced, that the facilities, which now exist, of moving human bodies from place to place, are among the curses of the country, the destroyers of industry, of morals and, of course, of happiness[2].

William Cobbett, you are an Englishman, and we love you!

NOTE I. The two standard biographies are:

E. I. Carlyle, *William Cobbett* (Constable, 1904).

Lewis Melville, *The Life and Letters of William Cobbett* (2 vols.) (Lane, 1913).

Neither throws much light on the American period, which is important to the understanding of Cobbett's character and opinions. Carlyle (pp. 30–31) explains why Cobbett declined the Court Martial. Melville brings out the many lovable features in Cobbett's private character by selections from his Letters to Lieut. Reid and William Windham and by quotations from Miss Mitford and others.

Melville (vol. I, chaps. 5–8 and 10, 11, especially the Letters to Windham) illustrates Cobbett's political tactics, but hardly touches his fundamental political opinions. Melville is again illuminating for the period after 1820 (vol. II, chaps. 18–20): and covers both public and private ground.

Carlyle (chaps. 3–5, especially chap. 4) completes Melville's picture for the period 1800–1807; but neither gives the full sequence of Cobbett's progress from the support of Pitt's War Government to the criticism of Finance and Political Corruption, and from these to the championship of the Labouring Classes.

NOTE II. Cobbett was the originator of *Hansard*—T. C. Hansard being the printer who produced Cobbett's *Parliamentary History of England* and the *Parliamentary Debates*, which were a continuation of the *History*. The series run:

Cobbett's *Parliamentary History of England from the earliest times to* 1803.

Hansard's *Parliamentary Debates*, 1803–1820, 1st Series, 1820–1830, 2nd or New Series—with General Index, 1803–1830; 1830 onwards, 3rd Series.

---

[1] *Rural Rides*, II. 57.　　　　　　　[2] *Ibid.* II. 50.

CHAPTER IX

THE OLD POOR LAW AND THE NEW

1. THE OLD POOR LAW

It is usual to speak of the old Poor Law in terms such as the following—At the end of the 18th century the wise controls provided by the Elizabethan Poor Law were withdrawn in a fit of mistaken philanthropy. Lax administration led to a demoralising extension of poor relief, which by 1834 had engulfed the whole of rural England. The new Poor Law of 1834 reverted to the policy of 43 Elizabeth, 1601, and thereby replanted independence and morality in the peasantry of England.

In support of this view a contrast is drawn between an Act of 1722 and a number of later Acts, together with a notable administrative decision, at the end of the 18th century. The Act of 1722 empowered parishes which possessed workhouses to refuse outdoor relief—to "put out of the book" all those who declined to be "lodged, kept or maintained" there[1]. The policy of this Act, it is argued, was reversed by Gilbert's Act of 1782, by the general Act of 1795, amending that of 1722, and by the Speenhamland decision of 1795. This interpretation was emphatically upheld by the Poor Law Commissioners in their Report of 1834. Let us therefore examine it in detail.

In the first place there is no evidence that Parliament in 1722 was consciously adopting the policy of using the workhouse as a deterrent to able-bodied pauperism. The intention of the Act was rather to enable parishes who had workhouses to fill them, as a matter of parochial economy, whether with the aged, the impotent, or the able-bodied.

In the second place there was a vast difference in the condition of England at the beginning and end of the 18th century. The

---

[1] Cf. *First Annual Report of the Poor Law Commissioners* (1835), p. 373. (All references to these Reports as well as to the Report of the Poor Law Commission (1834) are to the 2nd, octavo, edition.)

later legislation was passed under the shadow of scarcity and war. In 1783 the American War came to an end, and in 1793 the War with France began. Meantime, the population was increasing by leaps and bounds, enclosure was proceeding apace, and the country was suffering from a run of exceptionally bad harvests.

Gilbert's Act of 1782 effected considerable improvement in parochial organisation, but the provisions which made the Act famous were those excluding the able-bodied from the workhouse and ordering work to be found for them at or near their place of residence[1]. The importance of this Act has been exaggerated. For it only applied to those parishes which chose to incorporate themselves into Unions under the Act, and in 1834 only 924 out of the 16,000 parishes in England and Wales were so incorporated.

More important is the Poor Relief Act of 1795[2], which deliberately reversed the policy of 1722. Section 1 sanctioned the giving of relief in the poor person's home, while section 2 authorised justices to give orders for poor relief and instructed church-wardens and overseers to obey. The Act was passed on December 24, 1795, at the end of a year of exceptional scarcity and distress. At the height of this distress, in May 1795, the Berkshire Justices, assembled at the Pelican Inn, Speenhamland, decided to regulate relief by reference to the price of bread. For this purpose they framed "the original bread table, by which the parish allowance was systematically substituted for the wages of labour"[3].

The decision did not originate the practice of allowances in aid of wages; it systematised a practice which, because it was

[1] Section 29 of Gilbert's Act reserves the Poor House for the sick, aged and impotent and for orphan children.

S. 32 orders work to be found for "any poor person who shall be able and willing to work but who cannot get employment...near the place of his or her residence". The guardians are to maintain such poor till suitable work is found for them; and during the time of such work they are to apply the proceeds thereof towards their maintenance, "as far as the same will go, and to make up the deficiency, if any".

[2] "The great and fatal deviation from our previous policy", Poor Law Commission (1834), *Report*, p. 129.

[3] *First Annual Report of the Poor Law Commissioners* (1835), p. 207.

becoming widespread, needed to be conducted upon some regular plan.

We must agree therefore that there was a change in Poor Law Policy at the end of the century. But it was not the result of a fit of philanthropy or of foolish blindness to the wisdom of an earlier age; it was the almost inevitable result of the impact of economic forces, which the age of Elizabeth had never contemplated. These forces exposed all the weaknesses inherent in the Elizabethan Poor Law.

The Act of Elizabeth (43 Eliz. c. 2, s. 5) provided for the apprenticeship of poor children. Out of this, as reinforced by later statutes, developed the vicious practice of parochial apprenticeship, which produced such horrors in the early days of the factory system, when factories, for the sake of water power, were built in the sparsely inhabited valleys of Lancashire, Yorkshire and Derbyshire.

The Act of Elizabeth provided for the relief of the lame, impotent, old, blind and other poor not able to work (s. 1). The intention of the legislature was generous, but the results were meagre. This side of the Poor Law problem was allowed to drift, and among its legacies were the old mixed workhouses, which earned deserved obloquy in the 19th century. The Commissioners of 1834 did not look at it in this light. To them it was the one bright spot in Poor Law administration. "Even in places distinguished in general by the most wanton parochial profusion, the allowances to the aged and infirm are moderate"[1]. And why? Not because of a conscious policy of moderation in this one department, but for less worthy reasons. First of all, the number of old, lame and blind was limited by physical facts. No one would qualify for poor relief by putting his eyes out. Secondly, and this is the main reason, the England of 1760–1830 was definitely not what it is often assumed to have been. It was definitely not soft-hearted. It was as callous as it dared to be, and it took little heed of the needs of those who, because they were physically weak, had no power to create a disturbance.

The Act of Elizabeth, in dealing with the able-bodied poor,

[1] Poor Law Commission (1834), *Report*, p. 43 (octavo edition).

ordered those without maintenance to be set to work on materials to be provided by the parish. This looks like recognition of the "Right to Work", but it was not. The materials to be provided were such as would be appropriate to handicraftsmen. There is no word of supplying land for unemployed agricultural labourers. It never occurred to the Elizabethan age that this class of labour should be relieved in this way. If they were not working, it was because they were vagrants, and the proper place for them was the House of Correction or Common Gaol (s. 4). But at the end of the 18th century it was just this able-bodied agricultural labourer, who in the mass, was unable to live without assistance from the Poor Law; and unable, not because employment was wanting, but because it was paid at rates which under the new economic conditions were insufficient to maintain life.

The right solution would have been the enforcement of a legal minimum wage in agriculture. This the labourers demanded in the 1790's, appealing to the Elizabethan Statute of Artificers[1] (1563). But the appeal was useless, for the Wages sections were by this time inoperative, and they had never been used as a lever for raising wages beyond the prevailing competitive level. Samuel Whitbread was aware of this, and in 1795 proposed new legislation. But his proposal met with no response from a Parliament which regarded interference with wages as contrary to the Laws of God and of Political Economy. The right solution being declined, the only alternative, unless the population was to starve by thousands, was the system that the Commissioners of 1834 found in full force—viz., employment through parochial agency with parochial subsidies in aid of wages.

The parish intervened between the labourer and his livelihood in different ways. The least objectionable form was one common in small parishes, where the rate-payers bound themselves to provide employment at a given rate of wages for all who could not find it. This was called the Labour Rate. Then there was the

---

[1] "An act containing divers orders for artificers, labourers, servants of husbandry and apprentices". Sections 15–17 deal with the assessment of wages by the justices of the peace. See below, p. 216.

system of Roundsmen (most prevalent in Oxfordshire, Berks, and Bucks), by which the labourers went the round of the parish with a ticket ordering the farmers to employ them. Under this system the parish paid a portion, if not the whole, of the wages from the parish funds[1]. In the vicinity of Bicester (Oxfordshire) the labourers were put up to auction once a year. The farmer whose bid came nearest to the price fixed by the parish got the man he bid for, and the parish made up the difference. The parish's loss on good labourers was less than that on bad, but the labourers themselves received the same pay, whether good or bad[2].

As a last resort there was the parish pit. The labourers loathed it, but now and then they took it philosophically. At Mildenhall in Suffolk "the paupers form themselves into two gangs, which they denominate the House of Commons and the House of Lords. The House of Commons was engaged at the bottom of the pit, loosening the hard earth, digging the gravel, and throwing it up to the Lords, who were placed above them, and were occupied in sifting the refuse, and throwing what was useful to the top of the pit"[3].

If the labourers had been without wives and children, the intervention of the Poor Law might have been confined to the provision in exceptional cases of parochial or semi-parochial employment. But the wages that an agricultural labourer could earn, whether in ordinary private employment or in employment in which the parish was in some way concerned, were not sufficient to support a large family. Between 1795 and 1834 the rate of wages varied from 7s. 6d. to 12s. 6d. a week; and when food prices were rising, the price of labour never rose proportionately or as fast. It therefore became customary to assume that a man's normal earnings could not provide for more than five persons, himself, his wife and three children. Labourers with larger families received, as a matter of course, allowances proportionate to the excess. This system of family extras was

[1] Examples are given in A. E. Bland and others, *English Economic History, Select Documents*, p. 660.
[2] *First Annual Report of Poor Law Commissioners* (1835), p. 211.
[3] *Second Annual Report of the Poor Law Commissioners* (1836), p. 149.

the allowance system proper, the system which the Berkshire Justices had endeavoured to regulate by a sliding scale varying with the price of bread. It prevailed generally and it meant for rural England, as a whole, a complete confusion between wages and relief.

The light in which it was regarded by the magistrates and overseers may be seen from the following examples. In 1817 a Bedfordshire magistrate stated that in his county 2/6 was considered to be "what a family per head ought to earn" (*sic*), "any deficiency being made up by the parish"[1]. "We take a man's earnings", said the overseer of Burnham, Bucks, "at 12/- a week, and I have known instances where a man makes his earnings £1 a week at task work and he has four children; we pay him 3/- a week, reckoning his earnings only at 12/-"[2].

The recipients played up to the spirit of the administration. They called round on the overseer to enquire "what their money was" and considered, as did the overseers who paid the money, that they had "a right to so much"[3]. The Commissioners of 1834 were beyond measure distressed at this state of mind: "We deplore the misconception of the labourers in thinking that wages are not a matter of contract, but of right; that any diminution of their comforts occasioned by an increase of their numbers, without an equal increase of the fund for their subsistence, is an evil to be remedied, not by themselves, but by the magistrates; not an error, or even a misfortune, but an injustice"[4].

The Commissioners were Malthusians; the labourers mere labourers, who were fond of white bread and believed what Cobbett told them about their rights.

2. THE ACT OF 1834

"The Act of 1834", says Mark Hovell, "was the first piece of genuine radical legislation which this country has enjoyed; it was

---

[1] *Lords Committee on the Poor Laws* (1817). Evidence, p. 71.
[2] *Ibid.* Evidence, p. 99.
[3] *First Annual Report of the Poor Law Commissioners* (1835), p. 210.
[4] Poor Law Commission (1834), *Report*, p. 220.

the first fruits of Benthamism. For the first time a legislative problem was thoroughly and scientifically tackled"[1].

If we turn to the sections of the Poor Law Amendment Act in order to discover the principles underlying this "thorough" and "scientific" piece of legislation, we shall be disappointed. Section 52 contains the nearest approach to a generalisation. After reciting the evils of relief as at present administered to the able-bodied and their families and the difficulty of making any sudden changes in established practice, the section empowers the Commissioners to regulate the relief given to the able-bodied and their families out of the workhouse. In the last resort, after objections had been duly heard, the new Commissioners were given power to issue peremptory orders; and after this all relief given in contravention of the order was illegal, except in cases of urgency which must, moreover, be reported to, and approved by, the Commissioners.

To discover the new principles we must turn to the way in which the Act was administered. Two principles are then discernible:

1. The principle of "all or nothing" (or, as we said in the Army,—"either come on parade or go sick"). Mr Tidd Pratt, the Registrar of Friendly Societies, assured the Commissioners that in the Friendly Societies allowances in aid of wages were unknown. "I have known them", he said, "expel a party for stirring the fire or putting up the shutters of his windows, these acts being considered by them evidence of the party being capable of going to work.... They are perfectly well aware, from experience, that to give relief, in an apparently hard case, would open the door to a whole class of cases which would ruin them". The Commissioners translated this into the work-house test. An able-bodied man must be given relief, if he demanded it, but he must receive it in the workhouse. He must be altogether dependent or not at all.

2. The principle of "less eligibility". This was applied to all classes of pauperism, whether able-bodied or not. Since relief was given, as far as possible, in the workhouse only, the principle found expression in the workhouse regulations. By irksome

[1] *The Chartist Movement*, p. 79.

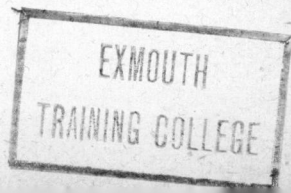

restrictions and the reduction of social amenities to a minimum, by depressing food and chilly religion, the state of the workhouse inmates was to be made less desirable than that of the most unfavourably placed independent worker.

Dicey tells us that the legislative tendency inherited from Benthamism was the constant extension and improvement of the mechanism of government[1], and he quotes, as an example, "the rigid and scientific administration of the Poor Law (1834)". This reads like a paradox—Individualism creates machinery which interferes with the individual.

The explanation is this. The legislature was prepared to give strong powers to a central authority in order to check the undesirable activities of numerous local authorities. As Hovell says: "Under the old system each parish had been an independent corporation, administering relief and levying rates with scarcely a shadow of control from the Central Government. Under these circumstances abuses and vested interests had grown up to an appalling extent. Parishes often fell into the hands of tradesmen, property owners, manufacturers, public house keepers, and the like, who exploited both paupers and public in the interests of their own pockets"[2].

The administrative chaos had been increased by half-hearted attempts at reform. The unions of parishes under Gilbert's Act of 1782 and the Select Vestries[3] created by the Sturges Bourne Acts of 1818 and 1819, though improvements in themselves, added to the complexity of poor law administration as a whole. The accumulation of population in towns like Manchester, which were still parishes, made it impossible to cope with the business of poor relief through the traditional officials, the churchwardens and unpaid overseers. These places therefore had paid overseers, and so burdensome was the office of churchwarden in Manchester that a "Tyburn ticket", exempting the holder from office, sold for £200–£300[4]. A Tyburn ticket was a ticket certifying that the holder was prosecuting a felony in the parish concerned. This

---

[1] *Law and Opinion*, p. 305.   [2] *The Chartist Movement*, p. 79.
[3] Cf. Webb, *English Local Government, The Parish and the County*, pp. 152–163.
[4] *Lords Committee on the Poor Laws* (1817). Evidence, p. 153.

by an Act of 1698 exempted him from Parish offices, and there-fore from the legal penalty attaching to refusal of such offices.

The Act of 1834 introduced a much needed uniformity. The Gilbert Incorporations, being unions of a sort, lingered till 1845, causing great inconvenience by their Salamander-like shape, but with the exception of these all the parishes of England and Wales were incorporated in 1834 into Poor Law Unions of parishes under the management of unpaid Boards of Guardians, elected from the combined parishes. These are the Unions and Guardians of to-day.

The increase in the size of the Poor Law unit was an advantage in two ways. It abolished parochial cliques, and it created a body on which the central authority could exert its influence. To have dealt with 16,000 parishes would have been impossible. By this means the real power was placed in the hands of the three central Commissioners, and to them it was due that the new Act was not a dead letter. Their position was parallel with that of the Factory Inspectors created by the Factory Act of 1833.

The Commissioners appointed under the Act—not to be con-fused with the members of the Royal Commission which drew up the report in favour of the Act—were T. Frankland Lewis, J. G. Shaw-Lefevre and George Nicholls, with Edwin Chadwick as Secretary. They were known as the three Kings of Somerset House, and their rule was vastly unpopular. They were held responsible for the hated Bastilles (as the workhouses were called), and it was widely believed that they were the authors of an anonymous pamphlet (probably a hoax) entitled *Marcus on the possibility of limiting populousness*, in which the "pain-less extinction" of superfluous babies was solemnly advo-cated[1].

The Commissioners were appointed in the first instance for five years, then like Peel's Income Tax they were renewed peri-odically till in 1847 (when it was clear that they had come to stay) their power was transferred to a Poor Law Board. This made their position more constitutional, for it gave the head of

---

[1] T. Mackay, *History of the English Poor Law*, III. 239.

the Board official representation in Parliament and took the sting out of the accusation that the Commissioners were a Secret Service directed by their Secretary, Chadwick, a "monster in human shape". In 1871 the Poor Law Board was merged in the Local Government Board.

Since 1834 there has been no general revision of the Poor Law. For Parliament, though ready to exert its sovereignty in railways, factories and mines, shrank from stirring up the local feeling which any prominent measure of Poor Law reform was certain to excite. It gladly allowed the central authority to introduce reform by executive instructions. The central authority has operated by various devices—advisory circulars, special orders applying to one Union, general orders applying to a group of Unions, and so forth. But from beginning to end the attempt to secure a uniformity of policy has been largely frustrated by the disobedience and neglect of the guardians.

The Royal Commission on the Poor Laws (1909) recommended sweeping changes. The majority report proposed the abolition of the Unions and the reconstruction of the Poor Law administration under the Borough and County authorities acting in co-operation with voluntary organisations. The minority report proposed the break-up of the Poor Law. Neither report was adopted at once by the Government.

3. The Law of Settlement

There is no better example of the limitations of legislation than the Law of Settlement. The Commissioners of 1834 were scientific radicals, and prepared to transport the village labourer anywhere and to any calling. They delighted in individual enterprise, above all when it took the form of mobility. And yet they failed ignominiously to abolish the restrictions on mobility which the Law of Settlement imposed. What was the reason of their failure?

For answer we must glance back to the History of Settlement in English parishes. In the middle ages the wanderings of beggars brought the problems of Poor Relief and mobility into contact. From early times the law presumed that each parish was responsible for its own poor. Its poor were those who were born in it or had lived there for a long time. The Statute of 1662, the basis of the Law of Settlement for the next two centuries, after reciting the evils due to the exploitation of well-stocked parishes by stranger vagabonds, authorised the magistrates, upon complaint made within forty days of arrival, to remove all persons, likely to become chargeable, to the parish where they were last legally settled. This provision was in time relaxed, at first in practice and later by Statute. The Settlement and Removal Act of 1795 protected persons from removal until *actually* chargeable. But in the lean years which followed, when an increasing percentage of the population was reduced to parochial dependence, few agricultural labourers were venturesome enough to abandon an undisputed settlement for the uncertainties and buffetings of town life.

By 1817 the Law of Settlement was as complicated as the Navigation Code. It needed a lawyer to interpret it. Surely here was a chance for the radical reformer! The House of Lords in 1817 did propose a radical reform, viz., to replace the complicated "heads of settlement" (qualifications for obtaining a settlement) by a single qualification of three years' residence. But the proposal was not adopted either in 1817 or in 1834. In 1834 the Commissioners progressed backwards. They removed heads of settlement[1] which had been introduced to aid mobility, and they did this because they found that ratepayers had reacted to the law's attempts to aid mobility by taking measures to prevent a right of settlement accruing in these new ways.

Not until 1876 was the three years' residence test enacted by Parliament, and then only because in the interval events had occurred which made the question unimportant. By that time the agricultural population had been re-absorbed into independent industry, and therefore settlement was no longer a prize valued by a large part of the population. Furthermore, the

[1] Poor Law Amendment Act, ss. 64–68. S. 64 repealed Settlement by Hiring and Service.

Union Chargeability Act of 1865[1] made the Poor Law Union
the financial as well as the administrative unit, and this removed
the incentive to inter-parochial dodgery, which was the main
cause of disputes about settlements.

The Law of Settlement remains approximately at the point to
which it was brought in 1876, and any possibility of hardship to
the pauper is minimised by the rule that, whether legally settled
or not, a pauper cannot be removed if he has resided for one
year. It has no appreciable effect on the mobility of labour. The
only objection to its complete repeal is the danger that vagrant
paupers might be attracted to a union whose method of treatment is above the average in leniency.

The history of the Law of Settlement is a strange one. The
first statute of 1662 was passed to remedy defects in administration. Then law necessitated law down to the end of the series.
All through the 18th and early 19th centuries England was
moving towards individual freedom, but the supreme freedom,
the freedom to come and go, was denied to the labourer. It
was, as Adam Smith said, "a most evident violation of natural
liberty and justice"[2], and yet the radical philosophers of 1834
failed to remove it.

Still more remarkable does this inaction appear when we remember that Adam Smith's own country had no such law. The

---

[1] The Act was the outcome of the Lancashire Cotton Famine (see page
280 below). As the historian of the Famine says: "If the Union Chargeability Bill had been in force in 1861, it would have sufficed to meet the
distress in many of the cotton manufacturing unions" (Dr John Watts,
Facts of the Cotton Famine, p. 299)—the point being this, that the wealthy
men of the locality resided outside the *parish* in which their manufactories
or warehouses were situated and in which the bulk of their workpeople
necessarily lived. The rich people however often lived in a different *union*,
and from this standpoint union rating was only a half-way house to county
rating, as contemplated by the recent Royal Commission on the Poor Laws.
The bill of 1865 was opposed in Parliament on the ground that it would
encourage expenditure and sacrifice country to town parishes. The answer
to the first objection was that in an industrial emergency liberal expenditure
was a social necessity. The second objection was factious. Parish rating,
in addition to fostering inter-parochial litigation, made it profitable to
demolish labourers' cottages, the parish trusting to get its labour from
neighbouring parishes. Union rating removed this incentive. A little rent
was better than none, when the sacrifice of rent ceased to save rates.

[2] *Wealth of Nations*, Book I. ch. x. pt II.

experience of Scotland showed, however, that free movement between two countries which have different standards of life is perilous to the country with the higher standard. The Irish, said a Scottish witness before the Emigration Committee of 1826–7, "gradually assimilate to the people of the country, and they cause the people of the country in some degree to assimilate to them. They have no notion of that degree of expense which is essential to a Scotchman's comfort"[1]. It had been held in the case of an Irishman named Higgins in 1824 that the Irishman had the same immunity from removal in Scotland as a native. "If the principle involved in that case", continued the witness, "were once established, as applicable to the maintenance, total or partial, of able-bodied demanding it as a right, then it seems to me beyond all question that Scotland will be placed under the same tremendous burden which England bears and has been struggling in vain to alleviate"[2]. In England the difficulty of acquiring a settlement afforded the locality a crude protection against the Irish influx. It cannot be denied that the old Poor Law demoralised the English labourer, but at any rate it demoralised him in white wheaten bread, and, through the operation of the Law of Settlement, it checked in some small degree the deluge which all but reduced England and Scotland to the potato standard of unhappy Ireland.

4. THE EFFECT OF THE NEW POOR LAW ON RURAL DISTRICTS

What was the result of the new Poor Law?

We must distinguish carefully between its operation in rural districts and its operation in urban and industrial districts.

In rural districts the new Poor Law achieved its purpose. It was conceived in terms of the agricultural labourer, and after it had been in operation for ten years the evils which it was framed to combat had disappeared. It ended the disastrous confusion between wages and relief, and cleared the way for the re-absorption of labour in agriculture or adjacent industries. The

---

[1] *Commons' Committee on Emigration* (1826–7), Q. 1791.
[2] *Ibid.* Q. 1794.

hardships that it caused were temporary, but they were an inevitable part of the price which had to be paid for an escape from the vicious stagnation of the old system. Men who from no original sin had been wasting their lives, gossiping in the parish pit, slacking on the farmer's land, drinking at the beer shop with the parish's money and there concocting schemes for burning their employer's hay-ricks, were squeezed out into the open and made to fend for themselves. We find proof of the re-absorption of rural labour not only in the Annual Reports of the Poor Law Commissioners, which are open to the charge of exaggerating the effects of the new law, but also in the evidence presented to Committees of both Houses of Parliament during the 30's—for example, the Committees on the State of Agriculture, 1836 (Lords and Commons) and the Commons' Committee on the Administration of the Poor Law Amendment Act, 1837. The re-absorption is all the more remarkable in view of the fact that it was accomplished in the face of acute agricultural depression.

From numerous instances the following are selected:—

A Sussex farmer said that before the Act of 1834 they had in the parish twenty to thirty unemployed men in winter and spring-time, for whom they provided in different ways, sometimes setting them to work on the roads, sometimes to grubbing on the land and sometimes "when we had nothing for them, we used to pay them money without work". But when the new Act came in, nearly every man found employment of some sort or other in his own parish, "except some three or four who went away to sea"[1].

And again, "in the old times the farmer used to fetch his men from the roads as he wanted them and send them back when the weather came on bad, but since the passing of the Act he found them employment on the farm during these intervals"[2].

Earl Radnor, a big Hampshire landowner, told the Agricultural Committee in 1836 that since the Bill there had been rather an outcry for labour than a deficiency. "Where there were men lounging about at the corners of the streets receiving

---

[1] *Commons' Committee on the Administration of the Poor Law Acts* (1837). Q. 15929–48.   [2] *Ibid.* Q. 17620.

2/- from the parish and doing nothing, these men are now all employed"[1].

But in other rural counties emphasis is laid on its unpopularity and immediate severity. Thus in 1836 a Cambridgeshire farmer draws a gloomy picture of his county[2]:—

"They have an amazing prejudice against the Poor Law Bill. Last year they were in a very deplorable state indeed,...the farmers frequently will employ the men with large families, to prevent their being relieved by a rate, and it makes the young men very desperate indeed....Several of the best and honest labourers have said to me that...before they will go to the Union Workhouse, they will rob on the highway".

The distress was increased by the penurious condition of the University. "Our University is spending a mere nothing now; the parents of the collegiates can afford to furnish them with so little money that they can spend nothing". The undergraduates of these days, let us remember, were mostly sons of landowners and clergymen—of landowners whose rents fell into arrears during a depression and of clergymen whose income was derived from fluctuating tithes and rate-burdened glebe.

Two circumstances, which were independent of any changes in the method of poor relief, had in certain districts borne heavily on the already depressed ranks of rural labour. A Sussex farmer told the Poor Law Committee of 1837 that the peace of 1815 contributed to the labour surplus: "The old soldiers and sailors were paid off and came home": and "we could not get vent for our young men in the army or navy"[3]. The labour market was further depressed by the fall in corn prices soon after 1815, which was "the ruin of a great many small farmers"[4], and forced them to swell the overcrowded ranks of rural labour or else to quit for foreign shores[5].

---

[1] *Commons' Committee on the State of Agriculture* (1836). Q. 16846 sqq.

[2] *Ibid.* Q. 2361 sqq.

[3] *Commons' Committee on the Poor Law Amendment Act* (1837). Evidence of Mr John Stapley, farmer of S. Birsted, a parish in the Sutton Gilbert Union, Q. 16879.

[4] *Ibid.* Q. 16880.

[5] Cf. S. C. Johnson, *Emigration from the United Kingdom to North America,* p. 41.

Taking rural England as a whole, we must admit that the introduction of the new Poor Law was *followed* with surprising quickness by local re-absorption or the migration of the surplus elsewhither. The new Poor Law, however, was not the sole cause. Its operation was greatly facilitated by the concurrent growth of new employments.

The Commissioners, in their reports for 1835 and 1836, made much of the success with which they had assisted the migration of agricultural families from rural employment in the East and South of England to industrial employment in the Midlands and North. After 1837 we hear no more of organised migration, and we may conjecture that the unaided migration was not very great. We know that some of those who were migrated by the Commissioners found factory life distasteful and the pace too strong[1]. Moreover the occupations to which they were sent, or to which they would find their way of their own accord, were unskilled and poorly paid. Except in a boom the ex-labourer from the South would have to fight his way to decent industrial employment through a host of competitors among the families of hand-loom weavers and Irish immigrants, many of whom had hereditary aptitude for textile work. The families most likely to succeed would be hand-workers coming from rural districts such as Norfolk and Suffolk, which had declining domestic industries. Nearer to the labourer's home and more akin to the work in which he had been brought up was the work provided by two new and expanding industries, viz., railway construction and coal mining. Evidence can be found of influx into both.

In Bedfordshire and Bucks, we are told in 1836, "an immense number of our labourers are employed on the railway"[2]. A farmer with several occupations in Bucks and Berks said: "From the great call there is for labour in the railways and other undertakings, at present we have no overplus of labourers as we used to have,—from that cause and the introduction of the Poor Law"[3]. "I believe", said Joseph Sandars, a Liverpool corn

---

[1] *First Annual Report of the Poor Law Commissioners*, p. 319.
[2] *Lords' Committee on the State of Agriculture* (1836). Q. 487.
[3] *Ibid.* Q. 849.

merchant, "that there are no less than 20,000 persons employed
on the rail road between London and Liverpool.... If the manufacturers had been in a state of distress and those railways had
not been in course of erection, the condition of the farmers'
labourers must have been wretchedly bad indeed"[1].

The railway navvy's life was rough and vagrant; but if
Malthus had been appointed to create a new employment for
the agricultural labourer, he would surely have selected this one.
For it discouraged marriage and took the male from home. Its
only drawback was that it did not take him far enough. "Our
paupers prefer going to rail roads (rather than to factories in
the North) as being nearer their parishes"[2]. Chicken-hearted
creatures, to value their home so much!

Evidence of the influx into mining is harder to find. For
mining was not an entirely new occupation, and a large part of
the new supply demanded by the expansion of coal mining came
from the natural increase of a notoriously prolific section of
the population. Nevertheless, it is possible to discover incidental
allusions in official papers.

Thus in 1843 the Staffordshire miners complained that the
butties were "very apt to take men into the pit from the plough
or other trades, who will come and work for 3d. or 4d. a day less
than the regular miners"[3]. "I am a native of Weymouth in
Dorset", said another: "there are a great many not born in the
county that have strayed about for work and go into the pit"[4].
In 1873 Durham reported a great number of Irish, "in the coking
districts principally"[5]. But the Irish stream was drying up. By
this time it was going to the United States. In the North Midlands (1873) "every available man has been sent to a colliery"[6].
The new collieries in North Notts were worked by men who had
been stocking weavers. "They made", we are surprised to read,

---

[1] *Lords' Committee on the State of Agriculture* (1836).   Qs. 4040–1.
[2] *Third Annual Report of the Poor Law Commissioners* (1837), p. 162.
[3] *Midland Mining Commission* (1843), *Report*, p. 59.
[4] *Ibid.* p. 71.
[5] *Commons' Committee on the Present Dearness and Scarcity of Coal* (1873).
Evidence of Alexander Macdonald, Q. 4596.
[6] *Ibid.* Q. 917

"good and steady workers"[1]. Finally, in the South Wales district, the last of the great coal areas to be opened up, we hear the same tale—there were no Irish, they were streaming westwards. Englishmen were deterred by the Welsh language. Some came from the West Midlands, but "we do not import many men from any other district; we get them from the agricultural districts in Wales"[2].

Thus coal (for railways are as dependent on coal as is coal mining itself) did what a thousand Poor Law Commissioners, operating on victims with the mental detachment of a super-Benthamite, would have failed to do.

5. EFFECTS ON URBAN AND INDUSTRIAL DISTRICTS

It is when we come to the towns that we see the short-comings of the new Poor Law. For the law was framed with reference to agricultural conditions, just when the problem of poverty was coming to be the problem of poverty in big towns.

In the North of England, the "Gehenna of manufacturing Radicalism"[3], the new Poor Law met with violent resistance from the working classes, and when the manufacturing districts had passed through the morass of semi-capitalism to full factory life, there still remained the chronic maladies of urban destitution— casual employment, under-employment, and the unemployment caused by cyclical depression. For these problems the medicine of the new Poor Law was a farce, as we have come at last to see. Though the members of the Royal Commission on the Poor Laws (1909) differed as to remedies, they were at one in their determination to depart from the inspiration of 1834.

Cobbett, the farmer, lived to represent the factory district of Oldham in the reformed House of Commons; and it was fitting that the opposition to a law which was attempting to foist its harsh solution for rural evils on over-employed townsfolk should

---

[1] *Commons' Committee on the Present Dearness and Scarcity of Coal* (1873). Q. 961.
[2] *Ibid.* Q. 1538.
[3] Carlyle, *Critical and Miscellaneous Essays* (Centenary Ed.), III. 159.

be inspired by him. The Act, he said [1], was an Act to compel the people of England to live on potatoes, a Coarser Food Bill, an Irish Wages Bill.

The agitation which he helped to kindle blazed up in 1836. There was an organised attempt to prevent the introduction of the new Poor Law in Lancashire and Yorkshire, led by John Fielden of Todmorden, Cobbett's colleague in the representation of Oldham. The violence of so benevolent a man pained and surprised the Commissioners, but he was not to be talked over. He presented countless petitions against it. "By his own exertions he prevented the introduction of the Act of 1834, or of the Registration of Births, Marriages and Deaths Act of 1837, which was closely connected with it, into the Todmorden area at all. It was a good generation later before Whitehall compelled the Todmorden Union to build a workhouse"[2]. So effectively was the resistance organised here and elsewhere that Lancashire and the West Riding of Yorkshire were administered under the old system for several years after the Act was in force in other places.

The organised resistance was reinforced by a popular clamour in which the leading voices were those of Richard Oastler, the "Factory King", and Joseph Rayner Stephens, a Methodist preacher. Oastler and Stephens breathed into the Ten Hour and Anti-Poor Law Movements the fervour of a religious revival. Both were thorough-going Tories, and so the bitterness of political hatred was added to the frenzy of religious enthusiasm. In Lancashire their eloquence and audacity raised them to a pitch of popularity such as few men have attained. Resistance to the law was preached as a sacred duty. "If Lord John Russell wanted to know what he (Stephens) thought of the New Poor Law, he would tell him plainly, he thought it was the law of devils...if vengeance was to come, let it come; it would be an eye for an eye, a tooth for a tooth, limb for limb, wife for wife, child for child, and blood for blood"[3].

The agitation spread rapidly through the North of England,

---

[1] *Legacy to Labourers*, passim.
[2] Hovell, *The Chartist Movement*, p. 87.   [3] *Ibid.* p. 90.

and for a moment it looked as though it would meet with the success which attended the agitation of the Short Time Committees and the Anti-Corn Law League. For a moment it looked as though the agitators had found their Cobden in Feargus O'Connor, the leader of the Chartists. But the agitation failed, and was bound to fail unless it was strong enough to triumph by revolution. For although aimed ostensibly at a single unpopular law, it was really part of a great cry issuing from thousands of desperate and excited men, who knew that they were miserable and struck blindly at the thing which insulted their misery. When the first phase of Chartism came to an end with the imprisonment of the Chartist leaders in 1840, the agitation against the Poor Law burned itself out, and its insults were forgotten in the easier years which followed factory reform and the repeal of the Corn Laws. What the new Poor Law had failed to do was realised more clearly forty years later when the country was confronted with unemployment in its modern form.

PART II

CHAPTER X

THE POLITICAL BACKGROUND FROM 1830 TO THE PRESENT DAY

1. FOREIGN POLICY: PALMERSTON, SALISBURY, GREY

THE interaction of foreign and domestic policy must now be traced over ground very different from that traversed between 1800 and 1830. After the latter date social reform was no longer cramped by the stress of European politics. The Government could not invoke the national security as an excuse for the suspension of civil liberties. At the same time the connection between foreign and domestic policy became less close. In domestic legislation public opinion became more potent, but no corresponding tendency is observable in foreign policy. When Lord Salisbury lifted foreign affairs out of the sphere of party contest, he also made them less amenable to direct popular control.

We may divide foreign policy since 1830 very roughly into two periods: the era of Palmerston from 1830 to the eve of the Franco-Prussian War, and the era of Salisbury and Grey from 1885 to the outbreak of the recent War. Between the two is an indeterminate period dominated by the figures of Gladstone and Disraeli. Gladstone thought in terms of Europe and non-intervention. Disraeli, a child of the East, dreamed of an Imperial Renaissance. When in 1875 he purchased the Khedive's shares in the Suez Canal for four millions sterling, he employed his imagination and business instinct to the very great profit of his country.

Lord Palmerston presided at the Foreign Office for most of the time between 1830 and his death in 1865 and even when he was out of office the influence of his policy was felt.

Following the tradition of Canning, he caused England to play the rôle of champion to the smaller nations—a rôle that was

popular in England, but provocative abroad[1]. "Stop that bullying", said Palmerston to Powers that were unlikely to fight.
The British citizen, even when represented by a Jew like Don
Pacifico[2] with a preposterous case, was to be protected by all the
resources of the State. "As the Roman, in days of old, held
himself free from indignity, when he could say *Civis Romanus
sum*, so also a British subject, in whatever land he may be, shall
feel confidence that the watchful eye and the strong arm of
England will protect him against injustice and wrong"[3].

Palmerston had the personality to persist in his policy, even
when it brought him into conflict with his party and his Sovereign. Queen Victoria objected strongly to the countenance

[1] Attention is drawn to a recently published essay by the late Captain
Sproxton, Fellow of Peterhouse, *Palmerston and the Hungarian Revolution*
(Cambridge University Press, 1919). The writer submits a strong case for
a material revision of the judgments previously passed on Palmerston. It
is argued that Palmerston's policy not only was carefully adjusted to
England's interest, but also took account of the permanent principles at
work in European diplomacy. Thus in 1848 he was favourable to Piedmont
and the revolutionary movement in North Italy, because he believed that
Austrian rule there was unnatural and could not last. But in the same year
he refused to recognise the independence of Hungary, in spite of his disap-
proval of the inhuman conduct of the Austrians, his reason being that the
separation of Hungary from Austria would overthrow the Balance of
Power in Europe. If the Austrian Empire "did not already exist, it would
have", he said, "to be invented" (Sproxton, *op. cit.* p. 20). He, therefore,
turned a deaf ear to the overtures of Kossuth in 1848, but in the year
following, after the danger to Austria had been removed by the intervention
of Russia, he strongly supported the Ottoman Government in its refusal
to surrender the Hungarian leaders who had taken refuge in Turkey. "The
man who had saved 'these miserable relicts of a lost cause' was Palmerston,
who had declared, again and again, that he knew nothing of a sovereign
independent Hungary" (*op. cit.* p. 145). Palmerston's policy, then, in the
critical years 1848–9 was consistent and well-considered; and he gave
evidence of sounder political instincts than the Queen and the Prince
Consort with their legitimist leanings. It cannot, indeed, be denied that
he had a tendency to schoolboy bluster, which at times produced unfortunate
results; but it is chiefly in the later years of his life that his policy is open
to serious criticism from the standpoint of European interests and deserving
of the reprobation which it has hitherto been usual to pronounce upon that
policy as a whole.

[2] Born in Gibraltar and for a time Portuguese consul at the Peiraeus.
When his house was plundered in 1847, he presented to the Hellenic
Government extravagant claims, including an item of £21,000 for the loss
of documents. The action of the English Government in supporting his
claim was debated in the House of Commons, June 28, 1850 (Hansard,
3rd S. CXII.).

[3] Palmerston. Hansard, 3rd S. CXII. 444.

which he gave to the cause of Italian independence and to his high-handed way of taking action without reference to herself. But though he was dismissed for a time, he was not out of office long enough for England to change its foreign policy and convince other nations of the fact. It was Palmerstonianism, if not Palmerston, which led England into the objectless Crimean War (1854–56); it was Palmerstonianism which connived at the discreditable wars with China, the Opium War of 1840 and the War of 1860, whereby the Court of Peking was forced into direct diplomatic relations with the European powers[1]. Such was the attitude of England towards the weaker Powers, but to the growing power of Germany England behaved with peaceful caution. No help was given to Denmark when she was invaded by Prussia in 1864. In 1866 Prussia humiliated Austria and in 1870 rounded off her Empire with the greater humiliation of France; yet on both occasions England maintained neutrality. Though there was considerable apprehension over the Peace of Frankfort (1871), English intervention before the catastrophe was rendered impossible by the bad odour into which the Emperor Napoleon III's imperialistic bombast had brought the French Government both in this country and elsewhere.

In her relations with America during and after the American Civil War (1861–65) England committed initial improprieties which she redeemed by common-sense. The ultimatum to the U.S.A. over the seizure of two Confederate envoys on a British steamer, the *Trent*, was toned down to a protest, which allowed of a compromise; and the depredations of the *Alabama* were referred to arbitration by the Treaty of Washington, May 1871. Similarly in the dispute between England and Venezuela (1895–97), when President Cleveland advanced a version of the Monroe Doctrine to which Lord Salisbury, with all his willingness to appreciate American opinion, was unable to agree, the matter was referred to an Arbitration Court at Paris, which upheld most of the points for which England had been contending; though at a later date Sir Edward Grey in effect conceded the claim of the U.S.A. to the diplomatic hegemony of the American Continent.

[1] See *Cambridge Modern History*, xi. chap. 28.

But if we were wise and conciliatory westwards, we were short-sighted and spasmodically militant in the near East, still suspicious of Russia and unreasonably credulous of the Sick Man's promise to amend his ways. As in 1853 on the eve of the Crimean War, so again in 1878 at the conclusion of the Russo-Turkish War England, in Lord Salisbury's words, "put her money on the wrong horse".

Canon Masterman condemns the Treaty of Berlin (1878) in these words:

"Instead of making a bold effort to settle, once for all, the problem of the Balkans, the Powers, hampered by mutual jealousy and distrust, fell back upon a patchwork solution that condemned Macedonia to thirty years more of Turkish misrule, left Bulgarian aspirations unsatisfied, sowed the seeds of hostility between Austria and Serbia, and committed Great Britain to the task of bolstering up Turkish misrule in Asia. Worst of all, it gave time for Germany to abandon her attitude of indifference to Balkan questions. Like the Congress of Vienna sixty-three years before, the Congress of Berlin lacked the courage and disinterestedness that were needed to effect a lasting solution of the problems with which it had to deal, and the history of South Eastern Europe ever since has been the history of the efforts of the Balkan States to set aside the results of the Congress"[1].

The Congress of Berlin closed the chapter of European history which opened with the Congress of Vienna. Henceforth the relations of the Powers were affected less by internal European questions than by the world-wide struggle for colonies and markets. Africa and "Kolonial Macht" became the topics of the day. In 1882 the German Colonial Society was founded.

During the last fifteen years of the century Lord Salisbury enjoyed the prestige which Palmerston enjoyed before him. Where Palmerston blustered, Lord Salisbury was pliant, but his was the pliancy of a wise man who had studied deeply the book of history and the geography of nations. Pacific in the

---

[1] G. P. Gooch and J. H. B. Masterman, *A Century of British Foreign Policy*, p. 28.

spirit in which Castlereagh was pacific, he was prepared to go to almost any lengths to maintain the friendship of the United States, and in Europe he gave proof of his willingness to co-operate with Germany by agreeing to the transfer of Heligoland (1890) in return for concessions in Africa.

But after 1900 (Lord Salisbury resigned office in 1902 and died in 1903), and especially during the tenure of Sir Edward Grey (1906–14), the seriousness of the situation created by the military strength of Germany became more and more apparent. By the end of the century not only was Germany the first military Power in Europe, but in addition she was rapidly con-solidating an economic hegemony over less powerful neighbours than herself—Sweden, Holland, Belgium and Italy. Finally, she had joined in the scramble for territory and acquired posses-sions in Africa and the Pacific.

The South African War (1899–1902) found England in a position of splendid isolation on the Continent, but when Ger-many showed a determination to challenge the sea-power of England, England and France felt the need of closer relations. They had already taken joint action in North Africa, England controlling the Suez Canal (which had been constructed in 1869 by French engineers), and sharing with France the control of Egypt. Territorial rivalry, however, had brought the two countries to the verge of war over the Fashoda incident in 1898, and it was not until the accession of King Edward VII that the Entente took solid shape, France receiving a free hand in Morocco (1904) in return for the strengthening of England's hold on Egypt. Germany observed with jealousy the Anglo-French Entente, to which Russia, under the influence of France, inclined. She feared a conspiracy by the rest of the world to throttle the Germanic peoples. In 1911 she challenged the Entente by sending a gun-boat to Agadir, to support Moroccan interests against France, but England openly stood by France, and Germany, not yet prepared for war, listened to the demands of her financiers and ate humble pie. Meanwhile, the annex-ation of Bosnia and Herzegovina by Austria (1908) had raised a new storm centre in the Balkans. Then followed the Balkan

War (1912–13), and the success attending Sir Edward Grey's efforts to confine the quarrel to the Balkan States led optimists to think that a new and better era was at last dawning in European diplomacy. But they were wrong. The international situation moved with irresistible drift from Agadir to Serajevo. In June 1914 the Austrian heir apparent and his wife were assassinated at Serajevo, and by the beginning of August the great Powers were at war.

2. COLONIAL POLICY, RESPONSIBLE GOVERNMENT AND FEDERATION

If the foreign policy of England is a record of a good beginning and a good ending with a long and ambiguous middle, her colonial policy during the same period presents a refreshing contrast. It is possible to argue that the statesmen who controlled colonial policy did not, at the time, see the significance of the steps which they were taking, but it is certain that these steps were those which, upon retrospect, were demanded by far-seeing statesmanship.

Under the inspiration of the theorists of 1830 (see above, page 17) England granted representative institutions to colonists of Anglo-Saxon race, and followed this up by interpreting these institutions according to the traditions of the British Constitution. In this way the English-speaking colonists became self-governing Dominions, enjoying responsible self-government.

In Canada the foundation of responsible Government was laid by the Act of 1840, which, with a view to harmonising the interests of English and French Canadians[1], united the Governments of Upper and Lower Canada. Between 1846 and 1854 Lord Elgin, Durham's son-in-law, was governor-general and he conducted himself as a constitutional sovereign, working as far as possible through ministers who commanded the confidence of the popular assembly. His tenure of office was marked by the complete transference of the Civil List to the Canadian

---

[1] "I found two nations warring in the bosom of a single state: I found a struggle not of principles, but of races" (Durham's *Report on the Affairs of British North America*, p. 8).

Government (1847), the ratification, in the face of loyalist clamour, of the Indemnification Act relating to the Rebellion of 1837–38 (1849), and the conclusion of a Reciprocity Treaty between Canada and the United States (1854).

The implications of self-government were brought to a head in 1859 when Canada successfully maintained its right to establish a protective tariff against the Mother-country. The Colonial Office at first supported the protest of the Sheffield manufacturers against the Canadian tariff, but they had to give way. The Canadian Parliament insisted that Canada could not be responsible for its debt and internal expenses unless it was allowed to raise the necessary revenue in the manner dictated by the economic interests of the country.

Canada now began to feel itself a nation, and this feeling found expression in the proposals for a confederation, which were formulated at Quebec in 1864 and became law as the British North America Act of 1867.   Only Newfoundland remains outside the Confederation.

The evolution of responsible self-government followed similar lines in Australia and New Zealand. The Australian Constitutions Act of 1850 empowered these colonies to create constitutions for themselves. The New Zealand Constitution Act of 1852 gave the same powers to New Zealand. The New Zealand authorities, appreciating the distinction between representative and responsible government, applied to the Home Government in 1854 to know whether they had power to establish responsible self-government.   Downing Street replied: "Her Majesty's Government have no objection whatever to the establishment. of the system known as responsible government in New Zealand". The despatch then proceeds to point out that no legislative enactment is required for this. "In this country, the recognised plan of Parliamentary Government, by which Ministers are responsible to Parliament, and their continuance in office practically depends on the votes of the two Houses—rests on no written law but on usage only"[1].

[1] Keith, *Documents on British Colonial Policy*, 1. 238—The Right Hon. Sir George Grey, Bart. to the Officer administering the Government of New Zealand (General Wynyard).

In 1900 Australia took the step taken by Canada in 1867. The Australian federal Commonwealth was created, New Zealand electing to remain outside it.

The course of South African history ran less smoothly; for through the 19th century there were two warring elements, the English and the Dutch. The Boers in 1836 trekked across the Vaal and founded the independent Transvaal Republic. The policy of England was half-hearted and vacillating. The independence of the Boers was recognised, then denied, then recognised again. With the regeneration of the Chartered Companies in British South Africa, British East Africa and the Niger the hold of Great Britain on South Africa was increased, but the continued independence of two unfriendly Republics within the circle of British interests arrested the development of South Africa as a whole. The discovery of gold on the Rand and the illtreatment of the Uitlanders by President Kruger led to the South African War in 1899.

In 1906 the Transvaal and Orange Free State were granted full self-government by Letters Patent, and in 1909 the third great Dominion in the British Commonwealth was created by the Union of South Africa.

The relation between the central and local authorities in the several self-governing Dominions varies. The Australian Constitution is nearest to that of the United States, for in both the federal authority only possesses the limited powers expressly assigned by the Constitution[1]. In Canada, on the other hand, all subjects of general interest not distinctly and exclusively

---

[1] Cf. Speech by the Right Hon. Joseph Chamberlain on the Introduction of the Constitution Bill in the House of Commons, May 14, 1900:

"I think it is true to say that, on the whole, this new Constitution...in the main, and more than any other, follows the Constitution of the United States of America. But it would be, perhaps, more interesting to us to contrast it with the Constitution of our own colony of Canada....While in Canada the result of the Constitution was substantially to amalgamate the provinces into one Dominion, the Constitution of Australia created a federation for distinctly definite and limited objects of a number of independent States, and State rights have throughout been jealously preserved. In Canada everything that was not given expressly to the provinces went to the Central Government. In Australia the Central Government has only powers over matters which are expressly stated and defined in the Constitution". (A. B. Keith, *Selected Speeches, etc. on Colonial Policy*, I. 346–7.)

conferred upon local authorities are vested in the "General" Government; that is to say, the federal authority is the residual authority. South Africa has gone one stage further in centralisation. The Union of South Africa is a unitary State. The provinces have no rights against the central authority.

The grounds for these differences are mainly historical. Canada created its instrument of government at a time when its neighbour, the United States, was resisting by civil war the claim of the Southern States to secede. It was, therefore, determined to run no such risk itself. The States of Australia developed in greater isolation. A vast Continent was parcelled out among a handful of settlers. When the States met together to form an Australian Government, they were so habituated to conducting their own affairs that they were jealous of surrendering more than was necessary to the central authority. In South Africa there was racial, as well as economic, jealousy, but the makers of the constitution realised that in the circumstances in which South Africa was placed a strong central authority was a *sine qua non* of permanent union. The white peoples were ready to sacrifice local interests to the supreme necessity of presenting a common front to the coloured population, which so largely outnumbered them.

3. IRELAND, HOME RULE AND LAND LEGISLATION

What is an Englishman to say of the deplorable condition of Ireland in 1800 at the time of the Union? Protestant Ulster, stubborn and hard-working, was laying the foundations of her industrial prosperity, but very different was the state of the great Catholic mass of this emotional and imaginative race.

Illiterate, because education had been forbidden; poor, because till very recently property owning had been criminal; ground down by Protestant landlords; represented in Parliament by Protestant nominees; ruled by a Protestant aristocracy; steeped, with her peculiar retrospective temperament, in the bitterness of the past; and regarding everything English through the bloody spectacles of Vinegar Hill, the scene of slaughter in the turmoil of 1798—Catholic Ireland was filled with a blind desire to throw off her burden of disabilities. But the people had no real political knowledge, no unity, no organisation, no leader; and they stumbled on in the dark, the hatred in their hearts expressing itself in secret oaths and agrarian crime, until a great man arose to champion them.

In 1824 Daniel O'Connell founded the Catholic Association, and rallied Catholic Ireland to the cause of emancipation. The clergy, always a formidable force, threw themselves into the movement, and very soon every Catholic parish had a branch of the Association. In 1825 the Association was suppressed by the Government, but not before it had done its work. The apathy, born of repression, gave way to a new current of national hope. For the next twenty years O'Connell dominated the Irish scene. In 1828 he was returned to Parliament, flouting the disabilities. In 1829 the Catholic Emancipation Act was passed, and Ireland went wild with joy. But the measure did not bring the expected peace, it merely loosened a nation's tongue; and the retrogressive step which accompanied the Act of Emancipation, the disfranchisement of the forty shilling freeholders, excited a fresh agitation for the repeal of the Union. Agitation was followed by agrarian crime, and Coercion Acts dogged the footsteps of both. On August 15, 1843, O'Connell's Repeal Campaign culminated in a vast gathering at the Hill of Tara (County Meath)[1]. The Government took fright, prohibited meetings, and threw O'Connell into jail. Then (1845–46) famine visited the island, leaving in its path a terrible death-roll and a ceaseless procession of emigrants. Over a million Irishmen took their hatred of England with them to the United States, and there founded that Irish American party which has been such a thorn in England's side.

On the death of O'Connell in 1847 the agitation fell into the hands of extremists, and in 1848 the wave of revolution in Europe caught Ireland and flung her once more against English bayonets. After this there was comparative quiet till the Fenian rising of 1867.

The failure of English statesmanship was proclaimed to the world. Continental nations, said Macaulay, regarded it some-

[1] Cf. *The Times*, Aug. 17, 18, 19, 1843.

what in the same light as the problem of Russia in Poland[1]. Successive Whig and Tory administrations were consistent neither in policy nor in strength of purpose. Repression was followed by concessions delayed until the virtue had gone out of them. The Whigs blamed the Tory high-handedness, the Tories blamed the Whig weakness, but the real difficulty was deeper than this. The English people profoundly misunderstood the Irish character, and the Irish, with long memories, profoundly distrusted the good intentions of England.

It remained for another great Irishman to bring the question of Home Rule into practical politics for a second time. Charles Stewart Parnell, "the uncrowned King of Ireland", founded in 1879 the Land League, and carried agitation to Westminster. He organised electoral Ireland, and the overwhelming Nationalist vote which followed the Franchise Reform of 1884–85 convinced Gladstone that some measure of self-government was necessary. Therefore in 1886 he introduced a Home Rule Bill, but 90 members of his party, led by Lord Hartington and Joseph Chamberlain, declared themselves Unionists and combined with the Tories to defeat the second reading. In 1893 Gladstone introduced a second Home Rule Bill, which passed the Commons but was rejected in the Lords by 419 votes to 41. After this decisive defeat the English public lost interest in the question, although the Irish never lost an opportunity of pressing their claims; and it was not until the Liberals returned to power in 1906 that Home Rule again received serious attention. A Home Rule Bill was on the point of becoming law when the War broke out, and was allowed to pass through Parliament on the understanding that it should not come into operation until the War was ended and an arrangement had been made which was acceptable to Ulster.

Though England refused to follow Gladstone in his effort to grant Home Rule, she was ready enough to grant reforms which stopped short of political separation. Gladstone diagnosed the three great troubles of Ireland—"the three great branches of the Upas Tree"—as the State Church, the System of Land Tenure and the System of Education. The State Church was

---

[1] House of Commons, February 19, 1844. Hansard, 3rd S. LXXII. 1186.

disestablished in 1869. The Educational System was remodelled in 1879 and 1892. But the experiments in Land Legislation, the Government's "planetary excursion into political economy", encountered grave difficulties. The dissatisfaction of the peasants with their economic lot had always been the basis of political agitation. In 1867 John Bright declared that a peasant proprietary was the panacea for Ireland, and the land legislation of the closing decades of the century had this solution in view. Between 1869 and 1895 a series of Land Purchase Acts were passed, but they were half-hearted measures, and in the sum they achieved less than Wyndham's Act of 1903, which was national in its scope and backed by the credit of the Imperial Government. This was granted on such liberal terms that the act of purchase involved an actual reduction in the annual rent charge. It is not surprising that property had its magic when purchase cost something less than nothing[1].

The legislation passed before 1903 prepared the way for the success of Wyndham's larger measure. The securing of tenant right, the protection from arbitrary eviction, and the fixing of rents by a Land Court gave proof that England was at last making a conscientious attempt to better the economic condition of Ireland. The establishment of a Department of Agriculture and Technical Instruction in 1899 was accompanied by the organisation of agricultural co-operation under the Irish Agricultural Organisation Society. Sir Horace Plunkett was the pioneer of the Irish Co-operation, and the substantial successes achieved in co-operative dairying and co-operative purchase of agricultural supplies led many to hope that the troubles of Ireland would be peaceably solved by economic reform. In the year 1916 the aggregate exports of Ireland showed a 40 per cent. increase in quantity and a 100 per cent. increase in value over the figures for 1904[2]. But there have always been people in Ireland anxious to speed up events, and to these malcontents was due the Sinn Fein Rebellion of March 1916.

[1] Cf. M. J. Bonn, *The Irish Agrarian Problem* (1906): "In Ireland the magic of property consists in the fact that it is cheaper by 25 per cent. to get it than not to get it. It is not the acquisition of property, but the refusal of it that is associated with sacrifices" (p. 151).

[2] *Economic Journal*, No. 114 (June 1919), pp. 250–1.

4. Fiscal Policy of the United Kingdom

The fiscal policy of England underwent no conspicuous change during the first few years of the reformed House of Commons. The Excise was overhauled[1], but the moderately protective tariff, constructed by Huskisson, was left intact, and it remained for Peel, an old colleague of Huskisson, to carry on his work, when the Tories returned to power in 1841.

In 1840 a Parliamentary Committee on Import Duties[2] made clear the distinction between the protective and the revenue-bearing functions of a tariff. They condemned all duties which were so high as to impede international trade; and Peel accepted their conclusions.

Faced with a permanent deficit in the revenue, he had the courage to carry out his Free Trade programme by re-imposing the "obnoxious and inquisitorial" income tax which had succumbed to a storm of abuse in 1816. In six years, 1841–46, he reduced the duties on manufactured goods from 30 per cent.—Huskisson's level—to 10 per cent., and abolished food taxes, duties on raw materials and certain export duties. He found a full-blooded protective system, he left only its skeleton. He found the country's finances in a state of chronic deficit, he left them with a revenue equal to the expenditure.

Gladstone completed Peel's work. Between 1853 and 1860, the remnants of protection, and with these the last of the imperial preferences, were swept away. The duties remaining were few in number, imposed for revenue purposes only and at a lower rate than heretofore. The Government reposed faith in Gladstone's creed of the resilience of the revenue through increased consumption, and their faith was justified.

Thus England became a Free Trade country; and Cobden prophesied that all Europe would quickly follow our lead. He was wrong. For half a century the Continent had been watching with envious eyes the growth of England's monopoly in large

[1] The Excise Commissioners, appointed in 1832 with Sir H. Parnell as Chairman, sat from 1833 to 1836 and published 20 Reports, which are summarised in the Report of July 1836.

[2] *Commons' Committee on the several Duties levied on Imports into the United Kingdom*, etc. (1840).

scale production for export, and, fascinated by English success, had modelled their policy on ours. But a reaction followed. The commercial classes of France, who should have acclaimed Cobden's Treaty of 1860, were hostile to it. The infant industries of the Continent had small chance of competing with the firmly established lead of England without protective assistance. The stiffening of the American tariff and its apparent success in developing home industry at the expense of British trade confirmed the new opinion; and by 1870 Cobden's prophecy was falsified. Behind new tariff walls industries grew up, using and improving English methods, and continental competition, even in England's specialities, became for the first time really serious.

During the last quarter of the century our trade statistics showed steady increases, but we were compelled to find markets further and further afield. American food-stuffs and German manufactures competed with English produce in English markets, and the foreign trade of America and Germany grew at a comparatively quicker rate. English manufacturers began to ask themselves whether Free Trade was the real cause of our mid-century prosperity, or whether that prosperity was not due to our virtual monopoly of large scale industry, at a time when rivals were crippled by wars and revolutions. The sting of the hostile tariffs and the lack of any weapon with which to reply were responsible for a revival of protection at the beginning of the new century. Chamberlain's movement for imperial federation in 1903 was captured by the forces of tariff reform, and the fiscal question loomed large in the political life of the first decade of the 20th century. Up to 1914, however, its advocates, the Conservative party, had not been returned to power.

The tariff history of the two great English-speaking nations affords a striking contrast. In England Free Trade was fully established before the American Civil War broke out. In the United States a protective tariff was maintained throughout the 19th century: at first to protect infant industries, then frankly to secure to American producers the monopoly of the American market. A graph of the tariff changes since 1800 would show a continuous upward trend, with occasional fluctuations downwards. In 1808 the average tariff was 15 per cent.; in 1897 it was

57 per cent. After 1900 public opinion in America forced the Government to recede somewhat from the policy of extreme protection; but it would appear that the financial interests which prop up the tariff wall are too powerful to be overthrown without a serious struggle.

5. TREND OF SOCIAL LEGISLATION IN ENGLAND

In Prussia the tradition of paternal government has run in a strong and steady current since the days of Frederick the Great, but in England the dominant political philosophy changed more than once during this period. In the first half of the 19th century the Manchester School, representing the new manufacturing plutocracy, challenged the political supremacy of the old landed aristocracy and imported into practical politics a *laissez faire* philosophy, which represented to them less the individualistic idealism of a Bentham than the pecuniary interests of their own pockets. *Laissez faire* was a doctrine of inevitability and the inference from it was that the Government was neither responsible for, nor capable of, improving the conditions of life—the English people must work out its own salvation. But the official disclosures of the '40's and the advertisement of the factory and mining horrors in the provincial press awakened in Victorian England a new sense of responsibility. Individualism, it was realised, had resulted in the enslavement of the weak. Slowly and painfully came the conviction that the State must intervene to save the health and vitality of the nation. To-day the belief in *laissez faire* is extinct, the State having committed itself to a comprehensive scheme for the endowment of citizenship, based on the maintenance of a national minimum of health, education and economic sufficiency[1].

The remedial legislation of 1840–50, and notably the Public Health Act of 1848, laid the foundation of the new system. But the Government moved cautiously at first, keeping its positive obligations within narrow limits. The classes enfranchised by the Acts of 1867 and 1884–85, though they exercised an immediate influence on the attitude of Government, were slow to build up

[1] See *Cambridge Modern History*, XII. chap. 23.

an independent Labour party. One of the results of the recent War was to increase the part played by the representatives of labour in the administration of departments of government directly affecting labour.

Legislation, however democratically meant, would have achieved little without appropriate machinery. Declining the alternative of bureaucracy, England appealed to the instincts of her citizens for local self-government. In the 18th century local institutions had fallen into sad decay. The Justices of the Peace ruled the country districts, and corrupt Corporations misruled the towns. In some places a modicum of authority was exercised by elected parish vestries, and certain indispensable services were discharged by Special Improvement Commissioners, nominally under local control; but the spirit of democracy in local government was faint.

The Municipal Corporations Act of 1835 marked the beginning of a general change. Power was gradually conferred on localities by the creation of representative authorities for special purposes—Boards of Guardians, Public Health Boards, School Boards, Rivers Boards, etc., and their functions were subsequently transferred to elective Municipal and County Councils (the latter established by the Act of 1888). In 1914, subject only to a central check on expenditure and efficiency, the Town and County Councils administered all local activities, with the exception of the Poor Law, and this anomaly was removed when the recommendations of the Poor Law Commission were carried out.

The local machinery thus created has proved to be a wise combination of local freedom and central control, and it has been strong enough to serve as an instrument for giving effect to the new social ideals.

The local authority is now the guardian of the public health within its area. It is concerned with the remedial treatment of epidemic disease, which includes free vaccination and compulsory notification: with drainage and the disposal of sewage: with street cleaning and smoke consumption: with the provision of free hospitals and clinics, of child welfare centres and a local nursing service. It has its own medical officer to assist it with expert advice.

The Education Act of 1902 transferred the power of the School Boards to the local authority. Elementary and Secondary Schools, Technical and Evening Schools, Art and Music Schools, Reformatory and Industrial Schools, Schools for Blind, Crippled and Epileptic Children, Schools of Cookery, Laundry, House-wifery, Gardening, Woodwork, are administered by a Committee of the Local Council representing the ratepayers whose children use the Schools. The Universities are subsidised, and the scheme of scholarships opens the way from the Elementary School to the University. The extension of educational activity brought the local authority into the medical sphere, and the Councils now undertake the medical inspection of school children and the provision of free meals in cases of necessity. The Education Act of 1918 raised the minimum age of employment to 14 and committed the nation to compulsory Continuation Schools and vocational training up to 18 years of age. The local authority will administer the scheme as soon as it is set in motion.

The provision of economic services by the local authority is constantly expanding. The local authority supplies water, light, tramways, public parks, plans the development of the town or district, and is at present engaged in coping with the shortage of houses. Many of the functions now discharged by it were left 100 years ago to private or semi-private enterprise.

Finally, the State has instituted national guarantees against economic hardships: Old Age Pensions (1908), Labour Exchanges (1909), National Insurance against Sickness and Unemployment (1911).

In this way, citizenship has been "endowed" both locally and nationally, the benefits being conferred on the individual as a citizen. The State, furthermore, has intervened with Minimum Wage Legislation in certain industries. The sweated trades are regulated by the Trade Boards Act of 1909, and the Coal Mining Industry by the Coal Mines Minimum Wage Act of 1912; but the significance of the two Acts is very different. The one is the official blessing of the chastened mood of the 19th century, while the other heralds the challenge of Labour to the 20th century.

CHAPTER XI

COBDENISM

I. "THE INSPIRED BAGMAN WHO BELIEVES IN A COTTON MILLENNIUM"

ENGLAND'S foreign policy, while liberal in its championship of small nations, was not liberal in the sense desired by Richard Cobden. He and his followers of the Manchester School were free traders, and as free traders they were whole-heartedly pacific. Let us see therefore what influence they had on international politics.

A society wit once called Cobden "the inspired bagman who believes in a cotton millennium"[1]. Does the cap fit?

He was certainly a bag-man, for he began life as a commercial traveller, and later won for himself the title of the "international man" by the frequency of his excursions to the Continent of Europe. To Cobden both Whigs and Tories were the slaves of shibboleths—balance of power, diplomatic interventions, armaments and the like. He, on the contrary, believed that the key to the international situation lay in trade—trade which had grown and was growing so rapidly that it was sweeping into its vortex all the elements of national life. In Cobden's view trade does not follow the flag—the policy of "the cudgel" is obsolete. So powerless were our cannon to open a single market that the calico printers of England were under-sold under the very guns of Gibraltar. "The fight is for commercial supremacy and the battle will be won by the cheapest"[2]. By cheapness we hold our home markets against the foreigner; by cheapness we secure the open markets of the world against rival importers; by cheapness we shall pierce hostile tariff walls.

The conflict between a policy of plenty and a policy of power is as old as economic history itself, and Cobden set the seal on the

---

[1] C. Gibbon, *Life of George Combe*, II. 309.
[2] Cobden, *Russia* (1836), chap. IV. (*Political Writings* I. 291.)

policy of plenty, which had been argued philosophically in *The Wealth of Nations* and was adopted by Parliament under Huskisson and Peel.

Cobdenism has a repellent exterior, but Cobden himself was no cold critic. We shall see in the next chapter how he roused his followers to a passion of enthusiasm for Corn Law Repeal, how he won over the agricultural labourers and even the farmers, and how he silenced the landlords by his eloquence and statistics. He was equally successful in the application of economic arguments to international politics. "I thank God", he said in 1864, "we live in a time when it is impossible for Englishmen to make a war profitable"[1]. It remained for Mr Norman Angell to convince his countrymen that because war is unprofitable and because credit is the life-blood of civilised society, therefore—

(*a*) As soon as we master these elementary truths, we shall cease to want war;

(*b*) High finance will forbid war—witness Agadir; and if war does break out, it cannot last for many weeks without destroying economic life.

In this mood many of us viewed the outbreak of war in August, 1914, and slowly recanted in the years which followed.

Cobden's millennium is derided as a cotton millennium. Cobden's firm made cotton prints, and the epithet is thus far apposite. But if cotton is meant to suggest something which is flimsy, then it is anything but apposite. Like the mid-Victorian England which he typified, Cobden was a hard-headed man of facts. Those who entered the lists against him found this to their cost. As he silenced the landlords, so also he worsted the Chartists when they matched O'Connor against him in 1843; and he was as successful in parliamentary debate as in popular oratory. When the Protectionists listened to him in Parliament in 1845 urging and proving the case for Corn Law Repeal, they whispered among themselves, "Peel must answer this". But Peel, so the story runs, crumpled up his notes, as he muttered, "Let those answer him who can"[2].

---

[1] Speech on Foreign Policy, November 23, 1864.
[2] John MacCunn, *Six Radical Thinkers*, p. 101.

If by cotton we understand something which is material and has no spirit behind it, then again we are mistaken in thus depicting Cobdenism. Indeed, the thing which most irritated his opponents, and which they not unreasonably designated as cant, was his habit of surrounding free trade in a halo of sanctity.

I believe that the speculative philosopher of one thousand years hence will date the greatest revolution that ever happened in the world's history from the triumph of the principle which we have met here to advocate[1].

And again,

It is because I do believe that the principle of free trade is calculated to alter the relations of the world for the better that I bless God I have been allowed to take a prominent part in its advocacy.... I see in the free trade principle that which shall act on the moral world as the principle of gravitation in the Universe—drawing men together, thrusting aside the antagonism of race and creed and language, and uniting us in the bonds of eternal peace[1].

Free Trade was the "international law of the Almighty"; and it was bound up in his mind with an ideal of human well-being, national and international. War was fatal to that ideal, and, therefore, although he was not for "peace at any price" and although on occasions he spoke strongly for Defence and the Navy[2], he hated war none the less with a perfect hatred.

Cobden was at one with Karl Marx in his economic interpretation of society; and even as Marx believed in the early advent of a new society, so too Cobden announced the certainty of his convictions, when he prophesied: "There will not be a tariff in Europe which will not be changed in less than five years to follow your example"[1]. The prophecy was signally false, but there were moments in the middle of the century when the world seemed to be following the fiscal lead of England and when the nations were disposed to flatter themselves that something like a millennium was at hand. Such must have been the feeling of many of those who were present at the great International

---

[1] Speech, January 15, 1846.

[2] "If the French Government showed a sinister design to increase their navy to an equality with ours; then, after every explanation to prevent such an absurd waste, I should vote 100 millions sterling rather than allow that navy to be increased to a level with ours" (*Speeches*, II. 249).

Exhibition of 1851 in London. The Prince Consort, an ardent disciple of the Manchester School, opened it; and Tennyson honoured it with the ode which contains the well-known lines:

Till each man find his own in all men's good,
And all men work in noble brotherhood,
Breaking their mailed fleets and armed towers,
And ruling by obeying Nature's powers,
And gathering all the fruits of earth and crown'd with all her flowers.

But these hopes melted like ice before the vainglorious imperialism of Napoleon III and the ruthless designs of Bismarck.

2. Commercial Treaty with France, 1860

Cobden's name is linked with France by the Commercial Treaty of 1860. This was a substantial achievement, even though it did not introduce a fiscal millennium, and it was a signal instance of the application of business capacity to foreign diplomacy.

By this Treaty England abolished the remnants of protective duties on imported manufactures, reduced the duties on wine and brandy and engaged not to tax or prohibit the export of coal. France lowered her tariff from a prohibitive level to a maximum of 30 per cent. The Treaty lasted till 1881, when it was ended at the desire of France, then reverting to protection. The French were only willing to renew it in return for substantial benefits, but England being wholly a free trade country had no substantial concessions to offer, and as her representatives were obliged to accept no alterations whereby any French duties were higher than those of 1860, the efforts at renewal fell through.

It is probable that the Treaty was more profitable to England than to France. French claret never became, as Gladstone hoped, a popular beverage in England; and the cessation of the Treaty checked English exports to France more severely than French exports to England. In this respect the Treaty of 1860 was a repetition of the Pitt-Vergennes Treaty of 1786, which flooded

France with English manufactures to the detriment of her nascent industries[1].

In 1860 there were special reasons inducing France to repeat the experiment of 1786 :—

(a) Napoleon III desired the friendship of England for political purposes; and under the new Imperial Constitution he had power to conclude a Tariff Treaty without the consent of the Assembly.

(b) Among the intellectuals in France, and to a certain degree in ministerial circles, there was a genuine free trade feeling, which had been absent eighteen years previously, when Peel, with larger concessions to offer, failed to make any impressions on the French tariff wall.

(c) England had in Cobden an exceptionally able negotiator. From the first mooting of the Treaty in 1859 to the signing of it on January 29, 1860, and for the seven months between April and November, 1860, when the French tariff was being altered in detail, Cobden was the driving force. Day after day he sat at Paris examining the schedules with the French Commissioners, exposing the fabrications of the French Protectionists and pulling the rates down to the agreed general level.

The Treaty of 1860 is a notable landmark in the history of commercial reciprocity. The Methuen Treaty between England and Portugal in 1703 was an exclusive bargain to the specified disadvantage of a nation outside the compact. Then "and for ever hereafter", it ran, the heavier wines of our traditional Ally, Portugal (Port and Sherry), were to pay not more than two-thirds of the rate paid by French wines. Pitt's Treaty of 1786 was not aimed against a particular rival, but its benefits were confined to the contracting parties. Huskisson's Reciprocity Treaties went a stage further. They came to this: "We, England, give to you, France, Austria, Prussia, etc., terms not less favourable than we give to others; and we shall continue to do so, so long as you do the same by us". In the Treaty of 1860 Hus-

---

[1] See *Economic Journal*, No. 113, Lilian Knowles, "New Light on the economic Causes of the French Revolution". The treaty came into force in May 1787.

kisson's method was adopted and extended. England said in effect: "We, England, make this Treaty with you, France; and the terms which we grant to you we grant to other countries, and we will take no preferences from them". France did not go quite as far, but the result was much the same. France said: "We, France, make this Treaty with you, England, and we propose to make Treaties with other countries to the same effect. If in so doing we are offered preferential terms, we shall accept them. Whether you also get those preferences, is your concern and theirs".

In this way what is known as "the most favoured nation clause", under which the two contracting powers engage to confer on the other any fiscal advantage which they may concede to any third power, became a regular item in commercial treaties.

By means of this network, of which few Englishmen seem to be aware, while fewer still know to whom they owe it, all the great trading and industrial communities of Europe, i.e., England, France, Holland, Belgium, the Zollverein (1870), Austria, and Italy, constitute a compact international body, from which the principle of monopoly and exclusive privilege has once for all been eliminated, and not one member of which can take off a single duty without all the other members at once partaking in the increased trading facilities thereby created[1].

So writes Cobden's biographer, quoting a diplomatic authority.

3. Peace and International Arbitration

Cobden died in 1865, five years before Prussianism triumphed at Sedan, but he lived long enough to protest against intervention in Denmark. Palmerston was ready, it was thought, to go to any lengths in the defence of Denmark, but Queen Victoria for dynastic reasons deprecated a breach with Prussia, and

---

[1] Morley, *Life of Richard Cobden*, p. 806. The position, however, in international law to-day is not so simple as this. Certain nations, the U.S.A. among them, have held that the clause does not entitle a party to privileges which some other state has gained by giving corresponding privileges in return, *unless the claimant also offers a fair consideration for them*. If the Reciprocity Treaty proposed in 1911 between the U.S.A. and Canada had been ratified, one part of the British Empire would have received preferential treatment which was not shared by the mother country; for England, having no negotiating tariff, was unable to offer to the U.S.A. concessions similar to those offered by Canada.

Napoleon III would only co-operate on conditions which we
could not accept. The policy of non-intervention therefore
carried the day.

Victorian England did nothing without a movement. When
Joseph Sturge and his supporters had brought their Anti-
Slavery campaign to a successful issue, they threw themselves
into the Peace Movement, reviving the activity of the London
Peace Society (which had been established in 1816) and con-
ducting a national propaganda in favour of disarmament and
non-intervention. Sturge's principal allies now were Henry
Richard, a Congregational pastor, who acted as Secretary to
the Peace Society, Elihu Burritt of the U.S.A., organiser of the
"League of Universal Brotherhood"—and Richard Cobden.

Cobden approached the subject from his own standpoint.
Believing that free trade was indispensable to peace, he stressed
the appeal to commercial interest. "Until", he wrote to Sturge
in 1850, "you can convince the public that they have no
pecuniary interest in violating the first principles of the New
Testament, you will not, I fear, make us a nation of Christians"[1].
Not that he was blind to the driving force of pure idealism. In
1853 he wrote to a political friend: "The soul of the Peace
Movement is the Quaker sentiment against all war. Without the
stubborn zeal of the Friends, there would be no Peace Society
and no Peace Conference"[2].

The first Peace Congress was held at Brussels in the stormy
year of 1848. Victor Hugo presided at the second in Paris in
1849. In 1850, when Denmark and Schleswig Holstein were at
war, Sturge and another Friend, William Forster, paid a visit to
the battlefield in the hope of persuading the combatants to make
peace. To the practical mind of Cobden it was a quixotic exploit;
but when the affair ended without ridicule or mishap, he was
ready to express his admiration: "You have done good service by
breaking through the flimsy veil with which the diplomatists of
the world try to conceal their shallow craft, and penetrating into
their mysterious domain, by your startling expedition to Rends-
burg and Copenhagen....If Russia, England, and France, or
either of them, had interfered with the sincere and disinterested

---

[1] Stephen Hobhouse, *Joseph Sturge*, p. 127.   [2] *Ibid.* pp. 127–8.

and single-minded aim which actuated you and your friends, peace would have been secured in a week "[1].

In 1853 Sturge undertook a second mission, this time to the Czar of Russia, to present from the Society of Friends an address urging him to avoid war. The Czar received him graciously, but declared that the honour of Russia was involved. In 1856, however, the Peace Movement obtained a substantial success. In response to a memorial from the Peace Society, Lord Clarendon, our representative at the Congress of Paris, induced the Powers to insert in the Peace Treaty a protocol in favour of settling disputes by arbitration. It was only the expression of a wish, but a publicly expressed wish was something; and Gladstone acclaimed it as "in itself a very great triumph: a powerful engine on behalf of civilisation and humanity "[2].

We noted (page 113 above) the value of arbitration in maintaining the peace between England and the United States on more than one critical occasion in the 19th century. The fruitful outcome of these precedents was the Peace Commission Treaty of September, 1914, by which the two Governments agreed that:

All disputes between them of every nature whatsoever, other than disputes the settlement of which is provided for and in fact achieved under existing agreements, shall, when diplomatic methods of adjustment have failed, be referred for investigation and report to a permanent International Mission (consisting of 5 members).

And they further agreed:

Not to declare war or begin hostilities during such investigation and before the report is submitted[3].

The report must be submitted before the close of a year; and this year will be an invaluable "cooling off period", during which the danger of war ought to be averted.

That Cobden would have rejoiced in this Treaty we may be sure. But what of the Treaty that has been concluded between the Allies and Germany? Could Cobden have digested the latter part of it? One wonders. At any rate he would have made an admirable Secretary General to the League of Nations.

[1] Stephen Hobhouse, *Joseph Sturge*, p. 138. [2] *Ibid.* p. 157.
[3] *Ibid.* pp. 157–8.

CHAPTER XII

THE ANTI-CORN LAW LEAGUE

1. THE OLD ENGLAND AND THE NEW

THE Anti-Corn Law League originated in a dispute concerning the apportionment of housing accommodation in a very desirable residence called Old England. The family had been away for a long time, warring with Bonaparte on the Continent. When they came back they expected to find things as they had left them, but the moment they entered the house they noticed differences. Bales of cotton littered the floor, and charts depicting the exports of British manufactures since 1800 covered wall space that had been sacred to the fox's brush. The library table was soiled by ink. Cicero and Bolingbroke lay flat on their backs in a corner of the bookshelf, and standing upright were huge folios marked "Ledger", "Cash Account", "Profit and Loss". From this sad scene they were hurriedly called away, and entering my lady's boudoir, found her prostrate over a dissenter's hymnal.

Clearly there must be domestic re-arrangements. But why could not the parties settle it quietly among themselves? Why must the poor at the park gates be dragged in? Why must a League be created, to educate the people in statistics and make them glow with a sense of their wrongs? The reason is this. The new-comers believed that they were fighting for a national cause intimately affecting those very poor. The old occupants stood for the England that had been, they for the England that was and was coming to be. The issue, as it happened, was fought out over the propriety of certain statutes affecting the importation of foreign corn, known as the Corn Laws. The intruders demanded total repeal, the old occupants scented a conspiracy to eject them from their home, and so a great campaign was waged over the length and breadth of the country. No such tumult attended the last days of the Navigation Laws.

2. The Policy of the Corn Laws

National policy expresses itself in laws. The purpose of the Navigation Laws was to build up a commercial marine and make England mistress of the seas. The purpose of the Corn Laws was to secure to England plenty and productive strength in the prime article of national subsistence. There were Corn Laws before 1688, but only after 1688 did they give expression to a deliberate national policy. Between 1688 and 1846, three periods may be distinguished: the bounty period, 1688–1774; the transition period, 1774–1815; the protective period, 1815–1846.

During the dark days of the Napoleonic Wars England looked back with longing to the peace and plenty of the bounty period. The bounty was given on export, when the home price of corn was below a certain figure. As Adam Smith showed[1], its economic effect can never have been very important. It made the price of corn a trifle higher than it otherwise would have been and raised landlords' rents a little, but the method on which it was given was far too clumsy to steady the market price of corn, and its amount, 5s. per quarter, was far too small to increase materially the home production.

In the transition period (1774–1815), the other side of corn law policy, plenty to the consumer, came into prominence. In the earlier period the interest of the consumer had been consulted by suspending the bounty in times of scarcity and prohibiting export. But from about 1770 onwards England was a corn importing instead of a corn exporting country. Therefore the duties on import, which had hitherto been of formal importance only (their purpose was to prevent the bounty being fraudulently obtained), began to wear a protective complexion. But the amount of protection was very slight, for prices now were rising steadily, and the price at which corn could be imported free was often less than the level of prices actually ruling. The Corn Laws of 1773, 1791 and 1804 were attempts to keep pace with a new situation, but the situation changed so rapidly

[1] *Wealth of Nations*, Book IV. chap. V.

that it was always ahead of the policy. On top of economic
changes came the Napoleonic Wars, when England was faced
with the peril of starvation. To meet the peril the Government
had not only to suspend the operation of the Corn Laws, but
also to take action for conserving and increasing the supply of
food. It seized food cargoes, gave bounties on importation, prohibited the distillation of spirit from grain, taxed hair powder
in which grain was used, promulgated through the bench and
the pulpit self-denying ordinances, forbade the use of new bread,
ordered the baking of "standard, parliamentary, wholemeal
bread, the whole produce of the wheat", and recommended
substitutes—oatmeal, soup, fish, potatoes and what-not. All
this it did by laws or orders in council in what Dicey calls "the
period of legislative quiescence".

The circumstances which led up to the Corn Laws of 1814
and 1815 are obscure. The original motive was apparently to
foster corn production in Ireland. The result was a complete
break in corn law policy. By the Act of 1814 all bounties and
restrictions on export were abolished, by the Act of 1815 the
Corn Laws were made rigidly and avowedly protective. No
duties were imposed on import, but until the home price of
wheat exceeded 80s. per quarter, no foreign wheat might enter
England. Above that price it might enter free.

Between 1815 and 1846 the Corn Laws were on sufferance. The
Government was engaged in repenting of the Act of 1815 and
trying to find a way out of it. The most obvious defect of the
Act of 1815 was its rigidity. Corn importers had a strong interest
in "cooking the averages", and when, as on one occasion (Nov.
1818), the average was declared at 80s. 2d., the suspicion was
justified. Huskisson tried to substitute something which would
work more smoothly. He therefore proposed a sliding scale
with a pivot price which gave moderate protection. For every
rise in price beyond the pivot point the duty on import fell
gradually to nothing. For this device Huskisson had precedents
in the high, medium, and low duty points of the old corn laws.
Huskisson, however, failed. The agricultural interest would not
be content with moderate protection. Wellington therefore

introduced a new sliding scale in 1828. This was the corn law in force when the Anti-Corn Law League came into existence. Nobody was satisfied with it. It did not secure high prices, for after a good harvest the home crop alone was sufficient to bring the price of wheat to an unremunerative level. So far from steadying prices it disturbed them; for, as the duty descended by unequal jumps, it encouraged speculation and manipulation of the market. At the same time it irritated the manufacturing and working classes. Its fluctuations disturbed the exchange of English manufactures for foreign corn, and its protective intention led the consuming public to believe that the bounty of Europe and the new world was being artificially withheld.

Peel tried to put matters right in 1842 by a sliding scale which, because it gave less protection, would work more smoothly. But he was too late. The agriculturalists were estranged by its moderation, the manufacturing classes by its pretension to improve a policy which they detested *in toto*. In 1846 under the stress of the Irish Potato Famine the Corn Laws were repealed. The Act of Repeal declared that from the date of its passing (June 26, 1846) to Feb. 1, 1849 the duties payable on imports of wheat were to range from 10s. per quarter, when the home price was under 48s., to 4s. when the home price was 53s. and upwards; there were similar scales for barley, oats, etc.; on and after Feb. 1, 1849, there was to be a uniform duty of 1s. per quarter. In 1869 the 1s. duty, which had been retained for purposes of registration, was abolished. "It is no more difficult," said Mr Lowe in that year, "to register the arrival of corn without levying a duty of 1s. per quarter on it than it is to roast a pig without burning down a house"[1].

3. The Story of the Anti-Corn Law League

Manchester sent two Radicals to the Reformed Parliament of 1832, but for six years the Corn Law question hung fire. The country was enjoying industrial prosperity, and Lancashire had its share of the good times. But in 1837 the trade boom began

[1] Sydney Buxton, *Finance and Politics*, ii. 93.

to crack, and in March 1838, Charles Villiers, the member for Wolverhampton, made the first of his annual motions for an enquiry into the Corn Laws. The House, however, would not give him a hearing, and the Government left the question an open one. Lord Melbourne declared that the Government would take no decided part till it was certain that the mass of the people wanted it. The challenge was promptly taken up with a fury which bewildered this easy-going champion of *laissez faire*.

In September 1838 a certain Dr Bowring happened to be passing through Manchester on his return from a commercial mission on the Continent. Invited by some Manchester Free Traders to address them, he opened with a reference to the desolation produced by the recent war between Turkey and Egypt and to the advantages that would be gained by a more general recognition of the principles of peace, and then proceeded to discuss the Corn Laws.

When I went into Normandy and Brittany, what said the Normans and Bretons? "Why", said they, "admit our corn and then we'll see whether anybody can prevent the importation of your manufactures into France". (Cheers.) "We are millions", said they, "willing to clothe ourselves in the garments you send us, and you have millions of hungry mouths to take our corn". The same language is held by every nation in trade....I have heard it said, and it seems to have had some influence upon the labouring people, that the introduction of foreign corn is the inevitable way to lower wages. I say that, if there be any certain means of raising wages, it is by the admission of foreign corn. (Cheers.) What are the two countries that have had the wisdom to avoid Corn Law legislation? They are Holland and Switzerland; in which wages are higher than in any country in Europe! (Hear, hear!) And that is invariably the case[1].

Wages in Lancashire were falling then.

After the address, one of the audience proposed the formation of an Anti-Corn Law Association in Manchester, and a provisional Committee met shortly afterwards to give effect to the idea. October was spent in forming a powerful Committee and collecting subscriptions; and on Thursday, October 25, 1838, Mr Paulton delivered his first Anti-Corn Law Lecture to an enthusiastic Manchester audience. When the Manchester

[1] A. Prentice, *History of the Anti-Corn Law League* (1853), I. 65–7. Prentice headed the invitation to Dr Bowring.

Chamber of Commerce held its meeting on December 13, the excitement was such that it had to be adjourned, and on December 20 an amendment drafted by Richard Cobden in favour of complete Free Trade was carried. Mr Thomson[1], their member—said Cobden—while representing the free-traders of Manchester, had attempted less than Huskisson had done while representative of the monopoly interests of the old borough of Liverpool.

By the middle of January 1839, the organisation of the League had been settled, and subscriptions were coming in. Other towns held meetings and sent delegates to a dinner given by the Manchester Association. On January 28, 1839, the Manchester Anti-Corn Law Association was officially launched. A few days later, in the elections to the Manchester Chamber of Commerce, the successful candidates were free-traders, and most of them were members of the newly formed Association.

Shortly after the opening of Parliament delegates from different Anti-Corn Law Associations met in London at Brown's Hotel, Palace Yard, and on February 18, 1839, Charles Villiers moved in the House that the petitions against the Corn Laws which had been entrusted to him should be referred to a Committee of the whole House. But the motion was negatived without a division.

Before leaving for the North the delegates recommended that the different Associations should be formed into a League, with federal headquarters at Manchester, and that a League circular should be issued. Both recommendations were carried out forthwith; and on Tuesday, April 16, 1839, the first number of the *Anti-Corn Law Circular*[2] was published at Manchester.

The League was now becoming important. The agricultural interest paid it the compliment of forming in defence a "Central

[1] Charles Edward Poulett Thomson, President of the Board of Trade, 1834–39.

[2] The Journal was published under three titles:

I. *The Anti-Corn Law Circular*, No. 1 to No. 57, Vol. 2, April 16, 1839–April 8, 1841. (Published in Manchester.)

II. *The Anti-Bread Tax Circular*, No. 58, Vol. 3 to No. 140, Vol. 4, April 21, 1841–September 26, 1843. (Published in Manchester, larger size.)

III. *The League*, No. 1 to end. September 30, 1843–1846. (Published in London, at the League's Office, 67, Fleet Street.)

Agricultural Society", and the Conservative press indulged in vituperation. The *Morning Herald* denounced the members of the League as "many of them unprincipled schemers, while of those members who may claim credit for honesty of purpose, there are few, of whom it may not be alleged that they are at best conceited socialists".

In May 1839, one of the League's lecturers ventured into the stronghold of Cambridge University; and No. 4 of the *Anti-Corn Law Circular* gives a report of the meeting in the theatre at Cambridge:

When Mr Smith appeared on the stage, he was met by applause from the townspeople and hooting and hissing from the gownsmen. Having commenced, his voice was immediately drowned amid shouts and the blowing of a guard's horn....

Mr Smith: I trust there will be no disturbance. I am anxious for peace. I am a stranger and in physical force you are a hundred and fifty on one.

Gownsmen: Ha! ha! Down with the Chartists.

Citizens: Put them out! Put them out!

Gownsmen: Damn you, come on! Will you fight? Curse the rascals, &c.

Mr Smith: Gentlemen, I implore you not to irritate the people.

Gownsmen: Three cheers for the Corn Laws. Huzza, huzza! While to the cries of the people, "Put them out" &c., they answered, "Damn your eyes—three cheers for Sir Robert Peel, huzza, huzza!" Here the gownsmen exhibited their bludgeons and put themselves in attitude for a battle. The townsmen rose from the pit, climbed into the boxes, amid the most fearful blows, and a regular battle was the result. Hats, gowns, surtouts and coats flew in all directions...and the issue was the complete overthrow of the gownsmen, and their expulsion from the theatre, amid deafening shouts of victory and three cheers for Mr Smith.

The *Circular* alluded to the incident in its leading article:

The labours of the Council of the Anti-Corn Law League were this morning interrupted by the arrival of Mr Shearman from Cambridge bearing a large blue sack, the contents of which upon being emptied upon the table, proved to be the remains of University caps and gowns (the former very much broken and the latter torn), together with the fragments of divers benches and chairs, which were gathered up by him after the riot in the theatre at Cambridge. As many of our plodding members have yet to learn how the members of our learned Corporations dress, we invite all who are anxious in matters of academic costume to inspect the contents of our blue bag. But still more do we invite those parents and guardians who may think of sending their youth to Cambridge, to inspect these evidences of the kind of discipline their minds are likely to undergo at that University[1].

Before the delegates revisited London the League secured official representation in Parliament and an official meeting-place in Manchester. When Poulett Thomson left for Canada in September 1839, R. C. Gregg, an active member of the League, was elected in his place; and shortly afterwards the Free Trade Hall was built in St Peter's Fields on a site owned by Cobden. The purses of the manufacturers and the "work of 100 men for 11 days"[2] avenged the massacre of Peterloo. This temporary pavilion was subsequently replaced by the present Free Trade Hall.

Villiers' third annual motion (1840) was dropped on adjournment, and the Whig Government continued to be lukewarm. But the League worked on for itself. Their delegates, back again in London, examined agricultural labourers from Bucks, Somerset, and other counties, with a view to proving that wages did not rise with the price of food. Lecture tours were arranged in the Provinces, and an Anti-Corn Law *Almanac* was circulated. The Report of Joseph Hume's Import Duties' Committee (1840) was a bull point for the League. Henceforward the repealers were able to cite the evidence of experts, like MacGregor, Porter and J. Deacon Hume, in favour of complete Free Trade. The estimated burden of the protective duties, as set forth in the Report, made first-class fighting material, which was reprinted and constantly quoted. However, the party leaders were too busy struggling for the Treasury to pay much attention to the Customs House. At the last moment, namely on May 7, 1841, Lord John Russell declared for a fixed duty of 8s.[3], but the deathbed repentance availed nothing, and on May 27, 1841, Peel carried a vote of "no confidence" by a majority of one.

At the ensuing General Election Cobden was returned for Stockport.

With the Tories in office under Peel, the tone of the contro-

[1] *Anti-Corn Law Circular*, No. 4.   [2] Prentice, I. 142.
[3] Cf. Spencer Walpole, *Life of Lord John Russell*, I. 369.

versy became more bitter. The League's *Journal* screamed and opened its columns to poetry. The Tories were insolent to the point of folly. In the debate on the Abolition of the Corn Laws (1843) Sir Edward Knatchbull said: "There are pecuniary liabilities created by family settlements, liabilities created under a system of protection, which could not be met if that Protection was removed. Did hon. Gentlemen mean to say that a sweeping measure of the Corn Laws was to make no provision for these liabilities?"[1] The League caused the country to ring with the name of "Dowry Knatchbull". If Peel's supporters (the young Disraeli among them) found some of his measures hard to digest, the League gave itself no such trouble. It labelled them all "poison" and spat. The new Income Tax was an imposition on the middle classes and introduced in order to perpetuate monopolies[2]. The new sliding scale, by a trick of the averages, would increase the degree of protection at the crucial point[3]. The reduction of the timber duties was a great sacrifice of revenue "wholly without necessity *at the present time*. People do not want houses *now*. There are 30,000 empty dwellings within 30 miles of Manchester and a like proportion of unemployed mills, manufactories and workshops"[4].

This is the language of hysteria, but there was cause enough for it. In the summer of 1842 the cloud of industrial depression settled heavily over the North. The air was charged with human electricity. Amid the solemn hush which preceded the storm of August 1842 (the month of the Turn Out), the manufacturers, assembled at Palace Yard, told London the tale of Lancashire's anguish. Sir James Graham, the Home Secretary, disgusted them by a statistical survey of mills recently erected, but Peel was visibly impressed and accepted a pamphlet: *How does cheap bread produce high wages?* At this moment of the League's history its members were citizens first and Leaguers second.

---

[1] Hansard, 3rd S. LXIX. 225.
[2] *Anti-Bread Tax Circular*, No. 84. No. 86 quotes from the *Liverpool Journal*: "We fully agree with the League in thinking everything bad of the Income Tax.... It is the very wickedest and most vexatious of taxes which the ingenuity of man ever conceived."
[3] *Anti-Bread Tax Circular*, No. 89.   [4] *Ibid.* No. 87.

At other periods of the long struggle they were trying to raise the country to their own high pitch by all the artifices that their shrewd minds could devise—by the passion of their speech and the satire of their pens, by prayers and statistics, by defiance and gibe, by thunderous iteration of their damning monotone—monopoly, landlords' monopoly. But now one great cry of national despair, unorganised, illiterate, with no statistics and with curses for prayers, monotonous only because the pitch was too high for the human ear to catch distinctions, made the League's agitation paltry by the side of its simple passion. The red-hot orators of the League were transformed into pale policemen. The delegates left London for the North, to keep there the peace of Her Majesty whom Peel and Graham served. "They wished for peace—they wished for no violence", said John Bright on July 14, 1842, "they would not have the Corn Laws or any other law removed by the shedding of one drop of blood".

By the summer of 1843 the tension in the North had eased and trade showed signs of revival. On July 25, 1843, John Bright took his seat in Parliament by the side of his friend, Richard Cobden, with whom he had made a compact two years before not to rest till the Corn Laws were repealed. But the year 1843 was a trying one for the League. Parliament was busy with factory legislation and the leading members of the League, being manufacturers and Nonconformists[1], cut a poor figure. In criticism of the educational clauses in the Factory Bill the journal of the League wrote:

Sir James Graham's plan may stuff the brains of the poor, but it will grind their faces and empty their stomachs. Where was the very peculiar need of this interference? Why pick out the factory poor? They are no worse taught than the agricultural poor. We would join heart and soul to aid an efficient plan of education; but no one can be blind to the animosity of this peculiar feeling for the factory districts. ...The whole thing is a masked battery against the march of the League[2].

But the heads of the League were resourceful men. They announced "new steps" (*inter alia*, the circularising of 300,000

---

[1] Cf. p. 264 below.   [2] *Anti-Bread Tax Circular*, No. 122.

electors[1]), and collected £100,000 to put them into effect. "They were not going to waste more time in petitioning Parliament, they would memorialise the Queen and appeal to the whole country". When Cobden made this announcement in Covent Garden Theatre, the audience, we are told, "almost in one mass, rose and burst into a series of the most enthusiastic cheers, which lasted for several minutes, accompanied by waving of hats and handkerchiefs and other tokens of satisfaction"[2].

The appeal to the country took the form of a rural campaign. Hitherto, said the *Circular*, we have been thinking mainly of the towns, now we appeal to the farmers: "A free trade in corn can alone save the farmers"[3]. Led by Cobden and Bright, they deluged the countryside with a rain of oratory and tracts. Cobden carried meetings in the strongholds of protection: in Essex, where the squires in vain "mounted their horses and posted up and down the country"[4]: in Buckinghamshire at the very gates of Stowe, whose ducal lord was derided for distributing prizes to servants who brought up their families without recourse to the parish[5]. Honest Hodge found tracts in his village inn and learned to spell the big word "MONOPOLY". Even the farmers were persuaded.

In 1844 the pace slackened. Parliament was preoccupied with other things, railways, banking, and factory reform. A new cry was wanted, and Cobden, taking a leaf out of Tadpole's[6] book, declared for registration. News went round that good free traders were to qualify as county voters by purchasing 40s. freeholds. "The registration movement", wrote Bright to his sister-in-law, "is creating a great sensation, and in truth I regard it as the ulterior measure of our contest. We shall make short work of some of the monopolist county seats at another election"[7].

---

[1] September 28, 1843. Cobden, *Speeches*, 1. 73.
[2] *Ibid.* Cobden, *Speeches*, 1. 65.
[3] *Anti-Bread Tax Circular*, No. 120.
[4] *The League*, No. 2, October 1843.
[5] *The League*, No. 10. Article on "Taming the Duke (of Buckingham)".
[6] Taper and Tadpole are the two "politicians" in Disraeli's novel, *Coningsby*.
[7] G. M. Trevelyan, *Life of John Bright*, p. 123.

In 1845 the tide turned, and when Parliament, after a six months struggle, dispersed for the summer holidays, the ship of the League was running on the flood. Disraeli averred that the League succeeded by a fluke just at the moment when the country was becoming heartily sick of it[1]. But the League knew full well that the country was behind it and listened with glee to the ferment which it was creating at last in Parliament. Its journal[2] reviews the Parliamentary proceedings of 1845. The session began with the retirement of "keep-your-station" Knatchbull from the Conservative Cabinet. On the day before the Queen's speech the Duke of Buckingham declared that the Cabinet would maintain the existing level of protection; Peel denied that the Government was under any such pledge. Cobden moved for a Committee of enquiry: "Give me this Committee and I will undertake to explode the whole delusion of agricultural protection". Sidney Herbert, for the Government[3], besought the landed interest not to come whining for protection. Mr Miles, goaded on by the Rump Parliament of No. 17, Bond Street (the headquarters of the Protection Society), bewailed the low price of corn and cattle. Low wages throughout the manufacturing districts, retorted Graham[4], was what depressed the price of meat. Reduced to desperation, the country gentlemen plunged their hands into grease and lard[5]. The Customs' Act, pursuant to the new budget, had placed lard and grease on the free list. Mr Branston complained that, if grease were admitted, butter would slip in under the name of grease. Mr Ward called grease protection "the policy of an area sneak". Colonel Windham, the Conservative free lance, who did not "like" free trade, now rounded on his own friends. "In 1841 the manufacturing members of Parliament were like Jacks-in-the-box, continually jumping up and down in their places... and he was now sorry to see his agricultural friends following their example"[6]. How Peel must have smiled! Not all the pricks of this session came from Disraeli's pointed tongue!

[1] Trevelyan, *op. cit.* p. 129. Cf. Disraeli, *Life of Lord George Bentinck*, p. 9.
[2] *The League*, No. 99.   [3] Hansard, 3rd S. LXXVIII. 818.
[4] Hansard, 3rd S. LXXVIII. 995.   [5] Hansard, 3rd S. LXXVIII. 1161 sqq.
[6] Hansard, 3rd S. LXXVIII. 1182.

The hold of the League on the British farmer was clinched by a final move. On February 27, 1845, Bright asked for, and was granted, a Select Committee to enquire into the operation of the Game Laws. The day before, Lord Ashley had written to Peel:

I have made up my mind to vote for Mr Bright's motion if it be fairly and decently introduced. This I much regret, because I had hoped that the subject might be handled by some respectable country gentleman; and I have no satisfaction in following a person who is almost unfitted by his manners for educated society, and of whom I never heard it proved that he was either honest or humane.

But the abuses of the Game Laws are so frightful, and so repugnant to public feeling, that I cannot undertake to refuse, so far as a single vote can go, the prayer that the whole evil be examined, stated, and, if possible, removed[1].

The Committee rejected the draft report written by Bright, who recommended the complete abolition of the Game Code. The time, he argued, was especially appropriate, since the cultivators of the soil were now about to be subjected to a free competition with the foreign grower. It was an ironical situation. John Bright proposes to relieve the special burdens of agriculture, in order that the agriculturalist may be able to sustain a free trade in corn.

Cobden, as he was never weary of informing an agricultural audience, was the son of a farmer. Near his house in Heyshott in Sussex were some allotments, one of which was cultivated by a labourer named William Elcomb. Elcomb stated to the Committee that the rabbits ate up all his turnips. They made "50 or 60 holes in which you could bury your fist"[2]. "That", he added unfortunately, "is what the gentleman told"[3]. The League was always thorough in its methods.

Meantime, between the first and last session of the Game Laws Committee the Corn Laws had fallen. In surrendering office on June 29, 1846, Peel made his apology for the step which his party condemned as "the great betrayal":

The name which ought to be, and will be, associated with the success of these measures, is the name of one who, acting, I believe,

---

[1] C. S. Parker, *Sir Robert Peel*, III. 179–80.
[2] *Commons' Committee on the Operation of the Game Laws* (1845), Part I. Q. 16370.   [3] *Ibid.* Q. 16371.

from pure and disinterested motives, has, with untiring energy, made appeals to our reason, and has enforced those appeals with an eloquence the more to be admired, because it was unaffected and unadorned: the name which ought to be chiefly associated with the success of these measures is the name of Richard Cobden.

Finally of himself he said:

I shall leave a name execrated by every monopolist who from less honourable motives clamours for protection because it is conducive to his own individual benefit; but it may be that I shall leave a name sometimes remembered with expressions of goodwill in the abodes of those whose lot it is to labour and to earn their daily bread by the sweat of their brow, when they shall recruit their exhausted strength with abundant and untaxed food, the sweeter because it is no longer leavened by a sense of injustice[1].

Who, or what, was really responsible for the repeal of the Corn Laws? The Duke of Wellington swore it was rotten potatoes. "Rotten potatoes have done it all; they put Peel in his d—d fright"[2]. Mr Croker declared that Peel's conversion was "nothing but the result of *fright* at the League"[3]. Rather, let us say that it was Time in his fulness, celebrating the majority of an infant registered in the Wealth of Nations, and fostered in his boyhood by two most estimable nurses, Mistress Huskisson and Dame Robert Peel.

4. CHARACTERISTICS OF THE AGITATION

The Anti-Corn Law League was strong in the personality of its leaders. In arguments and persuasive power Richard Cobden was easily first. After him came John Bright, after Bright the Rev. W. J. Fox. The rest also spoke. Before the crowded audiences in Covent Garden Theatre or the Manchester Free Trade Hall Cobden would lead off with what he loved to call "one short statistical statement"[4]. From statistics he passed to an exposure of the latest landlords' fallacy, and then he closed on a moral note, with a reference perhaps to the purity of the League's cause or the bribery and corruption which disgraced

---

[1] Hansard, 3rd S. LXXXVII. 1054. Speech on Resignation, June 29, 1846.
[2] C. C. F. Greville, *The Greville Memoirs*, 2nd part, II. 351.
[3] Croker to Duke of Wellington, April 5, 1846. *Croker Correspondence,* III. 65.
[4] Cobden, *Speeches*, I. 66.

the League's opponents. Bright followed, to do "a little prize fighting"[1]. But Bright's armoury was the Holy Bible. When the Corn Laws are repealed, "we shall see no more ragged men and women and children parading our streets,...but we shall have the people happy, 'every man sitting under his own vine and figtree'"[2]. Fox lacked the genius of Cobden and Bright, but he was grandiloquent and high-principled. "Our strength is in the principles we hold"[3]. "Our principles are not only the dictates of nature, but they are the morality of nations"[4].

The League was strong in the nature of its purpose. Its purpose was single and clear—the total and unconditional repeal of the Corn Laws. To the half measures of the Whigs it turned a deaf ear. The Complete Suffrage Movement, which divided the Chartists in 1842, was the work of a Corn Law repealer, Joseph Sturge, but Joseph Sturge was the first to remonstrate with the Editor of the *Anti-Bread Tax Circular*, when he dared to suggest that a fixed duty was better than a sliding scale[5]. Chartism was a welter of vague desire frothing behind a political document; the Anti-Corn Law League a palpably peaceful cause exuding sentimental earnestness.

Furthermore, the League's purpose was negative. There was no need for its spokesmen to understand the intricacies of agriculture. They left that to others. Their task was to thwart the wickedness of landlords and to rescue the country from the bondage of monopoly. Negative causes are often exhilarating, and the narrow platform of the Anti-Corn Law League assuaged a combination of desires. It offered to those who would tread it the satisfaction of their business instincts, the chastisement of their social superiors, the applause of the working man, and the undoubted blessing of Heaven.

The League was strong in the quality of its opponents. If the country gentlemen had been craven, there would have been no

---

[1] Trevelyan, *John Bright*, p. 97.
[2] Speech reported in *Anti-Bread Tax Circular*, No. 116.
[3] Covent Garden Theatre, February 15, 1844. Fox, *Collected Works*, IV. 69.
[4] Free Trade Hall, March 6, 1845. Fox, *Collected Works*, IV. 200.
[5] *Anti-Bread Tax Circular*, No. 73.

controversy at all, but being sensitive folk, who, according to their lights, did their duty by their property and dependants, they took up the challenge and fought a good case on weak ground.

The League can hardly be regarded as an exponent of class warfare, for they welcomed the adhesion of landlords to their cause. They sang the praises of free-trade Peers like Earl Fitzwilliam, Earl Spencer, the Earl of Durham, and Lord Kinnaird; and when their lordships presided at Anti-Corn Law Meetings, they were received with deference and applause.

In controversy the landlords usually got the worst of it. The League twitted them for the backwardness of their methods. "We have a right", said the League's journal virtuously, "to demand that the same degree of science, industry, capital and enterprise, so far as they are available, should be applied to land which have been so successfully devoted to manufactures"[1]. Only the landlords themselves knew the thousands they had sunk in drainage, but when Cobden, on a railway journey from Stafford to Manchester, espied some watery tracts, he entered it in his note book as material for his next big speech[2]. Indeed, according to the League, it was their prodding which kept the landlords up to the mark. "We", said Cobden, "are the great agricultural improvers of this country"[3]. So the League had the argument both ways. If swamps were undrained, the fault was the landlords'. If land was improved, the credit lay with the League. If the country gentlemen modestly referred to the achievements of progressive landlords, the League retorted with the example of Scotland, whose landlords were free-traders and more progressive and gave long leases to boot. If the agriculturalists protested that they suffered under special burdens, the manufacturers declared that they suffered under worse, for they suffered under the crushing burden of the Corn Laws.

The country gentlemen were persuaded that the object of Corn Law Repeal was cheap bread and low wages; and their

---

[1] *Anti-Corn Law Circular*, No. 9.   [2] Cf. *The League*, No. 4.
[3] Manchester, October 19, 1843. Cobden, *Speeches*, I. 104.

accusation was not unnatural. When repeal was first argued in Parliament by Villiers, his central argument was that the legislature had burdened manufactures with an immense weight of taxation, the direct tendency of which was to offer a premium on the consumption of foreign products and to induce British capitalists to seek an investment for their money in other countries[1]. Now, how could the Corn Laws be said to add an immense weight of taxation to the manufacturers, except by increasing their labour costs, and how would the repeal of the Corn Laws lighten this burden, except by reducing those labour costs? A reduction of labour costs is not the same thing as a reduction of wages, but the country gentlemen could hardly be blamed for connecting the two.

When the League started its propaganda, it saw the danger of this line of argument. Again and again the orators of the League repudiated the notion that they wished to reduce wages. Thus Cobden:

If the members of the Anti-Corn Law League, who are manufacturers, want a repeal of the Corn Laws with the idea that to cheapen food would enable them to reduce wages they are the most blind, and apparently the most besotted class of men that ever existed; for, if one may trust all experience, the effect of a free trade in corn must inevitably raise the money rate of wages in the North of England, at the same time that it will give the working classes their enjoyments, comforts and the necessaries of life at a cheaper rate than they have hitherto had them....I say, from the facts I have told you, that the effect of the repeal of the Corn Laws, if it be to cheapen the price of food, will be to lighten distress and to give a demand for labour by extending our foreign trade. If it reduce the price of bread, looking to all past experience, the effect in Lancashire, Yorkshire, and all the manufacturing districts, must be to raise the money rate of wages[2].

The League contended that the persistence of this charge was due to the mistaken idea of agriculturists, that in industry wages followed the price of food. They answered Ricardo out of Adam

---

[1] Hansard, 3rd S. XLI. 909, March 15, 1838.

Cf. also: "In France, in Switzerland and various other countries the manufacturers were now successfully competing with England in consequence of the cheapness of food and of production, and would in a short time completely exclude us from the Continental markets". (Ibid. 919.)

[2] Covent Garden, July 3, 1844. Cobden, *Speeches*, I. 200–202.

Smith: "Wages of labour do not in Great Britain fluctuate with the price of provisions"[1]. Then they went on to show by statistics that the labourers' comforts had been greatest when the price of corn was lowest, and that "every extreme rise in the price of food during the last 50 years had been attended with riots and blood-shed"[2]. They accused the Corn Laws, not only of raising the price of food, but also of producing an unnatural clash of interest between agriculture and manufacture.

I challenge anyone to point out an instance ever since these Corn Laws were introduced, wherein the agriculturalists and the manufacturers have had simultaneous prosperity. Now, I ask, is this a natural state of things? Is this alternation of distress—this intermittent fever, now attacking the one great portion of the body politic, and then the other...is this a natural state of things?...No; there is an unnatural cause for this unnatural state of things, and that unnatural cause is the law which interferes with the wisdom of the Divine Providence and substitutes the law of wicked men for the law of nature[3].

The charge which should really be levelled at the manufacturers is their exaggeration of the effects of the Corn Laws. It never seemed to occur to them that they had it in their own power, whether there were Corn Laws or whether there were not, to raise wages and improve the conditions of employment. They were not selfish, so much as enthralled; intensely practical in business, in their economic philosophy they were superstitious to the last degree. They cowered before bogies of Population and Foreign Competition; and had they but known it, they were suffering from the same malady as that which infected their arch-enemies, the Protectionists.

Cobden lived to see one great prophecy falsified (a Free Trade Europe), and a second apparently justified. His second prophecy concerned the effect of Corn Law Repeal on agricultural prosperity. "I have never been", he said in 1843, "one who believed that the repeal of the Corn Laws would throw an acre of land out of cultivation"[4]. He was right—for a time. The twenty

---

[1] *Wealth of Nations*, Book I. chap. 8.
[2] *Anti-Corn Law Circular*, No. 5.
[3] Covent Garden, September 28, 1843. Cobden, *Speeches*, I. 68.
[4] Manchester, October 19, 1843. Cobden, *Speeches*, I. 103.

years which followed the repeal of the Corn Laws were the golden age of English agriculture: and why? Just because that bounty of the New World, that "vast super-abundance", which the League promised would flow in, if import was free, from the granaries of the United States, did not flow in for another 20 years. The circumstances of the harvests and the stoppage of supplies, first from Russia, owing to the Crimean War, then from the United States, owing to the American Civil War, postponed the deluge. But in the late '70's, when America had recovered from the effects of Civil War and when cheap iron had reduced the cost of transport by land and sea, the deluge descended. By this time Cobden was in his grave, and the Anti-Corn Law League a memory; and the English farmer, with his landlord behind him, had to stand the shock, or make way for the hardy Scot. If England had possessed, as Cobden and Bright desired, a strong peasant proprietary, would the story have been the same, or would the country have saved its peasants from ruin by returning to that protection which Cobden and Bright destroyed?

Let us leave the controversy in the environment of the day.

In those days railways were new, and they were a boon to the League. The snorting monsters, whom the landlords were trying to keep away from their grounds, carried the lecturers on their tours, and the Manchester merchants to and from the Metropolis. To them time was money. The cheap press was a new thing; and the League was able to foster, in the columns of provincial newspapers, a strong free trade opinion. Not less important was the introduction of a cheap post. The League used the post for the exchange of correspondence among its own members and for the showering of Anti-Corn Law literature on the towns and villages of England. When the penny post came in 1839, the League's correspondence increased one hundred-fold.

In pictorial appeal later generations have left the League far behind. Big loaves and little loaves, manacled Chinamen and starving widows direct our judgment at the solemn moment of a General Election. Besides these the League's cartoons and

placards are paltry things. Thackeray drew for the *Anti-*
Law Circular of July 23, 1839, its one decent cartoon[1]. But the
League had allies which we are more shy of claiming. They had
God and the Bible. Corn, Church and Constitution were the
three C's dear to the Tory heart; and the League dealt in the
same coin. Its journal never wearied of recalling the Conference
of 645 Christian Ministers (of whom only two were members of
the Established Church), which met at Manchester, August 17–
20, 1841. "Our duty", they announced, "as ministers of religion is plain. On scriptural grounds we are called upon to
denounce all human restrictions upon the supply of food to the
people, and to employ all appropriate means to place the fatherly
provision of God within reach of his suffering and famishing
children"[2].

And having religion on their side, the Anti-Corn Law League
availed itself of the ornaments of religion. It issued an *Anti-Corn
Law Almanac*; and in July, 1842, it held at the Theatre Royal
in Manchester a National Anti-Corn Law Bazaar. "Women's
zeal", says the historian of the League, "was enlisted in the
cause of benevolence, and thousands of fair fingers were instantly
set at work"[3]. The receipts amounted to nearly £10,000. On
Stall 16 lay a memorial from the women of Manchester, containing 75,800 female signatures. Stall 10 was more attractive
still, for on it were Anti-Corn Law pin cushions. Take your
pick! Here is one showing a Sheaf of Corn with the motto "Let
me come free"; or perhaps you would prefer a Wind-mill which
says, "Freely give and freely I will grind".

Life was great in those days!

---

[1] Reproduced in Trevelyan's *Life of John Bright*, p. 56. A Russian and
a Pole, bringing corn for a family of starving English weavers, are repulsed
by the myrmidons of the Landlord State—soldier, policeman and beadle.

[2] *Anti-Bread Tax Circular*, No. 70.

[3] Prentice, *History of the League*, I. 206.

CHAPTER XIII

CHARTISM

I. LITERATURE AND SCOPE OF THE MOVEMENT

THERE has been a boom in the literature of Chartism. For many years we struggled along with Gammage's closely printed volume, refreshing ourselves with dips into Carlyle (*Chartism*, 1839; and *Past and Present*, 1843). In six years there have appeared in quick succession:

1913. E. Dolléans, *Le Chartisme*.

1916. Dr Schluter, *Die Chartistenbewegung*.

1916. (Composing Volume LXXIII of the Columbia studies in history, economics and public law):

    F. Rosenblatt, *The Chartist Movement*, Part I.

    H. U. Faulkner, *Chartism and the Churches*.

    P. W. Slosson, *The Decline of the Chartist Movement*.

1918. Mark Hovell, *The Chartist Movement*.

1919. M. Beer, *A History of British Socialism* (English edn). Vol. I deals with the origins of Chartism. Vol. II (announced) will deal with the Movement itself.

The difficulty now is what to leave out. The tale of Chartism, as the Chartists would have told it, is not very complex. But when we set Chartism in its social and economic environment, we find ourselves involved in the labyrinth of working-class life during the 20 years which followed the Reform Bill. The new poor law, the condition of the hand-loom weavers and frame-work knitters, religion, free thought, socialism, the evolution of industrial structure and the relation between food prices and social discontent, all become relevant. Numberless are the names we might include among the leaders of the Chartist army, numberless and of infinite length are the speeches which they declaimed.

2. RELATION TO THE REFORM BILL AGITATION

The Chartist movement derives from the Reform Bill agitation. The Rotunda Radicals[1] had watched with disgust the passage into law of the middle class Reform Bill. They thought it a "snail-paced shuffling squeamish mode of treating the subject", an anti-climax to Fox and Major Cartwright and universal suffrage. They were republicans; and let "Mr. and Mrs. William Guelph" and "Miss V. A. Guelph" mind what they were about! As for peers—

> What is a Peer? A useless thing,
> A costly toy to please the King,
>   A bauble near the throne.
> A lump of animated clay,
> A gaudy pageant of the day—
>   An incubus—a drone! etc.[2]

Between 1832 and 1836 political agitation was at a discount. The half measure of reform won in 1832 put further reform, for a time, outside practical politics. The country was passing through a period of industrial prosperity. When this came to an end, the dormant energy of the radical reformers awoke in sympathy with the outcry against economic hardships, and Chartism was born.

Chartism is a drama with a prologue and four Acts: 1836–39, the period of preparation (Prologue); 1839 and 1842, the two big years of Chartism (Acts 1 and 2); 1843–48, a period of distraction and desolation (Act 3); 1848, the last flicker (Act 4).

In 1836 the London Working Men's Association was founded, its objects being: "To draw into one bond of unity the intelligent and influential portion of the working classes in town and country. To seek by every legal means to place all classes of society in possession of equal political and social rights"[3]. It was organised by men who had been engaged in the various popular activities of the last 10 years, and included Henry Hetherington and John Cleave, the champions of a free un-

---

[1] So called because they used to meet weekly at the Rotunda in Blackfriars Bridge Road.

[2] *Poor Man's Guardian*, 1831, No. 15: published by Henry Hetherington.

[3] M. Hovell, *The Chartist Movement*, p. 60.

stamped press. William Lovett, a co-operator in the '20's, a radical during the struggle for the Reform Bill, the treasurer of the Victim Fund which assisted the prosecuted champions of cheap knowledge, and in the eyes of the Government a dangerous character, was its secretary. In 1837 Lovett drew up a petition, praying the House of Commons to introduce a Bill embodying the following Six Points:

(1) Equal representation.
(2) Universal Suffrage (women included).
(3) Annual Parliaments.
(4) No Property Qualifications.
(5) Vote by Ballot.
(6) Payments to Members.

In 1837, at the General Election following the death of William IV, the Association issued an address urging reformers to vote only for candidates who would support the "People's Charter", as the Six Points were now for the first time called. The Address was approved by the famous Birmingham Political Union, whose accession secured the support of radical opinion in the Midlands. Lovett, meanwhile, with the help of Francis Place, drafted a Bill in full parliamentary form, and this Bill is the document henceforth known as the People's Charter. The original draft contained a provision for Women's Suffrage, which was dropped owing to the fear that the demand might retard manhood suffrage. The Charter, prefaced by an address describing its origin, was published on May 8, 1838, and circulated widely in the Provinces, which were already in a state of ferment over the new Poor Law and Factory Reform.

3. The Chartist Drama

The task before the Chartists was two-fold. First of all they had to rally the country to the Charter, and secondly they had to force it upon Parliament. The conversion of the country was easy enough. Missionaries toured over England and Wales[1],

---

[1] Cf. a Letter from T. Philipps, Pontypool:
"There has existed in this town for some months a Chartist society, some of the members whereof make circuits periodically into the neighbouring

addressing willing converts. In the autumn of 1838 monster meetings were held in the North. At Manchester 300,000 collected, bearing flags and banners of a threatening character. "Murder demands justice" was a motto inscribed under a picture of the massacre of Peterloo. Another banner showed a hand grasping a dagger with a scroll, "O tyrants! Will you force us to this?" Similar demonstrations were held at Peep Green (between Leeds and Huddersfield) and at Liverpool. These were the big field days, but since demonstrations by day caused loss of wages, and the authorities thwarted indoor meetings by refusing the use of town halls, the Chartist leaders organised torchlight processions in the towns. At one of these, in Hyde (Cheshire) on November 14, 1838, the Rev. J. R. Stephens, surrounded by followers wearing and carrying upon poles red caps of liberty, branded the manufacturers as a gang of murderers, whose blood was required to satisfy the demands of public justice. The following week the Home Secretary instructed the Lancashire magistrates to announce the illegality of torchlight meetings and to suppress such meetings by every means.

The persuasion of Parliament was a task less easy. In fact, from the beginning the Chartists had not the remotest chance of making any impression on Parliament by peaceful means; and however violently many of them talked, their organisation was not a conspiracy to overthrow the Government by force.

Their big efforts in 1839 and 1842 both took the same form. Delegates from all over England met in London as a National

villages and mining districts to obtain signatures to the Chartist Petition and contributions to the national rent. The missionaries attend at public houses or beer shops where a party...has been assembled. The missionary expounds to them the grievances under which they labour, tells them that half their earnings is taken from them as taxes, that these taxes are spent in supporting their rulers in idleness and profligacy, that their employers are tyrants who acquire wealth by their labour, that the great men around them possess property to which they are not entitled, that these evils are to be cured by the Chartists, but that the people must sign the Chartist Petition and contribute to the Chartist rent, that if their demands are not peacefully conceded they will be justified in resorting to force and that they need not fear bloodshed because the soldiers will not act, and a letter is usually read to confirm the statement made with regard to the feelings of the soldiery" (*Home Office*, 40—1839, 45).

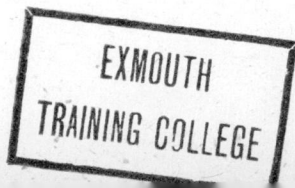

Convention. The task of the Convention was to present to Parliament a National Petition. The first petition was presented in 1839, the second petition in 1842. On the first occasion it was introduced in half-hearted language by Thomas Attwood, who put Currency before the Charter. On the second occasion it was killed by the eloquence of Macaulay: "What could follow but one vast spoliation?...Something like the siege of Jerusalem on a far larger scale"[1].

On each occasion the agitation culminated in disorders in the Provinces. Almost from the first meeting of the first Convention (February, 1839), a split was revealed in the Chartist ranks. On one side was the party of Moral Force, led by William Lovett; on the other side, the party of Physical Force led by Feargus O'Connor. From the outset the Moral Force party lost ground, and when the Convention moved to Birmingham on May 13, 1839, constitutional methods were drowned in talk of "ulterior measures". A manifesto was issued to Chartist Associations throughout the country, asking them if they were ready to adopt simultaneously the following:—

To withdraw savings from Banks; convert paper money into gold and silver; boycott non-Chartist tradesmen; defend liberty by arms; and abstain from work and intoxicating liquor in the event of a Sacred Month being ordered by the Convention.

Lovett was a party to this manifesto, having been goaded into violence by the arrest of his friend, Henry Vincent, on May 9. The manifesto of May was followed by disorders at the Bull Ring in Birmingham in July. On July 4 a detachment of Metropolitan police, headed by the Mayor and supported by the military, invaded the Bull Ring, where an assembly of working men were listening to the reading of a newspaper, and without any provocation on the part of the people launched an attack[2]. A week of

---

[1] House of Commons, May 3, 1842. Macaulay, *Speeches* (Popular Edn), p. 629.

[2] Cf. July 5.—Post Office, Birmingham, to Col. Moberly:

"A meeting of the Chartists took place last night in the Bull Ring in this town in defiance of the public authorities; and a strong body of Police who had been brought from London for the purpose, endeavoured to disperse them; on which a conflict ensued; and the Police, being greatly overpowered by numbers, were severely beaten. The military were therefore immediately

rioting ensued. Shops were sacked and their contents burned in the Bull Ring. The Government then struck heavily, arrested the Chartist leaders wholesale and by the end of the year had most of them in gaol, Lovett and Collins, the leaders of the Moral Force party, among them.

While the English crowds talked, eyeing with sullen hate the imported police and only striking back on provocation, the excitable Welshmen plotted rebellion. On November 4, 1839, thousands of men, armed with bludgeons, guns and pikes, "rushed like a torrent from the hills to lay in ruin the commercial emporium of their country". Their object was the release of Henry Vincent, imprisoned in Newport Gaol, and they found a leader in John Frost. The rebels mobilised on Sunday, November 3[1]; and that night, in drenching rain, men of all ages gathered at the appointed places, armed with weapons of every description. People not in the plot hid themselves in their houses and the neighbouring woods, many houses were searched and their occupants dragged from bed and forced to join in the march. The rain and darkness disorganised the attack, and only a bedraggled remnant arrived at the outskirts of Newport on the morning of the 4th. The Mayor and military barricaded themselves in the Westgate Hotel, and after the Riot Act had been read, the troops fired. Some 20 of the rebels were killed; and Frost and others in January 1840 received sentence of death, which was commuted at the last moment to transportation. "It

called out, and succeeded in dispersing the mob from the Bull Ring, but they afterwards assembled in great numbers on some waste ground at Holloway Head, on the outskirts of the Town, where about midnight they broke down about 20 or 30 yards of the Iron Palisades, enclosing St Thomas' Church, with which it is said they armed themselves, but they afterwards dispersed without doing further mischief". (*Home Office*, 40.—Birmingham, 1839.)

[1] Cf. Letter from Manager of British Iron Company (Aberyschan Works), Nov. 3, 1839:

"The Chartists are up in arms....I thought it prudent to decamp with my wife and children. What their plans are I do not know. Some say they are going to Monmouth to liberate Vincent and Edwards; others that they are going to Newport to seize the Magistrates who have been most active in arresting them....The whole of the Works in this neighbourhood are stopped. If this continues long the furnaces will get into a bad state". (*Home Office*, 40—1839. 45.)

is gratifying", says an anonymous writer, "to hear that this act of mercy is producing a moral revolution among the Physical Force Chartists in the manufacturing districts"[1]. Thus ended the first act of the Chartist drama.

Sobered by gaol, the Chartist leaders, Lovett and Collins, emerged in 1840 with a more moderate programme. They were still true to the Charter, but in their little book written in gaol, *Chartism, a new Organisation of the People*, 1840, there is more about Education and Temperance Halls than about politics, peaceful or revolutionary.

In the second act of Chartism the incidents of the first act were repeated in a hazier and more disjointed form. Lovett and his friends, in the hope of dissipating the prejudice created by the Chartist acts of violence, responded to the proposal of Joseph Sturge for a reconciliation between the Chartists and middle class reformers on the basis of Complete Suffrage. Accordingly in 1842 Conferences were held at Birmingham, but when Sturge and his followers, alarmed at the violence of O'Connor, demanded that the Bill drafted by the Complete Suffrage Union should be accepted as the basis of discussion to the exclusion of the Charter, Lovett refused to abandon the child of his pen; and the conference collapsed. After this Lovett took no further part in the Chartist movement.

The second London Convention (April–May 1842) and the rejection of the second National Petition (May 1842) were followed by the Turn Out of August 1842. We say, advisedly, "followed by"; for the Turn Out was not inspired directly by the Chartist leaders, and its course was beyond their control. They were sucked up into its flood.

On August 5, 1842, the factory hands at Ashton in Lancashire struck work, and their lead was widely followed in the textile districts of Lancashire and Yorkshire. The strikers broke machinery, raked out the fires from beneath the boilers and knocked out the boiler plugs—hence the name "The Plug Plot". On August 7 a great meeting on Mottram Moor resolved that all work should cease until the Charter became the law of the land.

---

[1] *The Rise and Fall of Chartism in Monmouthshire* (1840), p. 90.

From Lancashire the strike spread southwards through the Pottery towns and the Staffordshire coal fields. In this turmoil the Chartist leaders were engulfed.

Thomas Cooper has narrated his entry into it. From Leicester, where he was then living, he travelled up to Manchester, following the trail of tumultuous misery—from Leicester, where the frame-work knitters were starving, all work from the hosiery houses at an end, "Sunday come and naught to eat, and as the babe sought the breast there was no milk"[1], to Staffordshire, where the miners were on strike against a reduction of wages and swearing vengeance upon the Poor Law Bastilles. On August 15, he took the chair at a great open meeting at Crown Bank, Staffordshire. After rousing the passions of his savage audience, he tried to cool them and dissuade them from violence. That evening there were riots and fires, but of these Cooper saw nothing, for travelling all night on foot he joined the railway at Crewe, where he found some brother delegates also on the road to Manchester. As the tall chimneys of Manchester came into view, the travellers observed that smoke issued from none. "Not a single mill at work", exclaimed one of them, "something must come out of this and something serious too".

The Chartist leaders had come to Manchester to unveil a statue to Orator Hunt. Arriving on August 16, they found that a Trades Conference, assembled at Manchester the week before, had voted a general strike for the Charter and, if this failed, an appeal to arms. What line would the official Chartists take? The old hands hung back. O'Connor declared that the strike was a lock-out, engineered by the manufacturers in the interest of the Anti-Corn Law League. Even Julian Harney was opposed to intervention—"Julian, the indefatigable and eternal champion of physical force"[2].

But Cooper and others forced the pace, and the Chartist organisation issued a sympathetic resolution in the name of the Executive Committee. Arrests followed. Six months later, long after the strike had of its own accord collapsed, the Chartists

---

[1] Cooper, *Life of Thomas Cooper*, p. 170.
[2] Cooper's words: Dolléans, *Le Chartisme*, II. 203.

came up for trial before Baron Rolfe at the Lancaster Assizes. They were tried on a Monster Indictment, the gist of which was that the 59 accused, O'Connor among them, had endeavoured "by large assemblies of persons accompanied by force, violence, menace and intimidation, to produce such a degree of alarm and terror throughout the country, as to produce a change in some of the fundamental points of the constitution of the country"[1]. The judge gave the Chartists a fair hearing and enjoyed O'Connor's hits at the Anti-Corn Law League; and, as the country was now quiet, the sentences were lenient. But Cooper was tried at Stafford, and after being acquitted on the heavier charge of arson received two years imprisonment for sedition and conspiracy. He wrote in gaol his *Purgatory of Suicides*, a worthy contribution to the roll of prison literature, which extends from Bunyan's *Pilgrim's Progress* to the *De Profundis* of Oscar Wilde.

In South Wales the Newport rising of 1839 had its counterpart in the Rebecca Riots of 1842–43. The two were related to each other and to Chartism, as were the torchlight processions of 1838 and the Turn Out of 1842. In Lancashire the irritant had been the new Poor Law, and the objects of vengeance the Poor Law Bastilles. In South Wales the exactions of the Turn-pike Trusts, which took their toll of every vehicle and every beast, roused the inhabitants to an assault on the hated turn-pikes and side bars. In Pembroke and Cardigan not a gate was left standing. Wild proclamations were issued in the name of Rebecca in allusion to the verse of Genesis (Ch. xxiv. 60), in which it is promised to the wife of Isaac that her seed shall possess the "gate of her enemies". The armed mob, led by a man disguised in woman's clothes, claimed to be Rebecca and her children. By day all was quiet. But of a sudden, in the night-time, the luckless pike-keeper and his family "were roused by the blare of a multitude of cow-horns and the popping of a dozen guns; their door was burst open, and they saw a crowd, some on horses and some on foot—some in women's clothes and others with veiled faces—with the flaring torches and the glittering saws

---

[1] Extract from *Narrative of Proceedings* (Volume in the Goldsmiths Library).

and hatchets. The toll-takers must move out their furniture or lose it; and strong hands helped to carry bed and table and utensils into the field or the dry ditch, while others were sawing off the gateposts close to the ground and chopping up the gate. Then off came the roof of the toll house, and down came the walls, and up came the flags of the very floor; the road was made clear for passengers, and then the uncouth creatures leaped on their horses again, hallooed, blew their horns, fired their guns, and galloped off to some distant point which they would approach in dead stillness as in this case"[1].

The third act of Chartism is a record of disintegration (1843–48). Feargus O'Connor switched Chartism on to an agrarian side track. The National Charter Association of 1843 became the National Land Company. About the time that Robert Owen was presiding over the decease of the Harmony Community, O'Connor was raising funds for his venture at "O'Connorville" (an estate of 100 acres near Watford). He collected £50,000. The pence of the working men were to buy land, which was to be divided into small holdings and cultivated by selected members of the Association. The profits from the first estate were to be used for the purchase of a second estate and so *ad infinitum*. Thus O'Connor exploited the inspiration of Owen and traded on that vast fund of popular unreason which prostrates itself before the mystery of the rolling snowball and the progression of compound interest. In 1847 a Parliamentary Committee exposed the irregularity of the finances and recommended that the Company be wound up. The land venture estranged many of the old Chartists, Cooper, O'Brien, Macdouall, Harney; but O'Connor, supported by his latest recruit, the "young aristocrat" and poet Ernest Jones, retained the favour of the populace. The Parliamentary Committee had acquitted him of personal dishonesty; and relying on this he made a melodramatic apology to a vast audience at Manchester. After warming them with talk

---

[1] Quoted in Webb, *English Local Government*, "The Story of the King's Highway", pp. 218–9. Cf. *Report of Commission on the present state of the Laws in South Wales as to the maintenance and repair of Turnpikes, Highways and Bridges, and on the causes of the recent Acts of Violence and Outrage* (1844).

against "villains who quaff your sweat, gnaw your flesh and drink the blood of infants", and asking them if they supposed that he too "would crush their little bones, lap up their young blood, luxuriate on woman's misery, and grow fat upon the labourer's toil"[1], he flung himself on their mercy and said: "I have now brought money with me to repay every shareholder in Manchester". (Shouts of "Nay, but we won't have it!") "Well, then, I'll spend it all". (Cries of "Do, and welcome".) As a bank manager, on the eve of a crisis, O'Connor would have been worth his weight in gold. His character cleared, he stood for Nottingham against the Whig Minister, Sir John Cam Hobhouse, and was elected by 1257 votes to 893. In 1851 the Land Bank announced the suspension of payments, in 1852 O'Connor was confined in a mad house, and in 1855 he died. Wonderful is the demagogue and more wonderful still is Demos.

The flicker of 1848, the fourth and final act of the Chartist drama, was kindled by the success of the Revolution in France. For the last time the curtain was raised, and the familiar mummeries were repeated. The National Charter Association, changed back into a political organisation by a stroke of O'Connor's wand, arranged a National Convention. The National Convention was to present a National Petition. If this failed, a National Assembly was to present a National Memorial to the Queen, requesting her to "dissolve the present Parliament and call to her Council such Ministers only as will make the People's Charter a Cabinet measure". This was the Chartists' notion of "direct action"! But the petition was rejected, and the memorialists were refused a hearing. The demonstration of 1848 was the funeral of Chartism, with the Duke of Wellington as Master of the Ceremonies. 70,000 special constables were sworn in, and the whole of London was put in a state of defence. On April 10, 1848, a monster procession of 100,000 Chartists attended the last rites and was halted at Kennington Common; whence the corpse, stowed in three cabs and accompanied only by members of the family, the Chartist Executive, was borne to the House of Commons. The petition weighed 5 cwts. 84 lbs. Among

[1] R. G. Gammage, *History of the Chartist Movement*, p. 288.

the signatures were the 'Duke of Wellington' and 'Victoria Rex'! The lamentation in the House was very brief, and the body was removed amid jeers. R.I.P.

4. ITS FAILURE AND MEANING

Why did the Chartist movement fail? If by this we mean, why did not the Charter become the law of the land in 1839 or 1842 or 1848?, the answer is simple. Government, Parliament and everyone who possessed a vote regarded the People's Charter as a declaration of war upon themselves and all that they possessed. Nothing short of a revolution could have won it and everything was against this solution.

Geography was against it. The scene of a revolution must necessarily be the city which is the seat of government, but it was in the Provinces and not in London that the strength of Chartism lay. As Gammage says: "In all onward movements of the people Paris is France, for the rest of France moves at her bidding....London, on the contrary, whenever moved, is impelled by some external power; it is the provinces which give a direction to her efforts"[1].

The climate was against it. Revolutions flourish under hot skies. But the rains which rotted Ireland's potatoes and rained away the Corn Laws drenched the fire of revolution. "The rain poured in torrents during the meeting". "As soon as the meeting was assembled, the clouds gathered and the rain, driven by a sharp wind, began to fall". It was always the same, if we may believe Gammage; and moors in a rain storm are terribly depressing.

The tide of events was against it. After 1843 economic conditions improved. The working classes bettered their lot by the less hazardous enterprise of economic association in Friendly Society, Co-operative Society and Trade Union. Gammage, who never lost his faith in the Charter, returned crest-fallen from many a provincial gathering, which opened with a declaration

[1] Gammage, *op. cit.* p. 47.

in favour of the People's Charter and closed with a resolution for the opening of a Co-operative Store.

Above all, and this is the secret of Chartism, the leading spirits in Chartism were against it. Lovett, the self-taught apostle of moral force, advocated the Charter as a great instrument of popular education. Had he lived 50 years later, he would have been Organising Secretary to the Workers' Educational Association. Thomas Cooper was violent only when he was stung into violence by the sight of the misery around him. Henry Vincent, the leader whom the Welsh rebelled to save, was a slim handsome figure, passionate, eloquent, the darling of the women whose cause he championed, the "Demosthenes" of Chartism. He it was who wrote to the *English Chartist Circular* in 1841, "Your Unions ought not to assume the characters of mere talking clubs, neither should they become mere Petition Clubs: the object should be,—to *acquire useful information* in the sciences of Government and morals, and in the laws which regulate the production and distribution *of wealth*"[1]. John Frost, the leader of the revolt, is described as "an able and efficient magistrate, in manner mild and thoughtful". He had been a Poor Law Guardian and Mayor of Newport. The two Doctors, Taylor and Macdouall, were driven into Chartism by their contact with sufferings worse than those which made Charles Hall the first of the early Socialists. And among the leaders were some who had suffered themselves. Robert Lowery was a deformed emaciated tailor, like Crossthwaite in Kingsley's *Alton Locke*: Richard Marsden, an old hand-loom weaver, was by nature gentle, but ever for the most violent course; for his wife had come so near to starvation that when she tried to feed her infant it drew from her nothing but her own blood.

There were, of course, sterner types. Such were Julian Harney, a lonely bitter man, with hatred ever in his heart; Bronterre O'Brien, by far the ablest intellect in the movement and well-styled by O'Connor the "Schoolmaster of Chartism"; William Benbow, the shoe-maker and coffee-house proprietor, whose pamphlet, *The Grand National Holiday* (published in 1831),

[1] *English Chartist Circular*, No. 3.

enunciated in terms of class-conscious hatred the doctrine of the
General Strike. Finally there was Feargus O'Connor himself,
the "Lion of Freedom", the proprietor of the *Northern Star*,
with his huge frame and voice of thunder, a cowardly rogue and
yet overflowing with a big sympathy for his followers.

Holyoake says of him:

O'Connor was the most impetuous and most patient of all the
tribunes who ever led the English Chartists. In the *Northern Star* he
let every rival speak, and had the grand strength of indifference to
what anyone said against him in his own columns. Logic was not his
strong point and he had colossal incoherence[1].

It seems as though his dark nature made a mystic appeal to
his followers by its affinity with their own dark life. The strain
of real madness in him accorded with the spiritual madness in
them.

Chartism, in the last analysis, was neither a political, nor a
social, nor an economic movement. It was a religious movement.
It was a working-class interpretation of Christianity. "Charterism is not Christianity, but Christianity is Charterism and
vastly more"[2]. The Chartists had their Churches[3] and their
hymns. "If I am a Chartist", said one of their preachers, "I got
my principles from the Bible". To the Churches such language
was blasphemous in the extreme. The Church of England was
unanimously hostile. At Oxford the Tractarians denounced the
men who tempted the people "to rail against your rulers and
superiors"[4]. Disraeli started the Young England movement as
an antidote; but between Young England with its vision of
young noblemen playing cricket with the peasants on a Saturday
afternoon, and the school of Lovett with its insistence on the
intellectual independence of the working man, there was no
vestige of affinity. F. D. Maurice and Charles Kingsley from

---

[1] *Sixty Years of an Agitator's Life*, p. 106.
[2] *Chartist Circular*, No. 64.
[3] *Ibid.* No. 56. The number contains Model Rules for Christian Chartist
Churches. "It would be desirable that literary, political, and philosophical
associations, with good libraries, be connected with every Christian Chartist
Church and School....Let Christian Socialism, founded on brotherly love
and Chartist unity, be encouraged, taught and practised".
[4] *Tract*, No. 83, p. 229.

Cambridge came nearer to understanding it. The Chartists often called themselves "Christian Socialists"; and Kingsley hoping to turn their Socialism into the Christianity of professing Christians issued in 1848 the Appeal to the workmen of England, which was the origin of the propaganda known as Christian Socialism. The Wesleyans, too, were hostile. They mistrusted the infidelity and extreme democracy of many of the Chartists. Only by the left wing of Nonconformity, by Primitive Methodists and Baptists, was active sympathy given.

If you are to get the atmosphere of Chartism, you must look through the files of the Chartist newspapers. In the British Museum or the Goldsmiths Library or any of the big libraries in the North which have collections of Chartist papers you may read them for yourselves. The best known are:

The Northern Star (edited by O'Connor). Leeds, 1837–44, then London, 1844–52.

The Chartist Circular (the organ of the Scottish Chartists). 2 vols. Glasgow, 1839–42.

The English Chartist Circular and Temperance Record for England and Wales. 2 vols. 1841–42;

and there are many others.

Mr Faulkner's *Chartism and the Churches* contains an admirable bibliography; and from this work, which enters thoroughly into the spirit of Chartism, we take an extract in conclusion:

To advocate political freedom at a time when Europe was restless with revolution, secular education at a time when instruction was largely exploited by sectarian interests, teetotalism when intoxicating liquors were the ordinary beverage of all, and the suppression of church and state at just the time when the influence of the Oxford movement was beginning to make itself felt, was to arouse the bitter antagonism of all classes. The aristocracy and bourgeoisie found the whole subject too painful to contemplate and sought refuge in Government prosecutions and in the abridgement of common law liberties. Yet the Chartists, who had found in this agitation for political, economic, social and religious reformation a substitute for religious enthusiasm, firmly believed that they were not only trying to fulfil the teachings of Christ but were actually engaged in a work which rightfully belonged to the church[1].

[1] H. J. Faulkner, *Chartism and the Churches*, p. 58.

CHAPTER XIV

THE INDUSTRIAL SCENE, 1842

1. The Railway Navvy

LET us hover in fancy over the industrial scene in 1842, and photograph a stage of the economic conflict which the people of England were waging then with the forces which held them in thrall.

Our photograph would show us great white lines, continuous or destined to become continuous; they are numerous in Durham and Lancashire, and the newest lead up to and away from London. These white lines are the new rail-roads of England, and the myriad ant-heaps along them are the navvies. In the year 1848 their numbers had risen to 188,000[1].

What is a navvy and how does he live? The navvy is an inland navigator, who used to dig dykes and canals and now constructs rail-roads. The navvies work in gangs of a dozen or so. The Railway Companies give their contracts to big contractors who divide it among small contractors who subdivide the work among headmen of gangs, called gangers. In the '40's the navvies are getting 5s. a day, and for tunnelling and blasting even more, but they are a rowdy crowd, and many of them are Irish. The Sheriff substitute of Renfrewshire declared in 1827: "If an extensive drain, or canal, or road were to make that could be done by piece work, I should not feel in the least surprised to find that of 100 men employed at it 90 were Irish"[2]. So also now in rail-road construction, when they and the Highlanders are on the same job, it is necessary to segregate them in order to avoid a breach of the peace. The Irish sleep in huts and get higher pay than the natives who are lodged in the neighbouring cottages. The English navvy too keeps out the Irishman if he can. On a track

---

[1] Tooke and Newmarch, *History of Prices*, v. 356. They fell to 38,000 in 1855.
[2] *Commons' Committee on Emigration* (1826–7), Q. 1761.

in Northants, "there is only one Irishman on the work, for they would not allow any other Irishman"[1].

In the South of England wages are lower and the navvies are less expert. In South Devon, "very few North countrymen; they are men who have worked down the line of the Great Western; they have followed it from one portion to another"[2]. The riff-raff from the villages cannot work stroke for stroke with the navvy. "In tilting the waggons they could, but in the barrow runs it requires practice and experience"[3].

The high wages of the navvy are offset by the disadvantages of his employment. He is lucky if he gets the whole of his earnings in cash. In the Trent Valley they are paid once a month; "but every fortnight they receive what is called 'sub', that is subsistence money, and between the times of subsistence money and times of the monthly payment, they may have tickets by applying to the time-keeper, or whoever is the person to give them out, for goods; and those tickets are directed to a certain person; they cannot go to any other shop"[4].

The huts in which they live are little better than pig-sties and especially bad for regular navvies, who take their families about with them. In South Devon "man, woman and child all sleep exposed to one another"[5]. On a section of the London and Birmingham Railway fever and small-pox broke out. "I have seen", says an eye-witness, "the men walking about with the small-pox upon them as thick as possible and no Hospitals to go to"[6]. The country people, the witness continues, make money by letting rooms double. When one lot comes out, another lot goes in: and the cottagers' daughters pay the penalty.

Such is the navvy at work and at rest in 1842.

2. THE COUNTRYSIDE

If we can suppose that our camera is capable of distinguishing centres of industrial activity, then our picture will give us

---

[1] *Commons' Committee on the Condition of Labourers employed in the Construction of Railways* (1846), Q. 866.
[2] *Ibid.* Q. 217.   [3] *Ibid.* Q. 897.
[4] *Ibid.* Q. 733.   [5] *Ibid.* Q. 193.   [6] *Ibid.* Qs. 869–878.

"vital" patches which stand out against a background of deadness. This deadness is the major part of rural England.

What is the condition of the rural counties of Wessex?
"Everywhere the cottages are old, and frequently in a state of
decay". "Ignorance of the commonest things, needle-work,
cooking, and other matters of domestic economy, is...nearly
universally prevalent"[1]. To make both ends meet the wife has
abandoned her now useless spinning-wheel and hired herself out
to hoe turnips or pick stones. On the little farms inside the
factory districts of Lancashire and Yorkshire, on which the
country hand-loom weavers eke out a miserable livelihood by
cultivating patches of grass land, there is distress more acute
than ever was known in a Dorset village. But in the countryside proper of Northern England the picture is relatively bright.
"What I saw of the Northern peasantry impressed me very
strongly in their favour; they are very intelligent, sober, and
courteous in their manners.... The education in Northumberland
is very good; the people are intelligent and cute, alive to the
advantages of knowledge, and eager to acquire it; it is a rare
thing to find a grown-up labourer who cannot read and write
and who is not capable of keeping his own accounts"[2]. The
same sort of thing was said of Northumberland in 1869: "If all
England had been like Northumberland, this Commission ought
never to have been issued". The Commissioners[3] found that,
though the labourers worked harder and longer than in the
South, they were not working against starvation. They were
enjoying a rough plenty, which included fresh milk. The
rest of the family earned sufficient to leave the married woman
in her home, and no children under 12 were employed in field
labour.

Here then in the North there is a decent country life, but
elsewhere there is an atmosphere of deadness; and it is this
deadness of the countryside which explains the horror that new-

[1] *Report of Special Assistant Poor Law Commissioners on the Employment
of Women and Children in Agriculture* (1843), pp. 20, 25.

[2] *Ibid.* pp. 299–300.

[3] *Report of Commissioners on the Employment of Young Persons in
Agriculture* (1869), p. 64.

comers to industrial regions frequently expressed at the prospect of a forcible return to the parish of their origin.

"I was told", says a visitor to Lancashire in 1842, "that there had been several instances of death by sheer starvation. On asking why application had not been made to the parish for relief, I was informed that they were persons from agricultural districts, who, on committing an act of vagrancy, would be sent to their parishes, and that they had rather endure anything in the hope of some manufacturing revival than return to the condition of farm labourers from which they had emerged. This was a fact perfectly new to me, and at the first blush, truly incredible, but I asked the neighbours in two of the instances quoted...and they not only confirmed the story, but seemed to consider any appearance of scepticism a mark of prejudice or ignorance"[1].

3. RURAL INDUSTRY

Though there is little peasant life[2] in England, there is life of a feverish desperate order for many who live in country places. These people are not farm workers, nor yet are they artisans who supply the industrial needs of the village. They are feeders to the towns, engaged in what is misnamed (and yet what other term can we use?) "domestic" industry; and the life they lead is a sordid replica of an all too sordid original.

Cobbett in a tirade against the Lords of the Loom[3] idealised the old-time union of agriculture and manufacture. The men should work in the fields, while the women and children stayed at home by their spinning wheels, making homespun for the family garments. But the picture was a vanishing one even in his day. Domestic industry does not mean this. The rural distress revealed in the Hand-loom Weavers' Commission is the distress of specialised hand-workers, male and female, who are clinging desperately to the worst paid branch of a dying trade. The worsted industry of East Anglia is perishing, defeated by the resources of Yorkshire, of which the power loom is only one. The cloth trade in the Valley of Stroud is a shadow of its former

[1] Dr Cook Taylor, Letter to the *Morning Chronicle*, dated from Rossendale Forest (Lancashire), June 20, 1842.

[2] In many counties there were allotments, but the allotment was not made a stepping-stone to the small holding.

[3] *Rural Rides*, I. 219.

self. It has lost the power of recovering from a depression. The next period of slackness that comes along may bankrupt the business and rob a village of specialised hand-workers of their main employment.

In Devonshire, the serge trade, which used to give employment to looms in almost every town and village, has become so unremunerative that it has passed into the hands of the wives and daughters of mechanics and agricultural labourers. In Oxfordshire in 1834, we are told by the Poor Law Commissioners, glove and lace making were vanishing occupations. In the neighbourhood of Banbury "some make lace and gloves in the villages.... Formerly spinning was the work for women in the villages, but now there is scarcely any done"[1]. Since 1834 the process of disintegration has proceeded apace.

We must not, however, convey the impression that domestic industry in 1842 has all but vanished from the countryside. In its ancient strongholds it still endures, but it is in an unhealthy condition, and the towns are sucking its life-blood away.

To illustrate this, let us describe the course of a boom in domestic industry and study how the trade boom of 1833-37 spread to the country silk weavers in Essex and other places around London. The terms which we usually apply to the cultivation of land are apposite. The town workers represent the intensive margin of cultivation, the country workers the extensive margin. First of all the Spitalfields weavers, who have been short of work, have more work given to them. The weavers' wives also get work, and their boys and girls who never were on a loom before are now put to the trade. Fresh hands are introduced. From the Metropolis the demand for labour pushes outwards over the country. Recourse is had to "inferior soils". Old weavers in the villages get work, together with their wives and families. Even farm labourers are impressed. Blemishes for which at other times deductions would be claimed are overlooked. Carts are sent round to the villages and hamlets with work for the weavers, so that time may not be lost in going to the warehouses to carry home or take back work. Then comes

---

[1] *Poor Law Commission* (1834), App. B, Pt 1. 368 *a*.

the ebb. "The immediate effect is that all the less skilful work-men, the dissolute and disorderly, are denied work, the third and fourth looms, those worked by the sons and daughters of the weavers, are all thrown out of use". The intensiveness of culti-vation has been reduced in the towns, the least remunerative 'doses' no longer pay.

The ebb of the tide, which reduces the quantity of employ-ment in the towns, leaves the country districts high and dry. "At such times the country towns and villages, to which work is liberally sent, when there is a demand for goods, suffer still more. A staff or skeleton only is kept in pay, and that chiefly with a view to operations when a demand returns"[1]. A skeleton—well said!

Occasional cultivation is bad for land, and worse for human beings. The ribbon weaving villages North of Coventry are a disorderly eruption from the town. Coventry itself has the better paid "engine weaving"; the rural districts have the "single-hand trade". "The country workers", say the Com-missioners, "retain most of their original barbarism with an accession of vice". The yokels who went out to the French wars innocent boys returned confirmed rogues. Bastardy is greater than ever, despite the new Poor Law. "It may surprise the de-nouncers of the factory system, to find all the vices and miseries which they attribute to it, flourishing so rankly in the midst of a population not only without the walls of a factory, but also beyond the contamination of a large town"[2]. It may have sur-prised such people, but it does not surprise us, who are surveying the industrial scene and beginning to apprehend the rottenness of that worm-eaten structure which under the misnomer of domestic industry marks the half-way house to full capitalism.

4. THE FACTORY DISTRICTS

Let us journey now to the factory districts of Lancashire and the West Riding of Yorkshire, where town lies close upon town and the tall chimneys envelop in smoke the cottages in which

[1] *Hand-loom Weavers' Commission, Report* (1841), p. 19.
[2] *Ibid. Assist.'s Report* (1840), Part IV. p. 81.

hand-loom weavers work and the children of hand-loom weavers sleep. Let us suppose that we have found our position by Leeds. We should like to follow the track of the new rail-roads, for we have in our pocket a small green book:

> "*Bradshaw's Railway Time Tables and Assistant to Railway Travelling.*

"10th Mo. 19th, 1839.   Price Sixpence".

Bradshaw tells us that we can get from Littleborough to Manchester in 11 hours—*via* Rochdale, Heywood and Millshill, but it is not clear how we are to get to Littleborough. So we follow an alternative route, the canal. It is a fashionable method of transit for mineral traffic and paupers. Mr Muggeridge, the emigration agent, tells us how he transported the paupers in 1836. The journey from London to Manchester was made by wagon and canal, the agents assisting the emigrants on their journey[1]. When we got up our geography for this tour out of Thomas Dugdale's *England and Wales,* we read about canals at every turn—"Keighley: in the deep valley of the Aire. Its prosperity had been much increased by the Leeds and Liverpool Canal which passes within two miles". "Skipton: in a rough mountainous district. The trade has been greatly facilitated by the proximity of the town to the Leeds and Liverpool Canal". So the Leeds and Liverpool Canal shall be our guide.

We leave Bradford, Halifax and the worsted district to the left of us, and passing by Shipley, approach the cotton district near the Lancashire border. "The township of Shipley", says the Hand-loom Weavers' Commissioner, "is the western-most locality of the Leeds clothing district; it runs like a tongue into the worsted district. In like manner the worsted district blends with the cotton district at Steeton, Silsden and Addingham" (villages between Keighley and Skipton). We are passing from high wages to low. "The cloth weavers of Shipley work for wages but little, if anything, higher than those of the worsted weavers; while the worsted weavers north-west of Keighley are reduced down to the cotton standard"[2].

---

[1] *Second Annual Report of the Poor Law Commissioners* (1836), p. 468.
[2] *Hand-loom Weavers' Commission, Assistant Commissioner's Report* (1840), Part III. p. 551.

At Skipton we bend sharply south and soon reach Colne in Lancashire. Dr Cook Taylor describes the conditions there in the early part of 1842.

"I visited 88 dwellings, selected at hazard. They were destitute of furniture save old boxes for tables or stools, or even large stones for chairs; the beds were composed of straw and shavings. The food was oatmeal and water for breakfast, flour and water, with a little skimmed milk for dinner, oatmeal and water again for a second supply". He actually saw children in the markets grubbing for the rubbish of roots. And yet, "all the places and persons I visited were scrupulously clean. The children were in rags, but they were not in filth. In no single instance was I asked for relief....I never before saw poverty which inspired respect and misery which demanded involuntary homage".

The next stage is Burnley, where the weavers "were haggard with famine, their eyes rolling with that fierce and uneasy expression common to maniacs. 'We do not want charity', they said, 'but employment'. I found them all Chartists, but with this difference, that the block-printers and hand-loom weavers united to their chartism a hatred of machinery which was far from being shared by the factory operatives"[1].

From Burnley we follow the road to Accrington (for there is no railway yet, and the canal takes a winding course). Of its 9000 inhabitants not more than 100 were fully employed. Numbers kept themselves alive by collecting nettles and boiling them. Some were entirely without food every alternate day and many had but one meal in the day and that a poor one[2].

What a comment on England's industrial supremacy—England with her virtual monopoly of large-scale manufacture in Europe! It must have been a puzzle, too, for the Poor Law Commissioners who were then building workhouses in these parts for the purpose of depauperising hand-loom weavers on the less-eligibility principle.

But how was it, with such a Poor Law, that the hand-loom weavers did not die of starvation by the thousand? If we enter

[1] Letter to the *Morning Chronicle*, June 20, 1842.
[2] *Anti-Bread Tax Circular*, No. 91, June 16, 1842.

a cotton mill we shall see why. Within these gaunt walls, which are illumined at night by sputtering gas light, the children of these weavers work, earning twice as much as their parents, who are too old and too respectable to become factory hands.

By this time, perhaps, it is evening, but this matters nothing to the 'melancholy mad engines', which feed on water or burning coals. The young people will still be there, with eight hours work to their credit and more to go—"kept to work by being spoken to or by a little chastisement"[1].

"I have seen them fall asleep", said an over-looker in 1833 (he is referring to the days when there were no Inspectors), "and they have been performing their work with their hands while they were asleep, after the Billy had stopped"[2]. Put to bed with supper in their hands, they were clasping it next morning, when their parents dragged them out of bed. Half asleep they stumbled or were carried to the mill, to begin again the ceaseless round. "It keeps them out of mischief", said the opponents of shorter hours. Besides the conditions were no worse than any other industries! Factory work, however, as the doctors showed, was different from work in the mines. The heat and confinement of the mill caused precocious sexual development, whilst in the mines the result of exaggerated muscular development was to delay maturity[3].

In 1842 conditions are better than they were in 1833—thanks to the factory inspectors. Night work has been abolished for all under 18. Hours are shorter, though still far too long. There is little positive cruelty, and the sight of deformity—enlarged ankle bones, bow legs and knock knees, caused by excessive standing as a child—is rare. The problem is one of industrial fatigue. The children are "sick-tired".

[1] *First Report of the Factory Commissioners* (1833), p. 27.
[2] *Ibid.* p. 28.
By the Act of 1833 night work was prohibited for all under 18. The maximum hours for children under 13 were 9, and for young persons (13 to 18) 12. But until the establishment of a normal day, it was difficult for the Inspectors to prevent infringements of the maximum. Cf. Hutchins and Harrison, *History of Factory Legislation*, chap. VI.
[3] *Royal Commission on the Employment of Children etc.* (*First Report*), *Mines* (1842), pp. 194-5, footnote.

5. NOTTINGHAM AND LEICESTER

The Midlands of Leicestershire, Notts and Derbyshire are a region of red bricks and pantiles, dotted over vales of exquisite green. So let us leave the smoke of Lancashire and hover here for a while. Here dwell the stocking workers or frame-work knitters—the people who knit on frames stockings, gloves and other articles of hosiery. It does not look like a region of industry. There are only a few big towns, Nottingham, Leicester and Loughborough; and except for some lace factories in Nottingham, large buildings are rare. The town knitters either work in their own homes, or in shops with standings for perhaps as many as 50 frames. In the villages the knitting is nearly all done in the cottage, opposite long low windows, or in a small outhouse which might well be a fowl house.

But in the streets of Leicester we can see "life" of a sort. We can watch, for example, the procession to the pawn-brokers. Some of the knitters pawn their blankets for the day and most lodge their Sunday clothing during the week. Says a Leicester pawn-broker: "We regularly pay away from £40 to £50 (to some 300 persons) every Monday morning, or on the Tuesday. They will, perhaps, wash on the Monday and get their linen preparatory to the next Sunday, and in the course of the week they bring all the finer things they can spare. Friday is the worst; they will then bring small trifling articles, such as are scarcely worth a penny, and we lend on them, to enable them to buy a bit of meat, or a few trifles for dinner"[1].

They are too poor to indulge in church going or alcohol. They have no Sunday clothes. Their publican is the druggist, where they buy opium for themselves and Godfrey's Cordial, a preparation from laudanum, for their children. In the whole of Leicester, with its population of 50,000, there are but nine gin houses; and only on Sundays do they get any schooling. "We have only one bit of a cover-lid to cover the five of us in winter, ...we are all obliged to sleep in one bed"[2].

---

[1] *Report of Commissioner on the Condition of Frame-work Knitters* (1845), p. 109.   [2] *Ibid.* p. 115.

"A frame smith, making his usual inspection of hosiers' frames at workmen's dwellings in Nottingham, after thus spending a fortnight, found his health had begun to suffer from the squalid wretchedness of their abodes. Thinking to improve it, he went on the same errand into the country, but found the frame-work knitters there in a still more deplorable state. From the bad air and other distressing influences in their condition and that of their dwellings, in another fortnight he returned, too ill to attend to his business for some weeks afterwards. This occurred in 1843"[1]. So writes Felkin, the historian of the industry.

Nottingham, however, with its up-to-date lace trade was usually better off than this. The lace factories, like the cotton mills in Lancashire, eased the position of the hand-workers. In Leicestershire the knitters had no such alternative. The more their earnings were reduced, the more helplessly they were bound to their only trade.

6. THE BLACK COUNTRY (1871)

1842 is a long while ago! Let us go to sleep for 30 years and wake up in 1871, when the Truck Commissioners are publishing their report.

West of Birmingham lies the Black Country, an area of some 20 square miles. Here, if we have read the evidence of the Truck Commissioners, we can interpret a dumb show in Dudley, where the nail-makers dwell.

On Monday mornings the nail-maker emerges from a small hovel containing a smithy and walks into Dudley to call on a gentleman known as a fogger, a petty-fogger if he is a middle man, a market-fogger if he is a master. The nailer comes out with a bundle of metal which he takes to a second house and changes for a second bundle of metal, and with this he walks away. (The next nailer, not so lucky, hangs about till Wednesday morning, waiting for his metal.) On Saturday the nailer comes back with his nails, enters the fogger's shop, and emerges

[1] William Felkin, *History of the Machine-wrought Hosiery and Lace Manufactures* (1867), p. 458.

with 12s. in his hand. But he does not go home. He slips into a shop close by and parts company with the shillings. In return he gets a parcel, the contents of which are obviously displeasing to him. What has happened?

The nailer is a Government servant, but the Government employs him indirectly. It puts out contracts for rivets and nails to contractors who sublet their contract, so that the work reaches the nailer at third or fourth hand. The Government, in the interest of public economy, (Victorian England is famous for retrenchment) gives its contract to the firm making the lowest tender; and the policy of the lowest tender is responsible for the dumb show we have watched.

To begin with, the nailer gets metal which does not suit him, so he has to change it, and this he does at the price of 2d. per 10d. bundle, at a metal changer's—a relative of the fogger. (His friend, who has to wait till Wednesday for his bundle, is kept idling about in order that he may drink what is left of last week's earnings at a "wobble shop", which is owned by yet another branch of the family of Fogger.)

When the nailer and his family have worked 14 hours a day throughout the week, the nailer returns on Saturday with the nails, and receives 12s. for them. These shillings he takes to the fogger's store and exchanges for tea and other articles. The shillings are "nimble"—we commend the rapidity of their circulation to Mr Irving Fisher. The fogger who pays out the shillings from his metal warehouse receives them back again in a few minutes over the counter of his grocery store. "He will perhaps reckon with 7 or 8 hands at one time, and when he has reckoned with them, and perhaps paid them £6 or 7 or 8, he will wait until they have gone into the shop and taken the money there as they leave the warehouse. Then he goes into the shop himself for it, as he cannot go on paying without it"[1].

But surely this is truck! Certainly not. There may be "fearful cheating" with tea, but the nailer is not bound to go there. He is perfectly free. The only trouble is this: it is a case of tea or no work the week following. This is why, despite the Truck Act of

[1] *Evidence before the Truck Commissioners* (1871), Q. 37,500.

1831 and despite the known existence of the abuse, these practices are rife among the nailers as late as 1871. The plight of the nailers is not the plight of factory operatives or miners, it is the plight of the frame-work knitters, of men who are bound by the intangible fetters of economic need to the uncontrollable Devil of "semi-capitalism". How exactly the Devil played havoc with the frame-work knitter is an abstruse matter, which we reserve for analysis later.

CHAPTER XV

MINING OPERATIONS

1. Importance of Coal in English Industrial History

COAL was King of the 19th century. The first steam engine was built to pump water out of coal mines, the first canal was cut to carry the Duke of Bridgwater's coal from Worsley to Manchester. The first railroads were laid down around Newcastle to convey the coal from the pit mouth to the river. George Stephenson, the inventor of the locomotive, began life as a trapper in a Tyneside colliery.

Where would English industry have been without its King? In 1780 (in round figures) 5,000,000 tons were raised in the United Kingdom: in 1800, 10,000,000: in 1865, 100,000,000: in 1897, 200,000,000[1]. Coal enticed the cotton factories from the dales of the Pennines to the moist lowlands of South Lancashire. At every stage of their work the iron-makers depended on coal; and the great inventions in the iron and steel industry are landmarks in the expansion of the demand for coal—Cort's Puddling Process 1783, Watt's Steam Engine 1785, Neilson's Hot Blast 1824, Naysmith's Steam Hammer 1835, Bessemer's Steel Converter 1855, Siemen's Open Hearth 1870, Thomas' Basic Process for the treatment of highly phosphoric ores 1878. The steam ship, a novelty in 1820, ruled the seas in 1870; and ironclads followed steam ships. The smokeless steam coal of South Wales guarded the heritage of Trafalgar. By the end of the 19th century coaling stations were an important item of international policy.

Meanwhile the people of England, heedless of Malthusian forebodings, multiplied exceedingly. They lighted their streets and buildings with coal gas, and burnt coal in their grates. With coal they paid for the food and raw materials drawn from other

---

[1] Cf. Bartholomew, *Atlas of the World's Commerce, Coal Output of the United Kingdom*, and W. S. Jevons, *The Coal Question*, cap. VII.

lands. Imports of food and raw materials were offset by exports of coal and of textiles and hardware produced by coal. The spirit of invention is pushing on to electricity and oil, but coal is still the pivot of English industry and commerce. And therefore, inasmuch as coal has meant so much to England, what of the men who raised the coal? How did they live, what did they think about, what did they count for then, what do they count for now?

2. CONDITION OF THE MINING POPULATION, 1800–1850

In 1800 the miners counted for nothing in the nation's life. In Scotland they had just been emancipated from the status of villeinage. In Northumberland and Durham they were tied by yearly bonds. Elsewhere they were weak and isolated. In 1825 a "Voice from the coal mines of the Tyne and Wear" cried: "While working men in general are making 20/- to 30/- per week (*sic*), the pitmen here are only making 13/6 and from this miserable pittance deductions are made"[1].

In 1839, during the Chartist disturbances, a Welsh M.P. wrote to the Home Secretary begging for barracks and troops: "A more lawless set of men than the colliers and miners do not exist...It requires some courage to live among a set of savages"[2]. When the miners came out in 1844, there were thousands of cottages tenantless in Northumberland and Durham. For the colliery proprietors owned the cottages, and, when the miners struck, evicted them. So the miners set up house in the streets. "In one lane...a complete new village was built; chests-of-drawers, deck beds, etc., formed the walls of the new dwelling; and the top covered with canvas or bed-clothes as the case might be"[3]. Yet for all their griminess they had human hearts and voices. During the strike they obtained permission to hold a meeting at Newcastle; and the wealthy citizens who made their fortunes out of the coal trade trembled before the invasion of black barbarians.

[1] *Pamphlet of* 1825, p. 14.
[2] *Home Office papers*, 40—Letter from R. J. Blewitt, Esq., M.P., Nov. 6, 1839.
[3] Richard Fynes, *Miners of Northumberland and Durham*, p. 72.

But the meeting passed off in rain and peace. Thirty thousand miners marched in procession, "for near a mile flags in breeze, men walking in perfect order"; and as they marched, they sang, as only miners sing, songs and hymns and topical ditties:

> Stand fast to your Union
>   Brave sons of the mine,
> And we'll conquer the tyrants
>   Of Tees, Wear and Tyne!

Up and down the Durham coal fields tramped a misguided agitator (in after life the veteran servant of the Durham Miners' Association), by name Tommy Ramsey. With bills under his arm and crake in hand, he went from house-row to house-row calling the miners out. He had only one message:

> Lads, unite and better your condition.
> When eggs are scarce, eggs are dear;
> When men are scarce, men are dear[1].

This blasphemy appalled the Government's Commissioners. But the miners had a zest for religion as well as for strikes. During the strike of 1844, "frequent meetings were held in their chapels (in general those of the Primitive Methodists or 'Ranters' as they are commonly called in that part of the country), where prayers were publicly offered up for the successful result of the strike". They attended Prayer Meetings "to get their faith strengthened"[2].

Such ignorance could only be cured by education. Some worthy members of society had already recognised the fact. In 1830, a Cardiff "Society for the improvement of the working population in the county of Glamorgan" issued improving pamphlets:

No. 9.   *Population or Patty's marriage.*

No. 10.   *The Poor's Rate or the Treacherous Friend.*

No. 11.   *Foreign Trade or the Wedding Gown*[3].

---

[1] John Wilson, *History of the Durham Miners' Association* (1870–1904), p. 40.

[2] *Report of Commissioner on Mining Districts* (1846), p. 8.

[3] These pamphlets are in the British Museum. An extract from No. 9 will serve as a sample:

"John then went on to shew that if the labourers took care to have small families, they would gain another and a still greater advantage; not only

But the Northern miners were perverse people. In Scotland, according to one Wesleyan Minister[1], the miners read Adam Smith. In Northumberland, with still greater perversity, they preferred Plato. "A translation of Plato's *Ideal Republic* is much read among those classes, principally for the socialism and communism it contains; in pure ignorance, of course, that Plato himself subsequently modified his principles, and that Aristotle showed their fallacy and self-destructive nature upwards of 2000 years ago"[2].

3. Women and Children in Mines

The Royal Commission of 1842 on the Employment and Condition of Children and Young Persons in Mines disclosed facts which made Cobdenite England gasp[3]. The worst evidence came from Lancashire, Cheshire, the West Riding of Yorkshire, East Scotland and South Wales. In these districts juvenile labour was cheap and plentiful, and this was an irresistible argument for its employment; though the miners themselves disliked it. The meddlesome restrictions on the factories were a contributory cause. Parents, it was said in Lancashire, were pushing their children into colliery employment at an earlier age because of

---

would they have fewer children to clothe and feed; and therefore their money would go farther, but also their wages would necessarily be higher. The rich instead of having too many workmen would have too few".

[1] *Report of Commissioner on Mining Districts* (1850), p. 54.

[2] *Ibid.* (1852), p. 41.

[3] Cobdenite England, however, was not prepared to gasp if the injury manifested itself among *adults*. We must, therefore, relegate the following to a footnote.

Evidence from East Lothian:

"Between the 20th and the 30th year many colliers decline in bodily vigour and become more and more spare; the difficulty of breathing progresses, and they find themselves very desirous of some remission of their labour....At first, and indeed for several years, the patient for the most part does not suffer much in his general health....The disease is rarely, if ever, cured....The difficulty of breathing increases and becomes more or less permanent, the expectoration becomes very abundant, effusion of water takes place in the chest, the feet swell, and the urine is secreted in small quantity, the general health gradually breaks up and the patient, after reaching premature old age, slips into the grave at a comparatively early period, with perfect willingness on his part, and with no surprise on that of his family and friends" (*Royal Commission, First Report (Mines,* 1842), p. 189).

the legal restrictions upon sending them to the neighbouring factories.

A Lancashire woman declared in evidence: "I have a belt round my waist, and a chain passing between my legs, and I go on my hands and feet....The pit is very wet where I work, and the water comes over our clog-tops always, and I have seen it up to my thighs:...I have drawn till I have had the skin off me; the belt and chain is worse when we are in the family way"[1].

The children's office was a lonesome one. Children hate the dark, but being little they fitted into a niche, and so they were used to open and close the trap doors. A trapper lad in South Wales, William Richards, aged $7\frac{1}{2}$, said in evidence:

"I been down about 3 years. When I first went down, I couldn't keep my eyes open; I don't fall asleep now; I smokes my pipe; smokes half a quartern a-week"[2].

Except in the Northern Mining Districts, where there were good Day and Sunday Schools and Methodism was powerful, a pagan darkness prevailed. As the Derbyshire witnesses put it: "When the boys have been beaten, knocked about, and covered with sludge all the week, they want to be in bed all day to rest on Sunday"[3].

In the hopes of startling a religiously minded England, the Commissioners reproduced examples of working-class ignorance. James Taylor, aged 11, "has heard of hell in the pit, when the men swear; has never heard of Jesus Christ; has never heard of God, but has heard the men in the pit say, 'God damn thee'". John Ibbetson aged $13\frac{1}{2}$ declared, "I don't know who Jesus Christ was; I never saw him, but I've seen Foster, who prays about him"[4].

4. THE BUTTY SYSTEM IN SOUTH STAFFORDSHIRE

Just as in the East Midlands the frame-work knitters worked for middle-men or master middle-men, and just as the Dudley

---

[1] *Children's Employment Commission, First Report* (*Mines,* 1842), p. 27.

[2] *Ibid.* p. 21.

[3] *Children's Employment Commission, Second Report* (*Trades and Manufactures,* 1843), p. 147.

[4] *Ibid.* pp. 155–6.

nailers worked for petty-foggers and market-foggers, so too the Staffordshire miners worked for "butties". Here again the workers were exposed to the petty tyrannies of indirect employ-ment, and the immediate employers incurred the odium of a system for which their superiors, the coal owners and coal masters, were responsible.

Why the butty system prevailed in the Midlands—and in a modified form it prevails to-day—is not clear. In some places it seems to be connected with the smallness of the mining con-cerns or of the metal trades which they supplied. In South Staffordshire a contributing factor was the ancient and allied industry of nail making.

The conditions in South Staffordshire in 1843 are fully de-scribed by the Midland Mining Commission of that year.

The butty was a contractor who engaged with the proprietor or lessee of the mine to deliver the coal or iron stone at so much per ton, himself hiring the labourers, using his own horses, and supplying the tools requisite for the working of the mine. The contract price was known as the "charter price" or "charter". Thus by a freak of language the Staffordshire miner knew by the same word the "butty's charter" which was the symbol of his oppression, and the "people's charter" which was the goal of his desire.

"The butties", said the miners and their wives, "are the devil: they are negro drivers: they play the vengeance with the men"[1]. A collier related a case where "a pike man had worked only one half-day in the week and got 2/- for it, and because he did not spend 6d. of this at the butty's beer shop, the latter told the 'doggy' (the under man) to let the man 'play' for it"[2]. The men kicked when, after working a couple of hours, they were fetched up, without pay, on the excuse that there were no wagons to take away the coal. But the butty comforted them with a bottle of pit drink, and all was smooth again. The miners recognised that often the butty was not to blame. In the district

[1] *Midland Mining Commission—South Staffordshire* (1843), *First Report,* p. 34
[2] *Ibid.* p. 44.

North and East of Dudley, the butties received their "charter price" from the coal owners in the form of tickets on the coal owners' truck shop. What else could they do but hand them on to the men? "He used to be a very good butty", said one miner's wife, "till they haggled him and dropped his 'charter', so that he cannot pay his men"[1].

West and South of Dudley the butties, though they did not truck their men, kept public houses; and being employer and publican in one, they had a tight hold on the men.

Was the compulsion to drink an oppression? To our minds, yes; as also to the minds of the teetotal Chartists whom the Government imprisoned and of the strike leaders whom the Government's Commissioners denounced. But to the majority of the miners the abundance of beer was a delight. They objected to the butty's bullying, but they loved his beer, especially the feckless ones; for when wives were importunate, the drunkards pleaded necessity.

However, all the beer drinking could not be charged to the butties. The miners among themselves, in their own fellowships, were devoted to it; and the compulsion of friends was as severe as the compulsion of butties. Every approach to recreation, every act of mutual providence against accident or disease began and ended in beer. The day a man entered the pit's company, he paid 1s. for footing ale, and the doggy saw that no churl escaped. When a lad was old enough to have a sweetheart, he was toasted with the "nasty" shilling. The sins of the married men were washed away in half a crown's worth of ale. The beer shop was the headquarters of the Burial and Savings Clubs. The first charge on a Burial Club was a good oak coffin, the second charge drinks for the pall-bearers, and then a glass or two for the rest of the company. They had lotteries to which each man contributed 20 fortnightly shillings. Each week a name was drawn, and the lucky man stood a feast; while every member, in addition to a shilling for the box, produced 6d. for drinks.

In all these festivities the butty was in the offing. When they

---

[1] *Midland Mining Commission—South Staffordshire* (1843), *First Report*, p. 89.

would have him he presided; and so at his worst an obnoxious bully, at his best he was an accommodating landlord.

Direct employment, such as prevailed in the North of England, would have averted much of the trouble. There were no structural difficulties in the way of change. Direct employment would not have meant a change to another class of work (this is what it meant for knitters and hand-loom weavers). The butty system existed and persisted through slackness and irresponsibility. The owners paid compensation for accidents, when they might have diminished the number of accidents. They paid commissions to middlemen with whom they might have dispensed. The system made temperance impossible for the individual; and the masters, with the full approval of the Government, did their best to destroy the "pernicious combinations", by which alone a standard of sober decency could be promoted.

5. TRUCK

The Report of the Truck Commissioners (1871–72) enables us to complete the picture. It also enables us to understand why, at this late day, truck was rife in certain districts.

Truck and tommy, truck-shop and tommy-shop, are convertible terms. Truck is from the French *troc* = barter. Cobbett tells us how the word "tommy" was used. In his soldiering days the rations of brown bread, "for what reason God knows", went by the name of tommy. "When the soldiers came to have bread served out to them in the several towns in England, the name of Tommy went down by tradition, and, doubtless, it was taken up and adapted to the truck system in Staffordshire and elsewhere"[1]. From the textile districts it had all but disappeared in 1871. When the cotton manufacturers went to outlying dales for water power, they were almost compelled to open stores for their work people. Owen's store at New Lanark was, in effect, a well-managed truck shop; and the Truck Commissioners of 1871 reported that the New Lanark Company of

---

[1] *Rural Rides*, II. 353.

that day was breaking the law. But when the cotton industry was gathered in the towns, the need for Company stores ceased. Consequently, after the passing of the Act of 1831, which prohibited truck, the mill owners very generally abolished the stores of their own accord; and survivals were marked down.

A collection of Factory Scraps, preserved at the Goldsmiths Library in London, contains a copy of the Factory Bill of 1833, with some pencil notes in Oastler's handwriting which run:—

Cragg Dale Facts

Truck System: Little altered: men knew they were imposed. They pay in money now—but compel them to buy at their own shops.... Wholesale warehouses at Rochdale say, "Oh! put it sideways: it will do for Cragg Dale masters to sell among their people".
Song: "Lousy butter and burnt bread".

About 1842 a curious perversion of truck was prevalent in parts of Yorkshire. The trade depression in the Bradford district tempted disreputable woollen manufacturers to force on their operatives the products of the factory as part payment of wages. Combers were given pieces of cloth, workers in shoddy mills bundles of rags. But this utterly inexcusable fraud, no less than its specious complement, the employer's store, was rooted out by inspectors and factory reformers. In 1854, when the Government Commissioner was asked why "in the cotton manufacturing districts, employing a larger amount of population than even the iron districts, there is no truck?", he replied: "I think, in many instances, it is susceptible of very easy explanation. In order to carry on the truck system with effect on a large scale, the whole of the population must be situated near the works. In the great towns in Lancashire the workpeople employed at particular mills live in all parts of a large town, and they come from one or two miles, or more; therefore it would be manifestly impossible to carry the truck on in a case like that"[1].

---

[1] *Commons' Committee on Payment of Wages (Hosiery) Bill* (1854). Evidence of H. S. Tremenheere, Commissioner appointed to enquire into the State of Population in the Mining Districts, Q. 1181.

Truck, however, lurked in corners of Lancashire outside the factory districts. In Prescot, a small Lancashire town on the fringe of the factory district, the watchmakers in 1871 were being paid in watches. The masters alleged that they only gave watches to the workers when the latter had orders for them, but the evidence showed that these orders chiefly came to hand when the men were asking for fresh work. The pawnbrokers knew what happened. Watches, a pawnbroker's clerk admitted, passed from hand to hand as a circulating medium until they got very low in the market and were pawned[1]. The pawn shop in question had 700 watches on pledge, most of them belonging to workmen in the town.

During the boom in railway construction the truck-master reaped a rich harvest from the navvy. In roving employment of this type it is difficult to see how some form of contractor's shop could have been avoided. The navvy needed canteens or Y.M.C.A. huts, but such things had not been thought of then. However, when the big period of railway construction came to an end, the question lost its importance.

South Staffordshire and the Black Country were the ancient strongholds of truck. The campaigns against truck originated here. The nailers, the cash-paying masters and the respectable ratepayers joined together to promote the Truck Act of 1820. Lord Hatherton, a Staffordshire nobleman, after three years hammering at the House of Commons, obtained the Truck Act of 1831. But in 1843, the year of the Midland Mining Commission, truck was still rife in the coal fields. The well-known Tommy-shop scene in Disraeli's novel *Sybil*[2], which was published in 1845, is taken direct from the Commissioner's Report. Diggs, the butty of the novel, is Banks the coal proprietor of the Report. In the novel the people say of Master Joseph Diggs the son: "He do swear at the women, when they rush in for the first turn, most fearful. They do say he's a shocking little dog". In the Report, page 93, the miner's wife says: "He swears at the women when the women are trying to crush in.... He is a shocking

---

[1] *Evidence before the Truck Commissioners* 1871, Q. 33,670–71.
[2] Book III. chap. I.

little dog". One touch is Disraeli's own. He makes the miners keen to purchase "the young Queen's picture"[1]. "If the Queen would do something for us, poor men, it would be a blessed job". In the *Report* there is nothing about this, but there is a section dealing with Chartism.

However, between 1840 and 1870 the truck shop gradually disappeared from its ancient stronghold. Every year it became easier to expose evasions, and in good times the workers used their prosperity to slip from the Company store. In 1850 a final campaign was launched by five local Anti-Truck Associations, backed by the Miners' National Association under Alexander MacDonald. Truck-masters were prosecuted and truck was steadily dislodged from the coal fields and adjacent iron works. Only in the nail trade did it survive, for the reason that the complete subjection of the nailers made it possible to practise the essentials of truck without a formal violation of the law.

In 1871 in the different colliery districts truck was prevalent only in West Scotland and the newly opened coal field of South Wales.

In West Scotland it was yielding ground before the pressure of the Unions. The Companies only maintained it by active coercion. If a miner held out for money, they had to yield; and if they were malicious, they marked him as a sloper and dismissed him the first when a depression came. "Black Lists", said the Truck Commissioners, "are often kept of slopers; threats of dismissal were repeatedly proved; and cases of actual dismissal for not dealing at the store are not rare"[2]. However, the masters themselves were getting tired of it, since it led so frequently to strikes.

Truck in the South Staffordshire mines was bound up with the butty system; in railway construction with the system of con-

---

[1] Contrast the following extract from an Informer's account of a Chartist meeting on Nov. 3, 1839:

"Smallwood drew from his pocket a portrait of Prince Albert which after a little discussion it was agreed by those in the room to be burnt, which was soon carried into effect, amidst roars of laughter" (*Home Office Papers*, 40.—Birmingham, 1839).

[2] *Truck Commission* (1871) *Report*, p. 16.

tracting and sub-contracting; and similarly in the West of Scotland and South Wales, it was bound up with, and dependent on, the system of long pays. In order to carry on from one pay day to the next, the men got advances on the Company's store. In this way many lived permanently ahead of their wages. The thriftless and drunkards were always "advance" men, but the provident miners hated it and only dealt there on compulsion.

The Commissioners drew a vivid picture of Turn Book morning in South Wales at the close of the pay month.

At 1 or 2 a.m. the women and children begin to arrive with their Advance Books. Perhaps one hundred would be there, wet or fine, sleeping on the door steps or singing ballads until morning. At 5.30 a.m. the doors opened, and the assembly made a rush for the counter. Advance Books were produced, and goods handed over up to the amount of wages which would shortly fall due. The women took their pick of the articles, groceries, tobacco, occasionally a few shillings. "It is quite usual", said the Commissioners, "for shoemakers and other small tradesmen in the neighbourhood of Aberyschan to be paid by the workmen in goods....Tobacco, in several districts of South Wales, has become nothing less than a circulating medium. It is bought by the men, resold by them for drink, and finds its way back again to some company's shops. Packets of tobacco pass unopened from hand to hand"[1]. An Ebbw Vale grocer who took the Company's tobacco at a discount declared: "For years, when they were selling it for 1/4 a pound, I used to give 1/-; but I was so much over-flooded with it that I was obliged to reduce the price to 11d. That would not do still, and I had to reduce it to 10d. I told the men to take it to some other shop if they could get 11d. or 1/- for it. I was obliged to do that many a time, in order to get rid of the large stocks I held in hand. Tobacco will not keep for many months without getting worse"[2].

Weekly pays, therefore, were the constant demand of the miners' unions. In Northumberland and Durham, whence truck had disappeared long ago, pays were fortnightly, and the only

---

[1] *Truck Commission* (1871) *Report*, pp. 11–12.
[2] *Ibid.* Q. 19,239.

objection advanced by the owners against weekly pays was the
practical inconvenience of the pressure on the pay staff. In the
North of England iron trade weekly pays, the Commissioners
found, had just been introduced. In West Scotland some of the
coal owners were trying to recoup themselves for the loss of their
truck shop by charging poundage on the men's wages. But this
dodge, like the bigger grievance of truck, was stoutly resisted
by the local union. Indeed, in one coal field after another the
disappearance of truck and kindred evils coincides with the
appearance of strong county unions.

6. "A History of Working-class Currency in the 19th Century"

We understand that the miners of South Wales insist on
having their economics written by sound labour men. We therefore offer some suggestions for a "History of Working-class
Currency in the 19th century" from the worker's point of view.

i. In 1800 London relied for small coin on private enterprise.
Every week the Jews' boys collected from the shop-keepers their
bad shillings, buying them, at a heavy discount, with serviceable
copper coin forged in Birmingham (*vide* Patrick Colquhoun, *A
Treatise on the Police of the Metropolis*, 1800, Chapter VII). The
resumption of cash payments in 1819 was injurious; for owing
to the shortage of small coin, the wage earners were paid in bulk
with large notes, which they had to split at the nearest public
house. The Truck Act of 1831 prohibited wage payments in
notes on Banks more than 15 miles distant, but said nothing
about cheques—an oversight which the capitalists repeated in
their Bank Act of 1844.

ii. The general dissatisfaction with the state of the currency
led to attempts to dispense with coin. About 1830 Labour
Exchanges were opened in London for the exchange of goods
against time notes, representing one or more hours of labour.
The originator was Robert Owen, and the failure of the Exchanges was probably due to the fact that Owen was at heart
a capitalist. The National Equitable Labour Exchange at one

time was doing a business of over 20,000 hours per week, but very shortly after this, the President (Owen), had to report a serious deficiency of hours, many thousands having been mislaid or stolen. The Exchange in consequence had to close its doors.

iii. In the '40's the centre of interest is the Midlands, and the period may be termed the Staffordshire or beer period. The currency was very popular and highly liquid, but it was issued to excess and difficult to store. More solid substitutes were therefore tried; a Bilston pawnbroker[1] said that he had in pawn numerous batches of flour, which the men's wives had brought from the Truck Shops and turned into money, in order to pay their house rents. Flour, however, was not so hard as a Prescot watch.

iv. We come next to the Welsh or Tobacco period, when the currency was easily transferable, but liable to deterioration.

v. Finally, in the last quarter of the 19th century, the world of labour attained to a cash basis, and there was no Cobbett to denounce the resumption.

The authors will not be guilty of serious exaggeration, if they preface their history with the motto:

"*In the 19th century the Trade Unions and the Trade Unions alone made the nominal earnings of the working man a cash reality.*"

[1] *Commons' Committee on Payment of Wages (Hosiery) Bill* (1854), Q. 80.

CHAPTER XVI

THE HISTORICAL BASIS OF CAPITALISM (I)

1. THE CHALLENGE TO CAPITALISM

THE left wing of socialism informs us that it is working for the emancipation of the community from the capitalist system; because under capitalism "labour is bought and sold as an article of commerce, so that the workers are degraded to a condition of poverty and wage slavery"[1]. Whether this statement be right or wrong, one thing is clear: it is possible now to come to grips with capitalism in a way that was impossible 100 or even 50 years ago. Capitalism, with its complement, the wage system, has arrived. The system which prevailed in most industries 50 to 100 years ago was what we have called, for lack of a better name, "semi-capitalism". Its great feature was its indefiniteness. Truck and deductions ate into earnings, and earnings were not true wages. They were the price of goods rather than the wages of labour. The employer in many cases did not employ. He left this to intermediaries. The manufacturer in many cases neither made things with his own hands, as the word signifies, nor did he possess and manage premises on which others made goods under his supervision. He was a merchant rather than a manufacturer. Semi-capitalism differs from full capitalism as does a zone of improvised defences in open warfare from a clearly defined trench system; and every gunner knows which is the more difficult to attack.

2. EVOLUTION AND REVOLUTION

One aspect of the changes known as the Industrial Revolution has been adequately stressed by recent historians. They dwell

---

[1] Extract from the Objects of the Cambridge University Socialist Society, Lent Term, 1919.

on the gradual nature of the transition and on the foreshadow-
ings of the 19th century in the 18th, as of the 18th in the 17th,
and so on back to medieval times. They invite us to regard the
transition as a change in the scale of industry rather than a
revolution in system; and they show how difficult it is to prove
that at any given period in any given industry an economic
catastrophe occurred. All this needed stressing, but it can be
carried too far. We must not work evolution too hard. If we
take our stand at the end of the 19th century, we are justified in
saying that in the course of the century there occurred, first in
one industry, then in another, a revolutionary change of structure and personal grouping.

3. AGRICULTURE

Arnold Toynbee in the Christmas of 1881–82 delivered the
lectures which were afterwards published as the *Industrial
Revolution of the 18th century in England*; and he rightly assigned
pride of place to agriculture. For in this country agriculture was
the first industry to attain to full capitalism. The peace of 1815
found agricultural England with its present triple structure:
landlord, farmer and labourer. As an important class the
yeoman had disappeared. The predominant type of farmer was
the large scale farmer; and behind him, and in all matters of
labour policy supporting him, was the landlord. Landlord and
tenant farmer, enclosure and large scale farming, went hand in
hand.

The revolt of the agricultural labourers in 1830 was the revolt
of a proletariat, a revolt against capitalist employers by wage
earners who no longer possessed a stake in the soil. One of the
letters of the mysterious Captain Swing, who made himself the
terror of the countryside, ran:

We will destroy the corn stacks and the threshing machines this
year, next year we will have a turn with the parsons, and the third
we will make war upon the statesmen.

"We will destroy the corn stacks". This was a challenge to
property from labour. Stacks in which they once had a share

were now alien produce which it was criminal to touch and exhilarating to burn.

"We will destroy the threshing machines". They detested these, not because they were power machines which would drag them into "barn life", but because they were intruders which prowled round the village destroying the wages they hoped to earn by the lustiness of their arms. Extra wages from threshing furnished the labourers with the margin over subsistence which the copyhold and common had once provided. "An industrious man who has a barn never requires poor relief; he can earn from 15/- to 20/- per week; he considers it almost as his little freehold and that in effect it certainly is"[1].

"Next year we will have a turn with the parsons". The parsons were tithe owners, members of the possessing class. The agricultural labourers felt to them much as the miners feel to-day to the owners of mining royalties. A further offence, in the labourer's eye, was the parson's connection with poor relief. The Hampshire mob, after intimidating the vicar of Selborne, went on to the workhouse at Headley. "There was not a room left entire, except that in which the sick children were....The sick ward was full of infirm old paupers. It was not touched, but of all the rest of the place not a room was left entire"[2].

"The third year we will make war upon the statesmen". In the event, the statesmen made war on them. Half a dozen executions and some 400 transportations cleared the air. Dazed and stupified the ex-rebels arrived in Van Diemen's Land to die there in due course without realising that their children would enter on a heritage of freedom, such as they could never have enjoyed in the old country. As though to affix the official stamp of capitalism on the rural economy of England, the Government in 1834 swooped down upon the Dorchester Labourers in the village of Tolpuddle and converted the harmless ritual of a few wretched labourers into a landmark in the history of Trade Unionism.

[1] Letter in the *Kent Herald*, September 30, 1830, quoted in Hammond, *The Village Labourer*, p. 245.
[2] Quoted in Hammond, *Agricultural Labourer*, p. 261.

4. THE COTTON INDUSTRY

Outside agriculture the only industry which in 1815 was fully capitalised was the spinning branch of the Lancashire cotton industry. William Fielden of Blackburn told the Emigration Committee of 1826–27 how things had been done in the old hand-spinning days. "The raw cotton was taken out by the weaver, and spun in his own house, and the change to spinning mills was productive of considerable inconvenience in the first instance, great alarm was created and some spinning mills were destroyed at the time. Many persons were thrown out of employment; but at that time the manufacture of the United Kingdom was in a very limited state compared with what it is at present"[1].

Furthermore certain evils connected with the transition period, when the cotton mills relied on water, had disappeared by the time of the first big investigation into factory conditions, viz., the Factory Commission of 1833. The system of parish apprentices was coming to an end[2], and the Commissioners were satisfied that organised cruelty was no longer prevalent in the cotton mills. In comparison with the weavers and the knitters, the factory operatives were in every respect better off. Every

[1] *Commons' Committee on Emigration* (1826–27), Q. 1970.
Place drew up (Oct. 1837) some "Notes for the use of the Hand-loom Weavers' Inquiry", which contain a historical survey of the Cotton Trade:
   (i) Every weaver was his own master until 1740 when some of the masters began to give out work.
   (ii) Until the introduction of the mule (by Crompton, 1779) the yarn or twist for warp was spun from cotton on the water frames, whilst the weft was spun by the families of the weavers on the jenny, which requires no power but the hand of the spinner and is equally well calculated for the factory or the cottage.
   (iii) 1785 Rev. Edmund Cartwright, brother of Major Cartwright, invented a loom to be worked by water or steam.
   (iv) Power Loom dates from 1800. Big increase 1818–1833. 1802 high-water mark of wages. Thereafter decline. 1808, cotton weavers in distress.
Place was anxious to show that the distress dated before the Poor Law of 1834, which could not therefore be held responsible for it. (Place: British Museum, Add. MSS. 27,828, p. 203.)
[2] Individual apprentices came to a very speedy end. In Derbyshire at one time the death rate was so heavy that to escape notice the burials were distributed between two parishes, although the burial fees were double the charges in the neighbouring parish of Tideswell (*Memoir of Robert Blincoe*, published by J. Doherty, 1832, p. 35).

year their situation improved. They were over-worked and exposed to accidents, but they worked in a factory in which these
things could be marked down and removed. Responsibility was
located. The cotton manufacturer owned the mill and no other
was responsible. Furthermore the trade was a paying trade, and
therefore it could stand restrictions which might have smashed
an industry which was financially crumbling. The employer
being a definite person, the factory hands had a definite status
as employees. Clear issues could arise between them on questions
of wages. It was very natural, therefore, that the lead in the
militant trades unionism of the early '30's should be given by
the Lancashire cotton spinners.

By 1833 the cotton mills of Lancashire offered skilled employment to a limited number of mechanics and machine minders,
and steady though severe employment to a much larger number
of children and women. The case was different in Spitalfields.
In 1840 an observer reported—"In Bethnal Green Road (the
neighbourhood of Spitalfields) there is held every Monday and
Tuesday morning between the hours of 6 and 8 a children's
labour market,—that is to say, there is an open space to which
children of both sexes from the age of 7 and upwards resort, to
be hired by the week or month by any person who may require
their services"[1]. Spitalfields had no factories to absorb the
weavers' children. Furthermore in the cotton trade the pace
was set by the ablest employers. The success of the factory acts
after 1833 was in part due to the factory inspectors then first
appointed, but it was due still more to the big employers with
up-to-date factories, which served as a model to the factory
inspectors in their task of levelling up the rest. Such were the
Cobdens of Stockport, the Ashtons of Hyde, the Strutts of
Belper, Messrs Whitehead of Hollymount, and Messrs Wood and
Walker, the leading firm in the Yorkshire worsted trade. The
Commissioners of 1833 rightly emphasized the fact that "the
large factories, and those recently built, have a prodigious advantage over the old and small mills. The working rooms in the large

---

[1] W. E. Hickson, *Notes made during a Tour through the Weaving Districts*,
printed in Hand-loom Weavers' Commission (1840), p. 51.

and modern buildings are without exception more spacious and lofty; the buildings are better drained; more effectual expedients are adopted to secure free ventilation and to maintain a more equable and moderate temperature"[1].

5. DEBT OF THE CLASSICAL POLITICAL ECONOMY TO AGRICULTURE AND COTTON

The debt of the classical political economy to agriculture and cotton is a heavy one. The Malthusian labourer was an agricultural labourer. In the tales of Harriet Martineau and Mrs Marcet[2]—and it was by tale and tract that the classical political

---

[1] *Report of Factory Commissioners* (1833), p. 16.

[2] Miss Martineau was kind enough to append to her tales a "Summary of Principles Illustrated"—for example:—

A Manchester Strike (1833).

Mr Wentworth, the virtuous employer, the man of Political Economy, addresses a meeting of strikers:

"Keep on your strike a little longer, and the question will be of how many less shall be employed, at how much less, keep it on long enough, and the question will be entirely settled; there will be no wages for anybody. Do you understand me?...All that you can now do, is to live as you best may upon such wages as the masters can give, keeping up your sense of respectability and your ambitions to improve your state when better times shall come. You must watch every opportunity of making some little provision against the fluctuations of our trade, contributing your money rather for your mutual relief in hard times, than for the support of strikes. You must place your children out to different occupations, choosing those which are least likely to be overstocked; and, above all, you must discourage in them the imprudent, early marriages to which are mainly owing the distresses which afflict yourselves and those which will for some time, I fear, oppress your children", etc., etc.

The strike, of course, was a complete failure.

Principles illustrated:

"Combinations of labourers against capitalists cannot secure a permanent rise of wages unless the supply of labour falls short of the demand; —in which case, strikes are usually unnecessary.

Nothing can permanently affect the rate of wages which does not affect the proportion of population to capital".

(*Illustrations of Political Economy*, No. 7, pp. 96 sqq. and 135.)

Mrs Marcet's *Conversations on Political Economy* (1816) are a trifle less lugubrious. They conclude with a duet of sanctimonious gush.

Mrs B. "The grand object to be kept in view in order to promote the general prosperity of the country is the increase of capital".

Caroline. "Whoever, I conceive, augments his capital by saving from his income increases the general stock of subsistence for the labouring classes,

economy was interpreted to the people—the worker was a factory hand seduced by combination into interference with the laws of supply and demand. The labourer of the Iron Law of wages was a mechanical abstraction, a machine set in motion by capital and diminishing its effort if the amount of fuel ran short. Some of these machines were so constructed that they required a more generous allowance of fuel to keep them going; and therefore Ricardo's law was not so dismal as at first sight appeared. The inspiration of the popular political economy came, not from Birmingham with its forges and artisans, nor from Leeds with its clothiers and Cloth Hall, but from Manchester, from Cottonopolis, whose merchants sent their "shading trails to Agra's nymphs". The theory of foreign trade was conceived in terms of corn and cotton: corn for cotton yarns, cotton yarns for corn, a free trade, a ceaseless flow, the first and last of the commandments on the Tablets of the Economic Harmonies.

6. The Village Artisan

The artisan of the country went forth into the great towns, with bright eye and hope in his breast, to make his fortune.

"Turn again Whittington, Lord Mayor of London". When Hodge became a townsman he abandoned the only occupation at which he was skilled. When a manufacture was taken over by machinery, the children, whether they came from town or village, entered the factory ahead of their parents. In both cases, therefore, the change was reluctantly made. But from village to country town, from country town to the great

whilst he who spends part of his capital diminishes that stock of subsistence, and consequently the means of employing the labouring classes in its reproduction".

The *Dictionary of Political Economy* says of Mrs Marcet:

"It is probable that the work exercised considerable influence on the economic theory of the middle of the 19th century by helping to form the first impressions of young economists".

And of Miss Martineau:

"The success of these tales was extraordinary. Within a few years their circulation reached to 10,000. Cabinet ministers, newspaper editors and politicians appear to have vied for the privilege of having their proposals supported by the stories".

towns and finally to London, the artisan passed of his own free will; and it still needs all our educational ingenuity to equip the city child for competition with the artisan who is fresh from the all-round experience of provincial work. This drain to the towns is always going on, but as it is not associated with distress, the evidence for it is hard to find. We know much about the Irish in England, but little of the processes by which Scotchmen have gotten all the good jobs. In the early part of the century we find references to the inflow from English counties to the Metropolis, in connection with apprenticeship. In 1820 the Master Hatters of London complained that the journeymen would not "allow a finisher to work who has served his time in Manchester, Oldham, Denton, Ashton and other parts of Lancashire, by which they have prevented a supply of useful and industrious young men coming to London as finishers"[1]. It was a grievance with the shipwrights of London that young men were brought from the North, sometimes from Scotland, engaged as apprentices for 3 years, and in less than 3 months passed off as men who have served 7 years[2]. A London builder in 1833 declared: "A higher rate of wages has the effect of bringing up from the country in different seasons of the year a great number of countrymen"[3].

Jude the Obscure, when he had learnt how to use his village chisel, marched towards the glowing lights of Oxford.

7. The Nottingham Lace Trade

By 1815 cotton spinning was concentrated in Lancashire; and worsted and wool were rapidly acquiring the same predominance in Yorkshire. Similarly hosiery, a special branch of the textile finishing trades, was localised in the East Midlands. But there was a big difference between the Midlands and the North. In the North the localisation was clinched by the early introduction of steam power, in the Midlands the industry was localised and

[1] Place, Add. MSS. British Museum, 27,999, No. 84.
[2] *Ibid.* No. 35.
[3] *Commons, Committee on Manufactures, Commerce and Shipping* (1833), Q. 1679.

conducted on a large scale, as regards output, half a century before the processes were performed in factories with the aid of steam power.

To this general statement there is one partial exception. By 1815 the Nottingham lace trade was growing up. This trade was in a very literal sense an adjunct of hosiery, for about the middle of the 18th century "a number of appendages were applied to the stocking frame, one of which...by mere accident was applied to the making fabrics in imitation of lace.... This attempt was succeeded by another invention termed a point-net machine"[1]. When point-net went out of use about 1815, its place was taken by machine-made bobbin-net, which is the basis of Nottingham's lace trade at the present day. "Bobbin-net", said Dr Ure[2], "surpasses every other branch of industry by the complex ingenuity of its machinery". John Heathcote of Loughborough invented the first successful bobbin-net machine, and it was constantly improved by his successors, with happy results to Nottingham:

> For we'll all go a bobbin and carriaging,
> Oh yes! we'll go but—yes! we will all go,
> We'll go all together, a bobbin and carriaging.
> Hip. hip. hip. hip. hurrah![3]

The features of the lace trade in the period 1815–40 were:

i.   The lace machinery was propelled by human agency.

ii.   The machinery was so complicated that none but skilled men handled it.

iii.   In 1820 the machinery was in the possession of more than a thousand small owners, chiefly handcraftsmen, who employed some hundreds of agents in the disposal of their wares.

iv.   The agents took their goods in daily on pack-horses to London and the big towns, following the tradition of the Buckinghamshire hand-lace manufacturers.

---

[1] Extract from *Memorial to the Lords of the Treasury against the Exportation of Machinery*, 1834—quoted in *Report of the Commissioner on the Frame-work Knitters* (1845), p. 20.

[2] Felkin, *History of the Machine-Wrought Hosiery and Lace Manufactures*, p. 285.

[3] *Dictionary of Arts*, p. 730.

Between 1840 and 1860 these conditions altered:

i.   Steam power was introduced about 1840, but the machinery being still delicate and complex, skilled male labour was not displaced. When the Factory Commissioner visited Nottingham in 1860 he found women and children employed in the subsidiary processes only, in preparing and removing the bobbins and in mending the finished goods[1].

ii.   By 1860 the lace machinery was concentrated in fewer hands, and the places of work were large enough to invite regulation as factories.

iii.   By 1860 methods of marketing had also changed. Pack-horses had been succeeded by horse-drawn vehicles, and these in turn by railways. Improvements in communication widened the market. Travellers from the large mercantile houses waited on the Nottinghamshire manufacturers, who, in addition, had agents at home and abroad on the look-out for orders.

8.   THE FRAME-WORK KNITTERS

Thomas Cooper draws a picture of the hosiery trade in Leicestershire, when he lived there 1841–43.

At the head were the hosiers. They were called stocking and glove manufacturers, though no manufacturing took place on their premises. They let out knitting frames and supplied materials to be worked up on these at a certain price.

The Messrs Biggs, in my time, owned 1,200 frames, it was said. Perhaps 50 of these would be let out to William Cummins, thirty to Joseph Underwood, and so on to other "masters" or middlemen. The "masters" employed the working-hands, giving so much per dozen for the weaving of the stockings or gloves, and charging the man a weekly frame rent—which was, of course, at a profit above the rent "the master" paid the owner of the frame[2].

This was the trade as Cooper saw it, but in fact the bulk of it was organised in smaller groupings, and the towns differed from the villages; as we can see from the *Report of the Commissioner on*

---

[1] *Report of Commissioner on the expediency of subjecting the Lace Manufacture to the regulations of the Factory Acts* (1861), p. 28.
[2] *Life of Thomas Cooper, written by himself* (1873), p. 140.

the Frame-work Knitters (1845), and the *Report and Evidence of the Commons' Committees on the Payment of Wages (Hosiery) Bill* (1854) and the *Stoppage of Wages (Hosiery)* (1855).

In the towns, in addition to big master middlemen like the Cummins', there were small master middlemen who possessed premises with only a few standings. Nevertheless they too, like the Cummins', dealt regularly with one warehouse at regular prices, and sometimes they found time to work a frame themselves. Others in a still smaller way had no regular work. They took out any description they could get from any warehouse and at any price. They lived from hand to mouth, and the earnings of their journeymen were abnormally low.

In the country the knitters worked in their own cottages or outhouses. However small they were, they counted as "master stockingers"[1], if they worked under their own roof. One such master would have half a dozen journeymen, another his wife and child and a single journeyman, while a third would be master of no labour but his own. Mastership, however, did not save him from the middlemen. It did, indeed, if he lived close to a town and worked "direct to the warehouse", but the big houses found it inconvenient to deal direct with individuals scattered over the countryside, and therefore they employed a middleman, who was not a master-middleman, but simply a putter-out of work.

The status of the journeyman knitter was tolerably uniform. The essence of a journeyman was that he worked under another's roof. Most journeymen knitters lived in the towns, and their pay was better than that of journeymen knitters in the villages.

In these different structural types there is one constant feature—the material originates with the hosier; and therefore work does not begin until he has given the material out. Cutting across this traditional structure was the personage known as a "bag hosier", who made his appearance about the beginning of the 19th century. Certain master stockingers of Sutton-in-

---

[1] Cf. *Commons' Committee on Stoppage of Wages (Hosiery)* (1855). The master stockinger "is a man who lives at home with his wife and family at a cheap small house in a village with a small garden, and perhaps an allotment, and who keeps two or three journeymen and his family", Q. 6427.

Ashfield, we are informed[1], on the death of the hosier who employed them, bought their own materials and made them up
into stockings, which they carried in bags to Nottingham and
sold to the hosiers there for what they would fetch. They were
the first to introduce the "cut-up" work, which was prominent
in the troubles of 1809–19. But in 1845, and still more in 1855,
the term was losing its original contemptuous significance. For
the cheap work[2] which the bag hosier introduced was at these
dates being taken over by improved machinery which the hosier
kept under his own eye in his own factory. In this manner progressive hosiers ended by becoming bag hosiers themselves.

Let us now attempt to see the trade in motion over a period of
years. Three periods may be distinguished:

(a) 1809–19. This period was marked by Luddism. "Frames
were broken in 1811–15", said an old stockinger, "not on account
of disputes about wages, but of cut-up work, which lowered the
demand for fully wrought goods and so tended to reduce prices
generally"[3].

Respectable hosiers were in agreement with the knitters, and
in 1819 their joint petitions induced a Committee of the House
of Commons to recommend "by way of experiment" the prohibition of the "fraudulent species of Worsted Hose, which is
known as Cut-up Work" for three years[4]. But the recommen-
dation did not take effect, and in any case the relief would have
been disproportionate to the evil. For after 1815, although the
output of hand-made goods increased, the condition of the
knitters became steadily worse. The old standards having been
upset, the weak dragged down the strong.

---

[1] *Report of Commissioner on the Condition of the Frame-work Knitters*
(1845), *Glossary of Technical Terms*, p. 135.

[2] Cf. *Appendix to Report of the Commissioner, op. cit.*, Pt II., *Notts. and
Derby*. Q. 624. The "common manufacture" was "chiefly in the hands of
bagmen". Q. 625. "A large proportion of cut-up work" was in the same
hands, "especially in Sutton Ashfield and the neighbourhood". This perhaps was due to "the inconvenience of carrying in work from the villages
distant from Nottingham to Nottingham".

[3] Quoted in Felkin, *History, etc.* (1867), p. 237.

[4] *Commons' Committee on the Petition of the Hosiers and Frame-work
Knitters in the Woollen Manufacture of the town and county of Leicester* (1819),
Report, pp. 3–4.

In the years of rioting the custom of an agreed price list, which had obtained formerly, broke down. In a trial of 1821, in which certain delegates of the Nottinghamshire frame-work knitters were prosecuted for meeting together in violation of the statute against combinations, an old man was produced who was made to say that the knitters had forced him to sign a document. The document was an assent to resolutions passed by the knitters, to wit:

　i.　"That information be given immediately to those hosiers who refuse to give *the agreed price*, that their frames are at liberty.

　ii.　.　　.　　.　　.　　.　　.　　.

　iii.　That the thanks of the meeting be given to those gentlemen who pay *list prices*"[1].

　(*b*)　1837–45. This was the period of Chartism, and the old controversy over cut-up work and agreed prices was overshadowed by the grievance of frame-rents.

　Cooper puts it thus:

The knitter "had to pay not only frame-rent, but so much per week for the 'standing' of the frame in the shop of the master....The man had also to pay 3*d*. per dozen to the master for 'giving out' of the work. He had also to pay so much per dozen to the female 'seamer' of the hose. And he had also oil to buy for his machine and lights to pay for in the darker half of the year. All the deductions brought the average earnings of the stocking-weaver to 4/6 per week....But the foul grievance was this: each man had to pay a whole week's frame rent, although he had only half a week's work!"[2]

　Cooper is speaking of the journeyman knitter, but his plight was in substance the same as that of the small master stockinger in the villages. The frame rent controversy ranged together all frame letters against all frame users.

　The only possible justification for the frame rent was that it might have assisted the hosier to supervise and improve the frames on which his work was being knitted (this is the advantage which the American Boot and Shoe Machinery Combine[3]

---

[1] *Proceedings at the Town Hall, Nottingham, April* 30, 1821. (Foxwell Collection.)

[2] Cooper, *op. cit.* pp. 140–141.

[3] Cf. *Report of Committee on Trusts, Ministry of Reconstruction* [Cd 9236], (1919), p. 27.

claims for its Tying Clause system of leasing machinery); but it did not secure even this. "Butchers, bakers, publicans, gentlemen's servants, women of various classes and persons engaged in almost every trade, are found to be the owners of frames"[1]. Frame-investment by alien parties added the evil of sub-letting to the existing evils of leasing frames and putting out work; and all these factors acting cumulatively endowed the frames with a vicious vitality. They continued to multiply even when the trade was stationary or declining, for what was lost in profit could be recovered in rent. "Rent" was an appropriate term, since the price of hiring a frame was determined, not by the cost of reproduction of frames, but by the exigencies of the users. Frame rents were thus like slum rents. The users could not escape from them except by abandoning the access to their livelihood.

(c) 1845–60. About 1845 the knitting trade, which had become proverbial for its persistent depression, recovered unexpectedly, and the recovery was maintained.

The first sign of improvement was the abandonment of the rent system by progressive hosiers. "This rent system", said a hosier in 1855, "is a dead weight upon the community in the midland counties"[2]. He himself had given up frame rents and introduced the net system in its place, paying piece rates free of deduction. But in changing the method of payment he had also scrapped the old narrow frames and abolished the structure of which frame-letting was the corner stone. Henceforth he worked wide frames in his own factory. Similarly the master-middleman passes into a works manager. Says one of them, in 1855: "I have worked in a frame in my youth; I have been what is called a middleman; and I am now the superintendent of a factory"[3].

The inducement to structural change was not steam power. Steam power came last and confirmed the change. The inducement was the extension of the uses of the wide frame. This kind

---

[1] *Report of Commissioner on the Condition of the Frame-work Knitters* (1845), p. 56.
[2] *Commons' Committee on Stoppage of Wages (Hosiery)* (1855), Q. 379, Evidence of J. Biggs, Esq.
[3] *Ibid.* Q. 4782.

of frame had always been used for shirts, drawers and piece goods, which did not require "fashioning"; and it increased as the working class demand for these articles increased. The activities of the "bag hosier" further enlarged its field. Finally, the wide frame was adapted to take "straight down work", several stockings being knitted on the same frame. This gave scope for specialisation. One frame made tops, another middles, another bottoms. And specialisation necessitated co-ordination. It was therefore profitable to have the work done in a shop under the control of a master-middleman. But the work was still hand-work and the wages were low.

After 1845 came the changes which allowed of steam power. Rotary frames, in which the needles were placed on revolving cylinders, were introduced. Originally they were improved hand-frames, but they opened the door to steam power. For un-fashioned work of uniform size knitted on a wide frame by a circular motion was exactly suited to steam-driven machinery. Steam power accordingly was tried between 1845 and 1855, and gradually captured all the "straightforward work". To-wards 1860, when methods were devised for putting fashion into work by automatic action, without stoppage of the machine, steam power captured the wrought hosiery also.

With valuable machinery and central mechanical power, frame-work knitting became a factory trade. Full capitalism had arrived.

"The young and the strong and the active men", said A. J. Mundella in 1871, "have got into rotary frames..., and they are getting as good wages as in almost any trade in England. But the men who are compelled to adhere to the old wrought-hose frames, because they are not young enough and quick enough to work at the rotary frames, which can only be increased by slow degrees, are driven back on the hand-frames"[1].

Thus, by 1870, frame-work knitting had reached the stage which the Nottingham bobbin-net lace trade, with its initial complex machinery, reached in half the time. Frame-work knitting passed between 1815 and 1845 through a waste of dis-

[1] *Truck Commission* (1871), Q. 42,542.

order, without innovations either in technique or motive power.
The knitters were exploited, but the hosiers' profits were mean.
At last came the recovery, obscurely stimulated by mechanical
inventions, which were the precursors of steam power. When
steam power at last came, it was hailed with glee; for between
it and a better past lay an interval of nameless misery.

New methods brought new problems: unions, strikes, and
methods of averting strikes. After a strike in the autumn of
1860 Mr A. J. Mundella established a Board of Arbitration and
Conciliation in the hosiery trade. "Three of us", says Mr Mundella, "met a dozen leaders of the trades unions. We consulted
with these men and told them that the present plan was a bad
one, that they took every advantage of us when we had a demand, and we took every advantage of them when trade was
bad, and it was a system mutually predatory". Viewed at first
with suspicion by some of the masters, it soon won acceptance,
and the trying years of the American Civil War passed by without a strike. In 1867 its founder declared that the resolutions
of the Board had been loyally accepted both by masters and
men[1]. The United Frame-work Knitters' Society established in
1866 gave the Board its official support. "We recognise", they
said, "the power and assistance of the present board of arbitration in all its decisions according to the rules laid down by
that body for the guidance of manufacturers and workmen"[2].

The Nottinghamshire Board of Arbitration and Conciliation
points backwards as well as forwards. It points back to the days
of the agreed price lists and forward to the days of collective
bargaining in this and other trades.

---

[1] Quoted in Felkin, *History, etc.*, p. 485.
[2] *Ibid.* p. 489. Resolution passed at the foundation of the Society.
June 11, 1866.

CHAPTER XVII

THE HISTORICAL BASIS OF CAPITALISM (II)

1. THE CASE OF THE HAND-LOOM WEAVERS

HAND-LOOM weaving embraces the finishing or manufacturing end of various textile materials—silk, cotton, worsted, wool, linen and jute. It is therefore extremely difficult to draw any general picture of the transition to power weaving.

The main sources of evidence are four:

i. *Commons' Committee on Ribbon Weavers* (1818); *Lords' Committee on Bill to repeal the Acts relating to Wages in the Silk Manufacture* (1823).

ii. *Commons' Committees on Emigration* (1826 and 1826–27).

iii. *Commons' Committee on Hand-loom Weavers* (1834–35).

iv. *Report of Royal Commission and Assistant Commissioners on the Condition of the Hand-loom Weavers*, seven parts (1839–41).

The effect of mechanical invention in spinning was to increase the demand for weavers' labour, and this circumstance, together with the high prices ruling during the war, caused the period before 1815 to be regarded in after days as a Golden Age[1]. Witnesses before the Committee of 1834 recalled how weavers used to have their own houses and consume butter and ham and tea, and how 40 years ago they used to salt a little cow and eat it during the winter[2]. Scotland had memories of weavers who had risen to be Lord Provosts of Glasgow; Spitalfields had memories of the gifted men it had given to medicine and science, of its mathematical, historical and entomological societies, of its toy gardens and pigeon fancying. But in 1834 and in 1839–41 the tale was one of misery and decline. The weavers had a deadly interest in the price of their products. The prospect of next week's

---

[1] Cf. Place's Notes, p. 201 n. above.
[2] *Commons' Committee on Hand-loom Weavers* (1834), p. 53.

food and last week's house rent fluctuated with the fashions. Novelties gave a brief fillip to prices, but the general rule of all fancy goods was that they continued "to descend and descend, until the articles became so bad and the wages so low that they became stale and coarse and badly manufactured and they go out of use and some new article supersedes them"[1]. Substitution of coarser or cheaper material is of no moment to the factory operative, but it mattered vitally to the hand-loom weaver to whom it meant a progressive deterioration of earnings. The position was the same with the frame-work knitters, as may be seen from a comparison of the following tables:

Cotton-weavers' Weekly Wages[2]		Price per Dozen of Women's Worsted Stockings[3]	
	s. d.		s. d.
1795–1804	26 8	1815	7 6
1804–1811	20 0	1825	6 6
1811–1818	14 7	1826	5 6
1818–1825	8 9	1835	4 9
1825–1832	6 4	1836	5 0
1832–1834	5 6	1841	4 6

The marketing of the goods so produced was notorious for cut-throat competition. "In foreign markets" said a witness in 1834, "it is Bolton versus Glasgow rather than England versus France which pushes prices down"[4]. When cotton yarns were rising, the rise could be off-set by a reduction of wages. Said a yarn merchant to a manufacturer: "You can take just so much off the wages of your workmen as will amount to the increased price of the yarn, and you can sell your goods at the same price"[5]. There was much rotten finance in the business. There were firms in London known as slaughter houses, whose practice it was to make advances to small employers and demand re-payment at inopportune moments. The manufacturers conse-quently had to sell at slaughter prices. It was these slaughter

---

[1] *Commons' Committee on Hand-loom Weavers* (1834), p. 16.

[2] Table submitted by a Bolton weaver to the *Commons' Committee on Hand-loom Weavers* (1834).

[3] *Report of the Commissioner on the Condition of the Frame-work Knitters* (1845), p. 38.

[4] *Commons' Committee on Hand-loom Weavers* (1834), p. 47.

[5] *Ibid.* p. 47.

houses, so witnesses complained in 1834, which filled the ears of Government with fairy tales of trade prosperity[1].

2. THE SPITALFIELDS SILK INDUSTRY

At the beginning of the 19th century a number of familiar land-marks in the statutory regulation of wages disappeared. The Wages sections of the old Statute of Artificers were repealed in 1813, the Apprenticeship sections in 1814. But the Spitalfields Silk Acts of 1773 and onwards were in full force, and they were only abolished by Huskisson in 1824 in the face of strong opposition from many of the smaller masters and from all the silk weavers. What is the significance of this legislation?

At the beginning of the 19th century the Spitalfields silk trade was in a sense highly organised[2]. It was a specialised and localised trade. The official regulation of wages was an official assent to Piece Lists, which were revised by agreement from time to time: "never to my recollection", said a weaver in 1823, "by the authority of revision of the magistrates, always by the mutual consent of the parties concerned"[3]. But every year, as fashion changed and new varieties came in, the Spitalfields Book became a more complicated document.

Furthermore, the structure of the trade was changing. The official regulations were based on a traditional organisation of master weavers working with journeymen and a limited number of apprentices. But a new class of big manufacturers was arising, who combined the function of merchant and manufacturer, and to whom manufacturing meant giving out work to weavers. These manufacturers resented the restrictions of the Spitalfields Act. They complained that it put them at a disadvantage with their rivals in the Midlands and North, where such restrictions, never having had the sanction of law, had broken down; and that

---

[1] *Commons' Committee on Hand-loom Weavers* (1834), p. 348.
[2] Cf. Clapham, *Economic Journal*, No. 104, Dec. 1916; *The Spitalfields Acts*, 1773–1824. *English Economic History, Select Documents*, edited by A. E. Bland and others (1919), give the terms of the Act of 1773 (p. 547) and a Middlesex Wages Assessment under the Act (p. 551).
[3] *Lords' Committee on Wages in Silk Manufacture* (1823), p. 27.

the book of rates discouraged improvements, since masters had to pay the same rates whether labour-saving appliances were used or not. They resented the prohibition, which in practice they evaded, against putting out work in the country. They threw the blame of the traditional structure on the Act which perpetuated it. "The very touch of the magistrate", said one of them, "is paralysing"[1]. The Act was therefore repealed. Had it not been repealed in 1824, it would have gone without a doubt in 1826, when the silk manufacture was thrown open to French competition.

3.　Irish Immigration to the Weaving Districts of the North

In the North the burden was of a different kind. Here it was immigration from Ireland. This was emphasised by the Emigration Committee of 1826 and 1826–27, and in the Hand-loom Weavers' investigations. "The vast migration of unemployed Irish", it was said in 1834, "has been one of the means of reducing wages in England and Scotland"[2]. Mr Hickson, one of the Royal Commissioners, wrote in 1840: "From all I have seen I am led to believe that one half of perhaps the majority of weavers of plain fabrics, even in this country, are either Irish, or persons descended from Irish parents"[3]. At this time none but Irish were entering the trade as beginners.

Structurally the hand-loom weaving of Lancashire and Scotland resembled the frame-work knitting of the Midlands. In 1827 the Bishop of Chester, whose diocese in those days stretched over a great part of Lancashire, estimated the weaving population to consist of nearly one million souls[4], divided into two broad classes, town weavers and country weavers. Some weavers worked as journeymen under the roof of a master weaver on

---

[1] *Lords' Committee on Wages in Silk Manufacture* (1823), p. 162.
[2] *Commons' Committee on Hand-loom Weavers* (1834), p. 315.
[3] Hickson, *Notes made during a tour through the weaving districts* (1840), p. 55.
[4] *Commons' Committee on Emigration* (1826–27). Evidence of Bishop of Chester. Qs. 2250 sqq.

stuff provided by him. There were also weavers called custom weavers, who were employed to weave the yarns spun in private houses, but these, according to the Report of the Assistant Commissioner in 1840, though at one time numerous in Lincolnshire and Notts., had now nearly disappeared[1]. The great majority of weavers in Lancashire and Cheshire, whether town dwellers or country dwellers, worked in their own cottages on looms which they owned or hired. These were the hand-loom weavers whose problem came before the Royal Commission of 1839–41.

4. Proposals for a Minimum Wage

John Fielden of Oldham, "himself, by means of the power-loom and hand-loom, one of the most extensive manufacturers of the Empire", made a gallant attempt to stem the rot. He proposed minimum wage legislation in 1826 and 1834. In this he had the support of the better class of manufacturers. The Bolton manufacturers argued: "We cannot think that any circumstances can require or justify a permanent rate of wages, below what is necessary for the subsistence of the workman; because, when a manufacturer will not supply the labourer with food, it cannot long continue....Such superfluous labour will, of course, be ultimately checked both by the limit of natural strength, borne down by exhaustion, and by the limit of demand; *but while employment is thus largely sought on any terms, it draws capital to its assistance that would not otherwise be so employed,* and sales will be forced on the public by the temptation of cheapness, until the trade is so completely overdone as to be brought to a stand"[2]. Parliament, however, refused legislation, and, apart from the prejudice of the time, there were two good reasons against it. First of all, it would have made a call on administrative machinery which could not have been met. Secondly, the hand-loom section of the trade was a losing one and could not have survived regulation.

[1] *Hand-loom Weavers' Commission, Assistant Commissioner's Report* (1840), Part II. p. 352.
[2] *Ibid.* Part IV. p. 259.

5. INFLUENCE OF THE POWER-LOOM

The power-loom was invented by Edmund Cartwright and patented in 1785–87, but power-weaving was very slow in coming into general use. The position in 1840 was that it was fully established in cotton[1], not yet sensibly felt in linen, and in the experimental stage in wool and silk. In wool, however, Halifax was weaving worsted or "stuff goods" by power, and Leeds was similarly manufacturing broad-cloth.

William Fielden was justified in arguing in 1827 that "the manufactory by the power-loom is a very distinct one from that which is carried on by the hand-loom.... There are a great number of persons employed about the power-loom in various preparations of the article before it comes into the loom, and so many mechanics are employed in making the machinery and keeping it in order that I do not imagine from what I have understood, that more than from one-third to one-fourth is saved by the use of the power-loom"[2]. But from about 1840 onwards the power-loom steadily ousted the hand-loom in nearly every branch of weaving; and it was only in the woollen branch that the hand-loom survived for any length of time.

The moral of the hand-loom weavers is the same as that of the frame-work knitters. They were not overwhelmed by a sudden irruption of machinery. The power-loom came slowly and for long was complementary rather than rival. The tragedy of the weavers was the slowness of their passing.

6. THE IRISH INFLUX

The flood of Irish immigration extended further than Lancashire and Glasgow, and over more industries than hand-loom weaving.

It was noted by the Poor Law Commissioners in 1834 that the Irish who came over to seek manufacturing employment kept to

---

[1] Cf. p. 201 n. above.
[2] *Commons' Committee on Emigration* (1826–27), p. 181.

the big towns[1]; and a similar tendency has been observed in later times in the United States. In Manchester alone in 1835, "the Irish and their immediate descendants amount to about 60,000"[2]. In the factory districts they eschewed the mills. Those who entered rarely got beyond the Card Rooms; and employers who had experimented with Irish labour were disappointed. It was estimated in 1835 that there were not more than 100 Irish spinners in the county of Lancashire[3].

With another part of the flood—the Irish navvies—we have dealt already[4]. Similar to these were the gangs of agricultural labourers who came over for the harvest. The migrating harvester is a world-wide institution. Belgium and France have Flemings, Saxony has Poles, the Argentine has Italians, and England has the Irish. In the '30's some used to come by way of Liverpool in the company of fellow countrymen who meant to stay, while others came by the older route of the Bristol Channel, serving as ballast for the small Welsh collier on its return trip. From Bristol they walked or begged their way into the Midland counties, amassed a few pounds and returned home the way they came. Of late years the introduction of self-binding machines has considerably decreased the demand for Irish labour: "As the machines came in and the scythe took the place of the sickle, the Irish immigration dwindled away, and the whirr of the gearing supplanted the Celtic chatter"[5]. In the summer of 1899 28,000 came to England, and of these three-fourths belonged to the county of Mayo[6].

Liverpool, the port through which the Irish mainly passed, claimed as large a share as Manchester. The Liverpool docker to-day is mostly of Irish descent.

Others again found their way to London, where their favourite

[1] Cf. *Commons' Committee on Emigration* (1826-27). "The Irish concentrate themselves in the manufacturing towns and not in the manufacturing districts" (Q. 2095).

[2] *First Annual Report of the Poor Law Commissioners* (1835), p. 305.

[3] *Ibid.* p. 305.   [4] pp. 171-2.

[5] *Reminiscences of Albert Pell, sometime M.P. for South Leicestershire*, p. 145.

[6] *Board of Trade Report on Wages and Earnings of Agricultural Labourers* (1900), pp. 104-5.

occupation was building and transport. In 1833 they were reported to be earning 18s. per week at "carrying bricks, making
mortar, taking down and erecting of scaffolds and all those
employments connected with the building trade, which we can
get done by them in preference to the journeymen tradesmen"[1].
But they rarely became bricklayers, not coming over till they
were 25 or 26, when they were too old to learn the trade. These
were the families who contributed to make London's slums. In
1849 a cholera outbreak in London stimulated investigation into
housing conditions. The worst cases of overcrowding were
usually among the poor Irish. Thus at one lodging house in
Holborn Hill 68 were found herded together in three rooms. On
the second floor there lived a man, his wife and four children: a
widow and two children: one man: a man with his wife and child:
a man, his wife and two children: another man with his wife and
two children[2].

7. The Contractor in the Building Trades

The system of indirect employment in coal mining, the Midlands "butty" system, was, in principle, the same as the contract
system in railroad construction. Parallels can be studied in
other industries. The historians of Trade Unionism point out
that in the Trade Unionism of the '30's the building operatives
took a prominent part. Their grievance was the interference of
the contractor: "who, supplanting the master mason, master
carpenter, etc., undertook the management of all building operations. A placard issued by the Liverpool painters announced that
they had joined 'The General Union of the Artisans employed
in the process of building', in order to put down 'that baneful,
unjust, and ruinous system of monopolising the hard-earned
profits of another man's business, called 'contracting'"[3].

But in one corner of England the system which contracting

---

[1] *Commons' Committee on Manufactures, Commerce and Shipping* (1833),
Q. 1682.
[2] *Fifth Report of the National Philanthropic Association* (1850), p. 25.
[3] Webb, *History of Trade Unionism*, p. 114.

superseded survived down to the middle of the 19th century. In the Island of Portland, which Thomas Hardy has immortalised in *The Well-beloved*, island-custom died hard. The islanders worked in companies of seven or eight, agreeing with the stone merchants on the island to take their stone at a certain price, but it took them six months to clear away the rubbish and two years more to get the stone; and therefore in the interval the merchant advanced funds, which took the form of orders on the local shops. The latter were contrary to the Truck Acts, and that is why their story has survived. A stone merchant examined before a Committee of 1842 declared that there was no instance then of a capitalist making his contract with the merchant and hiring the men at so much a week. "It would not be suffered by the men"[1].

8. The Docker and Casual Labour

Similarly casual labour among dockers had its origin in the widespread phenomenon of indirect employment. From a Committee on Intoxication[2] among the Labouring Classes (1834) we learn something about the Liverpool dockers then. They were reputed to number 6000 and their wages varied from 1s. to 3s. per day. A Liverpool iron merchant, who had attempted in vain to better the dockers' lot, informed the Committee that:

There were about 120 of these persons called lumpers in Liverpool, men that took the jobs from the merchants, of loading and discharging the vessels for a certain sum, then go out upon the Quay and engage with a number of men to do the job for something less, and live upon the profits between the price they agree for and what they pay to the workmen. I find that there were not more than one or two out of the 120 that paid their workmen anywhere else than at a public house; some of them kept public houses themselves...; and it was,

[1] *Commons' Committee on Payment of Wages* (1842), Q. 2564.
[2]   "Those slight refreshments by the way
              Which were but meant his strength to stay
              So sank his soul in sloth and sin,
              He look'd no further than his inn".
                    Hannah More, *Works*, vol. VI. (1834).
It is difficult to understand how the labouring classes had the heart to get drunk amid all the excellent advice that dripped from the pens of sentimental females in this age.

and still is, the practice to meet the workmen at public houses early on Saturday evening, and to keep out of the way till 10, 11 or 12 o'clock...; then the shops would be closed before they could go to purchase the articles wanted for their families. In many cases half their wages were expended in the public houses before they received the rest. These lumpers were also in the habit of inducing their men during the week to send to their pay houses for the fetchings of drink, besides the money they were compelled to spend on Saturday night[1].

The worthy iron merchant is somewhat obscure, but here obviously is the seed of the dockers' problem. Casually he was employed and paid, casually therefore he lived. In 1834, as 50 years later, the rate of wage was a subordinate thing. As Sir William Beveridge says of the London Dockers' Strike of 1889: "The docker's tanner represents a tragedy of misdirected enthusiasm. Under-employment infringes upon the standard of life just as much as does under-payment"[2].

When we remember the origin of casual employment and the length of time it has persisted, we are not surprised that the docker, whom time has made, is restive under the process of scientific decasualisation.

9. Capitalism in the North of England

The North of England is the cradle of capitalism in the best sense of this ambiguous word. We have already studied the growth of the Lancashire Cotton Mills and observed that the large mills which employed directly hundreds of operatives, including not only children and women but also mechanics and machine minders, were the mills which offered the best kind of employment and rested on a strong financial foundation. When weaving passed into power shops, the weaving branch of the textile industries followed the same development. Let us now see how other industries in the North developed.

In Northumberland and Durham, from the beginning of the century, the collieries were large and the method of operation was direct. There were reasons for this. The collieries of North-

---

[1] *Commons' Committee on Intoxication among the Labouring Classes* (1834), Q. 3787. Evidence of John Finch.

[2] W. H. Beveridge, *Unemployment*, p. 207.

umberland and Durham in the first half of the century produced mainly for London. To this trade was added, in the second half of the century, an increasing volume of export trade. Furthermore, the allied iron and steel industry in the North of England was from the outset organised on a large scale. The influence of these factors may be seen by comparison with coal fields where the reverse conditions prevailed. The Lancashire collieries were opened in the neighbourhood of factories to supply a local demand. Of this district we read in 1873 that there has been a great increase in the number of small collieries: "every manufacturer who has had any chance of opening out a piece of coal upon the out-crop has opened it"[1]. Lancashire was one of the counties which in 1842 employed women and children under the worst conditions.

In the Midlands, where the butty system and truck prevailed, and in South Wales, the newest of the great coal fields to be opened, the collieries were frequently attached to particular iron works, and this restricted their size. But the iron masters in the North rarely possessed collieries or iron stone mines. "The North of England iron trade", said Sir David Dale in 1871, "is of modern establishment. There have been on the Tyne establishments existing for a great many years, but they do not exceed, I suppose, altogether perhaps four or five in number; and from that period and the discovery of iron stone in the Cleveland Hills dates the establishment of the North of England iron trade; and it so happened that those who have gone into it have been either individuals with large means or limited companies with large capital; and that there have not come to be erected any smaller works, and that the system of renting works has never crept in at all"[2].

Thus in Northumberland and Durham, both in mining and in the iron and steel trade big proprietors employed directly large groups of men. Contrast the pottery trade of Staffordshire and the cutlery trade of Sheffield. It was not in 1842 or in 1855,

[1] *Commons' Committee on Present Dearness and Scarcity of Coal* (1873), p. 147.
[2] *Truck Commission* (1871). Evidence of David Dale. Q. 44,603.

but in 1908 that these industries came under the notice of a Departmental Committee on Truck. The Committee found that work-shop inspectors had urged employers, often with success, to introduce net wages into the pottery trade, but in the cutlery trade of Sheffield the old customs persisted. The cutler rented a "trough" in a "wheel" (i.e. a side room in a factory), sometimes working solely for the owner of the wheel, sometimes solely for outside customers, and sometimes for both. "Originally", said the Committee, "the cutlery trade was carried on in works situated on the rivers which surround Sheffield and which afforded an abundant supply of water power. Here most of the workmen rented a little land which they farmed in their leisure and when the water ran dry in the summer. Working as they did in solitary grinding wheels on the banks of the streams, it was impossible for the rules and regulations which govern ordinary factory life to become traditional among them. On the other hand very informal habits were formed and a set of traditions handed down which it is easy to see arose entirely out of the peculiar circumstances under which they worked. To this cause we must attribute the freedom from restraint which is so characteristic a feature of the Sheffield cutlery workers of to-day. It is this love of freedom which makes him tolerate the practices which are the despair of those who wish to see his lot improved"[1].

In 1855 a Nottingham hosier had used language precisely similar. "When I ask the workmen what they think of the factory system, they deprecate it universally; the beauty of the stocking trade is its domestic character"[2]. For "stocking" read "cutlery" and an interval of more than 50 years is bridged. It is not strange in the light of history that in the list of sweated trades enumerated in the schedule of the Trade Boards Act of 1909, No. 3 should be "machine made lace and net finishing", and No. 4 "hammered and dollied or tommied *chain making*"[3].

---

[1] *Departmental Committee on Truck* (1908) *Report*, p. 45.
[2] *Commons' Committee on Stoppage of Wages (Hosiery)* (1855), Q. **6567.**
[3] Cf. Ashley, *The Economic Organisation of England*, p. 145.

10. The Characteristics of 19th century Capitalism

Direct employment, net wages, steam power, large scale industry, these are the things which capitalism, studied objectively, implies. Under it the standard of working class living steadily improved, and the owners of capital saved much more than they spent. But it does not follow that what worked in the 19th century will work in the 20th. For the conditions of competition on which the old system was based are being transformed by the Combine on the one hand and the Trade Union on the other. Furthermore the whole fabric of economic life has been stirred by the upheaval of war. Capitalism is now challenged less on account of its antecedents than on account of the outlook and supposed motives of those who are held responsible for it. The "Co-operative Commonwealth" is matched against Capitalism. It should be possible to do justice to these new aspirations without reading irrelevant notions into the history of the 19th century.

CHAPTER XVIII

A NATION OF SHOPKEEPERS

1. Origin of the Phrase

"The French", wrote Nelson in 1801, "have always, in ridicule, called us 'A Nation of Shopkeepers'"[1]. Possibly Napoleon himself wrote the unsigned article in the *Moniteur* of September 1, 1802, containing the sentence: "What a difference between a people who make conquests from a love of glory and a nation of shopkeepers turned filibusters". The remark reminds one of the answer given by the military representative of Portuguese East Africa a few years ago to a British staff officer who was trying to instruct him in the way he should not go. He replied: "We find it so hard to understand your English point of view, for, you see, we are a military nation".

But like many a good phrase, it goes back to Adam Smith, who said:

"To found a great empire for the sole purpose of raising up a people of customers, may at first appear a project fit only for a nation of shopkeepers. It is, however, a project altogether unfit for a nation of shopkeepers; but extremely fit for a nation whose government is influenced by shopkeepers"[2]. Adam Smith proceeds to argue that our shopkeeper policy in the Colonies was a narrow policy unworthy of a great Empire. It was a policy based on monopoly; and in the end, as Huskisson[3] well knew, it was destined to break down as completely as did the ancient policy of the Corn Laws.

[1] Letter of April 27, 1801 to S. Barker.

[2] *Wealth of Nations*, Book IV. ch. 7, part 3.

[3] "An open trade, especially to a rich and thriving country, is infinitely more valuable than any monopoly, however exclusive, which the public power of the State may be able, either to enforce against its own Colonial dominions, or to establish in its intercourse with other parts of the world" (Exposition of the Colonial Policy of the Country, March 21, 1825: *Speeches*, II. 321).

2. The Rise of Shopping

When did shops make their appearance?

Cobbett writing in the 1820's places the shopkeeper among the accursed novelties of the countryside. "I have often", he said, "had to observe on the cruel effects of the suppression of markets and fairs, and on the consequent power of extortion possessed by the country shopkeepers. And what a thing it is to reflect on, that these shopkeepers have the whole of the labouring men of England constantly in their debt; have, on an average, a mortgage on their wages to the amount of five or six weeks, and make them pay any price that they choose to extort. So that, in fact, there is a tommy system in every village, the difference being, that the shopkeeper is the tommy man, instead of the farmer"[1]. In the village of Cobbett's dream there would be no tea kettle, no "straight-backed bloated" publican, and no "extortioner" under the name of "country shopkeeper"[2].

In the towns great improvements were effected at the beginning of the 19th century in road construction and the lighting of houses and streets. Both classes of improvement must have contributed to the growth of shopkeeping and shopping.

3. Fairs

The fairs, which Cobbett spoke of as being suppressed, died of degeneration. Of the latter days of the Fair which had once been the most celebrated in England, Stourbridge Fair, we catch a glimpse in the Reminiscences of Henry Gunning, Esquire Bedell of the University of Cambridge, published in 1854. The Fair was proclaimed on the 18th day of September by the Vice-Chancellor and officers of the University. Mulled wine and sherry in the Senate House were followed by oysters and bottled Porter at the Tiled Booth, and a dinner of goose and apple pie to finish. In Gunning's earlier days (he became Bedell in 1789) the Fair was an event of mercantile importance.

---

[1] *Rural Rides*, II. 355.   [2] *Ibid.* p. 356.

As soon as you left Barnwell, there was a small public house on the right hand side called the Race-horse; here the Cheese[1] Fair began; from thence till you came opposite the road leading to Chesterton Ferry, the ground was exclusively occupied by dealers in that article. It was the great Mart at which all the dealers of cheese from Cottenham, Willingham, with other villages in the county and isle (sc. of Ely) assembled; there were also traders from Leicestershire, Derbyshire, Cheshire, and Gloucestershire. Not only did the inhabitants of the neighbouring counties supply themselves with their annual stock of cheese, but great quantities were bought and sent up to London, the practice of employing travellers being at that time scarcely known. In the neighbourhood of the Chapel, which is still standing (1851) there were about a dozen Booths, called "Ironmongers' Row"; these, among a great variety of other articles, furnished the goods required by saddlers and harness-makers, together with every description of leather in great abundance....

Another row of Booths, reaching from the Chapel to Paper Mills turnpike was called "The Duddery". These contained woollen cloths from Yorkshire and the Western counties of England; but this part of the fair was beginning to be on the decline. There was a very large piece of ground set apart for the sale of hops. A considerable part of the Common was occupied by earthenware and china from the Potteries and by the coarser wares from Ely. On the left-hand side of the road leading from the Newmarket Road to the Ferry, was a row of Booths extending to the Common; they consisted of silk mercers, linen drapers, furriers, stationers, an immense variety of toys, and also of musical instruments....Besides the tradesmen there was the usual mixture of dwarfs and giants, conjurers and learned pigs[2].

Stourbridge Fair alas! is no more.

4. Markets

Markets, on the other hand, have survived, because they continued to fulfil useful trading purposes. In old times markets were either in public or in private hands, but during the first half of the 19th century most of the private markets passed into the hands of the local authority, which was re-invigorated by the Municipal Reform Act of 1835. In recent times, except in cattle markets, the taking of tolls on the quantity of goods exposed for

[1] On the left, as you go out of Cambridge along the Newmarket Road, there is a street leading on to the back of the Gasworks, called "Cheddars Lane".

[2] Henry Gunning, *Reminiscences of the University, Town and County of Cambridge* (1854), I. 153–6.

sale has been superseded by charges for stall space. The small producer has disappeared from the market, and retail and wholesale markets have been separated, the wholesale markets growing relatively to the retail. In 1891 the Royal Commission on Market Rights and Tolls was informed that Covent Garden was the only Metropolitan market at once retail and wholesale[1]. East and South London got perishable articles of food from the costermongers' barrows—excellent stuff at a low price. This fact has been confirmed by social investigators. "In no place", writes Mr Aves, the colleague of Mr Charles Booth in his monumental work, *Life and Labour in London*, "does the force of retail competition make itself so effectively felt as in the Metropolis,—the cheapest as well as the dearest place in the world in which to live"[2]. Mr Aves is accounting for the fact that "London as a whole is as yet almost untouched by co-operation".

5. BREAD

Bread is the most important item in the town wife's expenditure; and as the price of bread was regulated by law until well into the 19th century, the position of the baker at that time is less obscure than that of other shopkeepers. The assize of bread was abolished in London and the surrounding neighbourhood in 1815, and in the Provinces some years later. The assize fixed the amount of bread that the baker had to sell for the price of a quarter of wheat, and made him an allowance to cover expenses and profit. The legislature intended him to be a servant of the community, working on commission and unconcerned with fluctuations of price, but the intrusion of the miller between the producer and consumer destroyed the traditional relationship. The baker became dependent on the miller, and in the famine years at the close of the eighteenth century, 1795–6 and 1800–1, the baker bore the brunt of the popular clamour. When the opera-

---

[1] *Royal Commission on Market Rights and Tolls* (1888–91). Evidence of C. Prior Goldeney, City Remembrancer. Qs. 352 sqq.
[2] Ernest Aves, *Co-operative Industry* (1907), p. 61.

tion of the assize was examined by Parliament in 1815[1], it was found that in those parts of England where the assize had been discontinued or had never existed the price of bread was lower than in London, though the price of wheat was the same. The Committee ascribed this to the lack of competition, and abolished the assize with the express purpose of giving the baker an interest in prices. They expected also that the removal of regulation would cause business to be concentrated in fewer hands. But this did not happen. Baking continued to be a small-scale business in disorganised subservience to milling. The old-fashioned bakers tried to retain their status by catering for the high class trade, but these "full price" bakers, as they were called, failed to control the trade. Some of the millers bought the leases of bake houses and installed journeymen as managers. Others sold flour for ready money to a new class of bakers who cut prices and retailed for ready money. Competition, therefore, brought, not one price, but many. There were 500 different prices among the bakers of London, it was said in 1824; ever since the abolition of the assize the trade had been at sixes and sevens. "I believe the 'full price' bakers are not all of a price and the cheap bakers are not all of a price: they are all dissatisfied"[2].

The towns which the Committee of 1815 congratulated on their exemption from the assize were the centres of a rapidly growing industrial population—Birmingham, Manchester, Newcastle-on-Tyne. The Committee implied that the Northern towns were ahead of the Metropolis in their escape from medieval restraints (Huskisson argued for the repeal of the Spitalfields Silk Acts in the same strain); but the contrast was superficial. For in the North of England it was customary for the inhabitants to prepare their own bread. In Manchester in 1815 half the inhabitants used the public ovens buying their flour from the millers and flour dealers who came in from 40–60 miles around[3]. In

---

[1] *Commons' Committee on the Laws relating to the Manufacture, Sale and Assize of Bread* (1814–15).

[2] *Commons' Committee on "Allowances granted to Bakers in those places where an Assize of Bread is set"* (1824). Evidence, p. 6.

[3] *Commons' Committee on...Assize of Bread* (1814–15). Appendix, p. 147.

Newcastle-on-Tyne, not one-tenth part of the inhabitants on an average used bakers' bread. "Common bakehouses are numerous, and the principal part of the inhabitants buy their own flour and meal, make it into bread themselves, and get it baked at the common bakehouses"[1]. Thus Parliament, in 1815, invited the Metropolis to follow the example of the North and to establish a free trade in bread. Thirty years later the North came thundering at the doors of Westminster, demanding the repeal of the laws which restricted the importation of foreign grain; and once again London followed Manchester's lead.

But in the '40's a movement was growing which was far more important to the working man than the repeal of the Corn Laws. The co-operative store was spreading fast. It is significant that the earliest form of co-operative store (the Hull Anti-mill Society, 1795, the Hull Subscription Mill 1801, the Devonport Union Mill, 1817) was formed by the poor inhabitants of towns for the purpose of providing themselves with cheap flour. During the century, and as a result of the expense of up-to-date milling machinery and the establishment of bakeries by co-operative stores, nearly all the early Milling Societies disappeared or changed their form. The bulk of co-operative corn milling is now in the hands of the co-operative wholesale federations, which mill corn for their members, the co-operative stores. The stores, in turn, pass it on to their members, the individual consumers, in the shape of flour or of bread made in the bakery belonging to the store. The Lancashire house-wife now buys at the "Co-op." the bread which her grandmother made at home, but those who have not forgotten the ancient art have recently had reason to congratulate themselves.

6. Clothing

New clothes are not necessaries. The statisticians of the 19th century many times computed the exports of calicos and cotton yarns, and many Committees and Commissions examined the condition of the textile workers; but no one paid much attention

[1] *Commons' Committee on...Assize of Bread* (1814–15). Appendix, p. 147.

to the style in which the people of England were clothed or to
the process by which the premier manufactures reached the
Englishman's wardrobe[1]. The merit of English fabrics lay in
their cheapness and durability rather than in their beauty or
delicacy of finish. But these matters were seldom discussed in
public. When the orators of the Anti-Corn Law League talked
of clothing, they dwelt on the luxuries which free trade brought
in from other lands: "Her modest blushes (W. J. Fox was
speaking of the English lady) concealed beneath a veil of
Brussels lace, French gloves on her hands and an ostrich plume
waving over her head, which never grew in an English poultry
yard"[2].

7. IMPROVEMENTS IN SHOPKEEPING

In 1833 a Parliamentary Committee took stock of the state of
manufactures, commerce and shipping. Several witnesses described the state of shopkeeping at this time. One[3] represented
a London firm of wholesale drapers: a second[4] was a builder of
shops and warehouses in London; a third[5], a retired operative of
Stockport, said that he wrote "far more private letters for all
the lower classes of the people than any person in that part of
the Kingdom".

In 1833 London was at the dead end of a shop-building boom
and builders were chary of erecting shops for traders with little
capital, but the depression was weeding out the unsubstantial
men and retail business generally was more stable than it had

---

[1] Francis Place, in a review of the Causes of Improvement among the
working classes, mentions under the heading of Cleanliness the following:
"A great change was produced by improvements in the manufacture of
cotton goods. It was found to be less expensive to wear cotton gowns and
cotton petticoats than stuff gowns and quilted petticoats, and as it was
necessary to wash these cleanliness followed, almost as a matter of course.
It was impossible that the women should improve in this particular without
producing a very beneficial effect upon the men". This change, Place goes
on, permeated downwards through all classes of females, so that, when he
wrote, "all wear washing clothes". Place, British Museum Add. MSS.
27,827, p. 51.

[2] Rochdale, Nov. 25, 1843. W. J. Fox, *Collected Works*, p. 443.

[3] *Commons' Committee on the Manufactures, Commerce and Shipping*
(1833), Qs. 1333 sqq.

[4] *Ibid*. Qs. 1659 sqq.   [5] *Ibid*. Qs. 10,515 sqq.

ever been. "I should say", said the first witness referred to, "that the retail dealers of this country are in a condition to pay closer than ever I knew them; they have been gradually improving their method of managing their business and are now enabled to pay for their goods in about half the time that they used to pay some twenty years ago". In London "there are some very large establishments grown up in the last few years, and business perhaps is more concentrated in large establishments than it was some eight or ten years ago". The practice of marking the price of goods by tickets had made its appearance. There was more ticketing in Oxford Street than in Regent Street, and more still in Shoreditch and Whitechapel. As R. S. Surtees reminds us in one of his novels: "'2d. posters', circulars and ticket shops used to be held in about equal repugnance"[1].

The improved system of business was visible in the more rapid turn-over of stocks, the giving of shorter credits and the reduction of losses from bad debts. The wholesale houses settled with manufacturers once a month for cash; and retail houses either paid cash or took shorter credit than formerly. In the latter case a wholesale house would draw a three month bill dating from the beginning of the month following that in which the goods were sold to the retailer. The retailer either accepted the bill or paid the account on the day the bill became due, without waiting to be asked. Hence the work of a commercial traveller was now (1833) "not settling accounts, but taking orders".

According to the Stockport letter writer, about 50 per cent. of the commodities purchased by the labouring population of that town for domestic purposes were purchased on credit[2].

---

[1] *Ask Mama* (1858), p. 437. If you want to get the atmosphere of the life of the English country gentleman in the middle of the 19th century, read any and all of Surtees' novels.

[2] In the *Co-operative Magazine* of 1826 a member of the London Co-operative Society writes:

"There is scarcely a married working man within the bills of mortality, who is not in arrears with his landlord, his chandler and his coal merchant. ...The pawnbroker has his wardrobe within his grasp in nine cases out of ten. Few of the working classes occupy more than one room to a family

Clothes were paid for on the easy payment principle, and this added considerably to their price. "The clothing is generally bought from Scotchmen who travel; they call upon the families once in three weeks and I should think that half of the population get their clothing in that way".

These allusions show us that shopkeeping too had its industrial revolution and that by 1833 it was beginning, at any rate in the Metropolis, to find its legs. Whether private shopkeeping could have provided ultimately an efficient system of retail distribution in the working class districts of industrial England we shall never know. For the wage earners of these districts elected to become their own shopkeepers. The wage earners' reply to the company's truck shop was the Co-operative Store, registered at law as an Industrial and Provident Society; even as in Germany the peasants' reply to the money lending cattle dealer was the Village Bank, organised by Raiffeisen on co-operative lines.

and the whole contents of such a room is seldom worth more than £3 at a fair valuation: estimate the duplicate of things pledged at £3 more, allow £3 for the threadbare garments of the father of the family, including the tatters on his miserable wife and children, and we shall have nine pounds as the average capital of each working man in the state of holy matrimony. Now out of this £9 his debts are to be paid, for instance his landlord a quarter's rent, his chandler a month's score, his hawking linendraper, his doctor, his shoemaker, his taylor—say £10 for the whole tribe of clamorous creditors; and we shall find the unhappy man just one pound worse than nothing. This is not any exaggerated statement, an overstrained estimate; experience fully tells me that I have but fairly described the condition of more than ⅔ of all the married operatives in the Kingdom" (p. 309).

CHAPTER XIX

THE CO-OPERATIVE MOVEMENT SINCE 1844

1. Source and Scope of the Movement

THE co-operative movement in England was a confluence of three streams. The first was a trickle along the dry bed of State control (the assize of bread): the second a flood from the well of Owenite enthusiasm: the third a work of irrigation constructed by working men in the factory and mining districts of industrial England. We have followed the course of the first two[1]. It remains to trace the remarkable expansion of the co-operative movement in England after 1844, the year in which the Equitable Pioneers began business in Toad Lane (T'owd Lane), Rochdale.

In England to-day there are three types of co-operation: agricultural co-operation, labour co-partnership, and consumers' co-operation, i.e. the co-operative store. The first is a 20th century product and has a separate organising authority, the Agricultural Organisation Society. The Labour Co-partnership Societies have their own Labour Co-partnership Association, but they are members of the Co-operative Union, which embraces both wings of industrial co-operation.

2. Christian Socialism and Labour Co-partnership

The propaganda known as Christian Socialism originated in 1848, when Frederick Denison Maurice and Charles Kingsley, supported by a small band of brilliant young lawyers—Thomas Hughes, the author of *Tom Brown's Schooldays*, J. M. Ludlow and Vansittart Neale—addressed themselves to the task of arresting the irreligious tendencies which appeared to them to mark the Chartist revival of 1848 and the revolutionary Socialism of France. In 1850 they established in London a Society for

---

[1] Cf. pp. 60–2 and 230–2 above.

promoting Working Men's Associations, and set up or encouraged a number of small productive societies which, for various reasons—over-assistance, isolation, and want of funds—soon came to an end. Further efforts were made in the next 20 years, but many of these were not genuinely co-operative, and the frequency of financial failure caused co-operative productive societies to be eyed with suspicion by the rapidly growing co-operative stores.

In the '60's Messrs Briggs, a firm of Yorkshire colliery owners, started a scheme of profit sharing with their employees, which was successful for some years, but in 1875 the scheme collapsed after a strike in which the miners, having to choose between profit sharing and their union, stood by the latter.

The Labour Co-partnership Association, established in 1884, broadened the basis of co-partnership. It includes to-day workers' co-partnership societies (co-operative productive societies, as they used to be called) and firms practising co-partnership, such as the South Metropolitan and other Gas Companies, William Thomson & Sons, woollen manufacturers of Huddersfield and Messrs J. T. and J. Taylor, Ltd., woollen manufacturers of Batley. Co-partnership, as understood to-day, recognises the necessity of the Trade Union and aims at giving the workers a share in control as well as a share in profits. Thus the South Metropolitan Gas Co. has three working men directors, while in the firm of William Thomson & Sons the Committee consists of the manager, two employees of the Society (for the firm in 1886 was converted into a Society registered under the Industrial and Provident Societies Act), three representatives of share-holding Co-operative Societies, one representative of the Huddersfield Trades Council and the Secretary of the Weavers' Association.

Similarly the basis of the workers' societies has been broadened. The societies are not managed by the workers exclusively, nor do they obtain the whole of their capital from them. In 1910, 80 of these societies were doing a trade of nearly one and a half millions sterling per annum. Some of them, among which is the Walsall Locks and Cart-Gear Society, founded as far back as

1873, produce for the open market, but the majority of the bigger societies sell most or all of their output to co-operative stores. The capital of the workers' societies is provided in part by the workers themselves and in part by co-operative stores and persons interested in this side of the co-operative movement. The interest on capital is a first charge on profit and usually limited to 5 per cent., and a part at least of the surplus profit is allotted to the workers proportionately to their wages. Where the stores are themselves big customers, the rules of the society sometimes assign them a dividend on purchases proportionate to the workers' dividend on wages.

The constitution of the workers' societies is thus a mixed one. The workers founded the societies, the stores backed them up with capital and custom. The workers have their own representatives on the committee of management, while the existence of other share-holders, whether represented on the committee or not, corrects any tendency to one-sidedness and makes it easier for the manager to exercise that full authority which is necessary to the successful execution of business enterprise. The stores offer a good market, but a market which is not guaranteed. The workers' societies have to compete with the productive departments of the Wholesale Societies (p. 240 below) and with outside competition as well. A rivalry between the workers' societies and the Wholesales is a healthy stimulus to both parties, and it operates in the area in which the co-operative stores are furthest removed from the checks of market-price. The workers' societies are strongest in the textile and leather trades, clothing and boots being in constant demand by the stores. The Midlands district about Kettering and Leicester seems to possess an atmosphere congenial to labour co-partnership. One success helps to another, but its peculiar strength in the boot trade suggests that the technique of the industry is exceptionally amenable to democratic organisation. It has been suggested that the gaps between the different grades from the least skilled man to the top are not great in the boot trade, and that this enables the workers to understand different processes and thereby to make an intelligent use of their influence in the control of the business. There seems to be no hostility between the trade unions and the workers' societies, and there is no ground for any. The members are generally union men, working standard hours and drawing standard pay.

The societies continue to flourish, but it need not be a matter for surprise that their numerical increase is slow, for they set out to do a very difficult thing. Their members are the enthusiasts of co-operation in England, and their work has a bracing effect upon the co-operative movement as a whole[1].

3. G. J. HOLYOAKE

If Robert Owen was the father of English co-operation, George Jacob Holyoake was its historian and apostle. The figure of Holyoake spans the century. Born in 1817, he died on January 22nd, 1906, in the month when Liberalism and Labour were triumphing at the polls. A young mechanic at the Eagle Foundry, Birmingham, he learnt his first lesson in politics in the Reform Bill days. He soon left the forge for the Lecture Hall and in 1842 he was imprisoned for atheism and blasphemy. His offence was an answer to a question put to him after a lecture at Cheltenham. He had been advocating home colonies. The questioner said that the lecturer had "told them a good deal about their duty to men —what about their duty to God"? Holyoake replied: "I appeal to your heads and your pockets if we are not too poor to have a God?"...."Religion, in my opinion, has ever poisoned the fountain springs of morality"[2].

Such was the man who went up to Lancashire in 1843 to lecture on "self-help" to the weavers of Rochdale. The result was the Rochdale Pioneers. "The owd weavers' shop", said the mocking crowd, "is opened at last". The growth of the co-operative movement from this year onwards is to be read in the many writings of Holyoake. In 1857 he published his *History of the Rochdale Pioneers*, and the book was soon translated into every language in Europe. Holyoake was above all things an

---

[1] Cf. C. R. Fay, *Copartnership in Industry* (1913) (*Cambridge Manuals of Science and Literature*).

[2] J. McCabe, *Life and Letters of George Jacob Holyoake*, I. 64.

idealist. With his stalwart friend, E. O. Greening, and his old religious opponents, the Christian Socialists, he preached the educational value of co-operation. When the Rochdale Pioneers and the federal society, the English Wholesale (C.W.S.), abandoned profit sharing with their employees, he and his colleagues saw in this a falling away from the ideal; and the question of profit sharing was a constant battle ground between the two wings of the movement, the Southerners or "profit sharers" led by Holyoake and Judge Hughes, and the Northerners or "federals", led by Mitchell, the Chairman of the C.W.S. After the establishment of the Labour Co-partnership Association in 1884, the situation eased. Co-operators came to realise that the two wings were promoting different forms of co-operation and that there was scope for idealism in both.

Holyoake was a prominent figure at the Co-operative Congresses, which have been held annually under the auspices of the Co-operative Union since 1867. He was venerated as the grand old man of co-operation, and his death was mourned by all Europe. "Holyoake, the glorious pupil of Robert Owen, the world known orator, the formidable propagandist, the historian of the Pioneers, the friend of Garibaldi and Mazzini, the lover of humanity, the venerated master is no more"[1]. In these words the co-operators of Milan announced his death.

4. THE WHOLESALE SOCIETIES

In 1863 the North of England Co-operative Wholesale Industrial and Provident Society, Ltd. was established at Manchester. In 1867, largely through the efforts of the Christian Socialists, legislation was obtained which permitted one Society to have shares in another. This power was indispensable to federal expansion. In 1873 the Society took its present title the Co-operative Wholesale Society. In 1868 the Scottish Wholesale Society was formed on the same lines. The two Wholesale Societies are the crown of the co-operative movement on its commercial side. Practically all the stores are

---

[1] McCabe, *Life and Letters of G. J. Holyoake*, II. 317.

members; and the Wholesales deal only with store members.
They began as wholesale merchants. Early attempts to boycott
them only increased their strength. In the '70's they went on to
production and now they have productive departments for most
of the goods which the stores sell. The English Wholesale has a
banking and insurance department; and the two Wholesales are
joint owners of tea estates in Ceylon and corn lands in Canada.
Their tale is truly a tale of millions, and they have provided an
elastic outlet for the co-operative investment of the funds lodged
with them by the Co-operative Stores.

5. THE CO-OPERATIVE STORES TO-DAY

A general survey of the Co-operative Store movement is given
in the author's *Co-operation at Home and Abroad*, published in
1908. The figures which follow indicate the material progress
made between 1908 and 1918:

Stores in United Kingdom	(a) 1908	(b) 1917
Number of Societies	1,428	1,366
Membership	2,404,595	3,788,490
Share and Loan Capital	£34,595,373	£55,746,493
Sales	£69,783,278	£142,003,612
Profit or Surplus	£10,773,005	£15,916,591

(a) *Co-operative Congress* 1909 *Report*, pp. 596–97.
(b) *Ibid.* 1918 *Report*, pp. 810–11.

English Wholesale

	Year	Member-ship	Share and Loan Capital	Wholesale Trade	% of Retail Trade	Value of Production	Net Profit
(a)	1908	1,139	£4,328,099	£24,902,842	45·24*	£5,749,046	£448,128
(b)	1917	1,192	£6,937,325	£57,710,133	50·94	£18,581,555	£1,315,155

Scottish Wholesale

	Year	Member-ship	Share and Loan Capital	Wholesale Trade	% of Retail Trade	Value of Production	Net Profit
(a)	1908	275	£2,760,768	£7,531,126	51·08*	£2,270,103	£283,296
(b)	1917	263	£4,257,818	£17,079,842	59·51	£6,294,857	£500,915

(a) 1909 Report pp. 596–7.   (b) 1918 Report pp. 683, 686, 811.

* These percentages are obtained from Holyoake House as they are not
recorded in 1909 *Congress Report*.

The general progress of the last 10 years may be studied under three heads:

> (*a*)   Local Store Policy.
>
> (*b*)   General Social Policy.
>
> (*c*)   General Industrial Policy.

(*a*)   Efforts have been made to decrease the amount of credit trading, and to minimise over-lapping by adjacent societies. Hence the recent reduction in the number of societies, *pari passu* with the large increase of total membership.

(*b*)   General social policy is directed by the Co-operative Union. The Central Education Committee of the Co-operative Union, "the keeper of the educational conscience of the movement", organises educational classes, issues pamphlets, text-books and a quarterly magazine, *The Co-operative Educator*. It has charge of the scheme for the erection of a Central Co-operative College, as a memorial to co-operators who have fallen in the war.

The Women's Co-operative Guild, founded in 1883, has proved to be one of the most progressive elements in the movement. The work of the Guild, while primarily concerned with co-operation, has a further side which embraces questions of industrial and social reform affecting its members as married women. The Women's Guild has been prominent in the establishment of a minimum wage for all co-operative employees, the anti-credit campaign, the extension of co-operation in poor districts, the provision of school clinics, the abolition of half-timers, divorce law reform, the insertion of maternity benefit in the Insurance Act of 1911, and the promotion of other measures, many of which are outside the ordinary course of co-operative business, but all of which help to keep the co-operative movement true to its past. For the "Co-op." has always set out to be something more than a Civil Service Store for the working classes.

(*c*)   The expansion of the Wholesales inevitably brought difficult problems. The C.W.S. is now one of the biggest trading and manufacturing bodies in the United Kingdom, and its members, the retail stores, are faced with similar problems on a smaller scale. Of these the most pressing are:—

i. *The relations of the stores and the wholesale societies with their employees in the distributive and productive departments.*

The co-operative employees belong to the Amalgamated Union of Co-operative Employees (A.U.C.E.). For some years a Joint Committee of Trade Unionists and Co-operators has undertaken the work of promoting harmonious relations with employees and securing the settlement of differences by arbitration. In 1915 Congress adopted a general scheme of Conciliation Boards, supplemented by District Hours and Wages Boards. These are now in operation and high hopes are entertained of them. They were subjected to a severe test in the summer of 1919, when a disagreement between the Co-operative Union and the A.U.C.E. led to a stoppage of work in a number of stores. The stoppage, happily, was not prolonged; and the Conciliation Boards rendered service in bringing about a settlement, in which most of the employees' demands were conceded.

ii. *The relations of the stores and the wholesale societies with agricultural co-operation.*

No satisfactory solution has yet been found. The stores have in many places their own farms, on which they raise produce for their members. Ought they to extend their agricultural activities, or ought they to wait for agricultural societies to organise co-operation from the farmer's standpoint? The arguments on either side and a possible middle way are outlined in the Supplement to the 2nd Edition of the author's *Co-operation at Home and Abroad*[1].

iii. *The relation of the Co-operative Movement to the State.*

In 1905 at the Paisley Congress the proposal to join the Labour party, which was then being formed, was defeated. In 1917, however, at Swansea, the Co-operative Congress resolved that "The time has now arrived for the co-operative movement to take the necessary steps to secure direct representation in Parliament". In the General Election of December, 1918, ten co-operative candidates were nominated and one seat was won, the Kettering division of Northamptonshire.

The institution of food control during the war brought the

---

[1] C. R. Fay, *Co-operation at Home and Abroad*, P. S. King & Son (1920).

Co-operative Movement into closer relations with the State, and the Food Controller acknowledged the importance of the services rendered by Co-operative Societies. Law and opinion are now marshalled against the profiteer; and the rapid extension of Combinations and Trusts makes it all the more necessary that the working classes should employ to the full for the protection of themselves as consumers the democratic organisation which they have built up in the course of a century.

Co-operators are often told that co-operation is nothing but business. We all know the tale about the new-born baby. "Where did you get it from"? asks the small boy of the family. "From the doctor's", replies the father. "But why didn't you get it from the 'Co-Op.'?—then we'd have had divy on him". It is for co-operators to prove by fresh efforts and a progressive policy that they are worthy of the heritage bequeathed by Robert Owen, the father of co-operation, and registered in the book of history by George Jacob Holyoake, after whom the Co-operative Union has fittingly named its new house in Hanover Street, Manchester.

CHAPTER XX

THE REVIVAL OF SOCIALISM

1. The Blank in English Socialism, 1850–1880

WHY is there a blank in English Socialism between 1850 and 1880? The answer is fourfold:

i. The almost complete failure of the revolutionary movement in Europe (1848–51) and the absolute failure of Chartism in England brought disappointment and disillusionment. Revolutionary politics lost their attractiveness.

ii. The general industrial situation improved. In this improvement the main factors were:

(a) The increasing strength of the nation's industrial structure.

(b) The abundant supply of precious metals from 1850 onwards.

(c) The removal of restrictions on trade—free import of food and raw materials, reduction of taxation and a more scientific adjustment of the taxes which remained.

These factors, in conjunction, made possible a long spell of industrial prosperity between 1850 and 1880. There were commercial crises in 1857 and 1866; in 1861–63 Lancashire was severely hit by the cotton famine consequent on the American Civil War; between 1874 and 1879 there was considerable depression, and in the mining districts of the North successive deductions in the price of coal led to successive reductions in wages. But each crisis or depression was weathered with less difficulty than the one before; and industrial England responded with elastic vigour to the first signs of reviving trade. The late Viscount Goschen, in a famous essay, *Seven Per Cent.* (1865), showed the importance of the Companies (Limited Liability) Act of 1862 in promoting enterprise at home and abroad. He dwells on the way in which the promotion of Limited Joint Stock companies sucked into the money market and condensed

" into large and available streams countless rills of savings, scattered up and down the country which were not reached before "[1].

iii. The working classes turned from political to economic association. These years were marked by an uninterrupted increase in the membership and financial strength of Friendly Societies, Co-operative Societies and Trade Unions.

iv. The middle classes stood between the working classes and a policy of class-warfare.

De Tocqueville headed a chapter of *L'Ancien Régime* "Comment on souleva le peuple, en voulant le soulager". Why was there no manifestation of this in England when the economic situation improved in the '40's? Chartism was an instalment of class-warfare, the Chartists were pioneers of the new working class associations, why then were not these the breeding ground of social revolution? We shall see the reasons in detail when we examine in the next chapter the agencies that were contributing to social reform. The same agencies were at work in the purely political field and produced an alliance between the middle and working classes, whereby Chartism was merged in the Radicalism of Cobden and Bright. Bright claimed that the issue lay between the landed aristocracy and the rest of the nation. In this spirit he led the agitation for the extension of the franchise in 1867. "The class", he said, "which has hitherto ruled in this country has failed miserably....If a class has failed, let us try the nation "[2]. The bulk of the politically minded members of the working class accepted Bright's lead. In the autumn of 1866 huge Reform Meetings were held at Birmingham, Manchester, Glasgow, Leeds and London. "At all these places the order of the day was a mass meeting on some moor outside the town, of 150,000 to 200,000 citizens, a march past of the Trades Unions and Trades Societies before Bright, and in the evening one of his orations delivered in the largest Hall of the city to as many as could find room therein. On the next day all England would be reading admirable reports of his speech "[3].

---

[1] Viscount Goschen, *Essays and Addresses*, p. 17.
[2] Trevelyan, *Life of John Bright*, p. 368.   [3] *Ibid.* p. 362.

It is true that the Anti-Corn Law League owed its strength to the manufacturers and their middle-class followers and that the Chartists and Factory Reformers resented its rivalry. Nevertheless the Anti-Corn Law League had a strong popular following, especially among the artisans and those who in the Reform Bill days accepted the leadership of Attwood and Place. The continental Socialists looked with envy on the results which the working classes had thereby obtained. Lassalle in his message to the German working classes in 1863 said: "Look at England. The great agitation of the English people against the Corn Laws lasted for over five years. And then the laws had to go; a Tory Ministry itself had to abolish them....Debate, discuss, everywhere, every day, without pausing, without ending, as in the great English agitation against the Corn Laws, now in peaceful public assemblies, now in private conferences, the necessity of universal direct suffrage"[1].

2. KARL MARX

The outstanding industrial events of the '80's were—the profound trade depression of 1884–86, which was the subject of investigation by a Royal Commission in the latter year; and the birth of what is known in Trade Union History as the "New Unionism", that is to say, the growth of a corporate life in industries hitherto unorganised and the expression of that life in militant form. In this decade Socialism was born again.

The theoretical inspiration came from abroad, from Karl Marx and from the American, Henry George.

Marx's extraordinary influence on English working class thought is attributable to a variety of causes:—

i. Marx based his appeal on history. He drew on the rich stores of English Parliamentary Papers and clothed his theory with an atmosphere of reality which was lacking in the Ricardian socialists, whose only facts were the statistical tables of Colquhoun.

ii. Marx offered a science of evolution to a generation which

---

[1] Quoted in R. C. K. Ensor, *Modern Socialism*, p. 46.

remembered the futility of revolution and economic Utopia. He based his philosophy neither on religion, nor on politics, but on economics. The course of evolution, he argued, would be painful. It would be a struggle—that was its revolutionary aspect—but it was sure to prevail—and this gave confidence to those who knew how the dreams of early socialists had come to naught.

iii. Marx fortified his economic arguments with the technical apparatus of philosophy, developing thesis, antithesis, and synthesis on the lines of Hegel. Feudalism (thesis) had been vanquished by the bourgeoisie (antithesis); and in its turn the bourgeoisie would be overthrown by the proletariat which it now plundered and oppressed (synthesis).

iv. Marx was neither an anarchist nor a bolshevik. He did not belittle the State nor propose to use it in the interests of a minority. It is true that the severities of the Continental Police System forced him into the category of revolutionaries, hunting him in turn out of Germany into France and out of France into England; and that in 1848, and again in 1871, the year of the Paris Commune, he was roused to the hope that political revolution would be the lever to social revolution. (Hence the countenance which he lent to the dictatorship of the proletariat.) But the main trend of his teaching was economic rather than political. The struggle would be a struggle of classes and very bitter, but it would be a struggle forced on by circumstances and carried through by the force of circumstances. As Engels, his life-long friend, wrote in old age: "We have a huge international army of socialists, marching onwards and daily onwards". Socialism will march onwards to inevitable success. That is the spirit of the Marxian revival.

v. Marx' appeal was international. He was chief of the "International", founded in 1864, from which came the watchword: "Proletariats of all lands unite". Bright took the sting out of the left wing of Radicalism by winning the franchise for all householders who did not as yet possess it, working class and middle class alike. Marx cut clean through national divisions and made the line of cleavage horizontal—proletariats of all lands against capitalists of all lands.

vi. Marx' theory of surplus value, as developed in *Das Kapital* was, indeed, world-famous, but only because the world had forgotten what English socialists had written nearly half a century before. His further theory that the poor were becoming poorer and the rich richer was difficult to maintain in the face of statistics, and his coldness to Trade Unions and Co-operative Societies was due in part to the suspicion that their successes contradicted his philosophy.

3. HENRY GEORGE

Henry George is known to the world by a single book, *Progress and Poverty*, published in 1879 and soon translated into all the languages of Europe. "What I propose", he said, "as the simple yet sovereign remedy, is to appropriate rent by taxation". He is thus the father of "single taxers"; and the 1909 edition of the *Dictionary of Political Economy* says of him: "the danger of these opinions has become more apparent as time goes on"! Like Spence before him, Henry George owed his fame to the simplicity of his appeal. He directed popular thought to a very old grievance—the contrast between the bounty of nature, when rightly used, and the anti-social gamble of speculation. He propounded a simple remedy—taxation. He pleaded for the conception of land as a social asset, and thereby won the sympathy of the thousands of dwellers in great towns who were becoming alive to the fact that urban values were created, not by the enterprise of those who benefited by them, but by the presence of those who dwelt there.

Thus Marx, with his theory of surplus value, supplied the argument for the abolition of profit, and Henry George, with his plan of taxation, the argument for the abolition of rent. The teachings of the two familiarised the working classes with the idea that economic society might be based on some other motive than competition, namely the motive of social use rather than of private gain.

4. THE FABIAN SOCIETY, THE I.L.P. AND THE LABOUR PARTY

In the year 1880 a Parliamentary Labour Party did not exist or show signs of coming into existence. By the year 1906 it was an organised group with 31 representatives, made up as follows:

1. Independent Labour Party (17), plus Fabians (2) = 19
2. Social Democratic Federation   = 1
3. Trade Unionists co-operating with the I.L.P.   = 11

$$\text{Total} \quad 31$$

After 1906 the miners and textile workers came in.

The Fabian Society, established in 1883, moulded the thought of the Socialist revival. It was said of Quintus Fabius "Unus homo nobis cunctando restituit rem"; and accordingly the Fabian Society planned the gradual and successive undermining of the capitalist citadel and the permeation of its garrison with a new spirit. It pioneered the extension of municipal enterprise in the '90's and accustomed people to contemplate without dismay the assumption of economic functions by the central authority in the State.

Three phases of its development may be distinguished:

(a) From the publication of the Fabian Essays (1889) to about 1900. In these years the groundwork of Collectivism was sketched out. The arguments leading up to it were set forth in the Essays. The Ricardian law of rent was put in the foreground, and applied to incomes from industry and business as well as to incomes from land. The conclusion was reached that the "unearned" or socially created element in wealth should be socially appropriated by the nationalisation (or municipalisation) of land and of such industries as this method might practically suit.

(b) From about 1900 to 1911, at the inspiration of the leaders of the Fabian movement (Mr and Mrs Webb), the programme was amplified. Disciples were invited to tread "the fourfold path": (i) the method of Collective Ownership (i.e. the method of the original programme): (ii) the method of Collective Regulation—i.e. Factory Acts and similar machinery designed

to secure a National Minimum: (iii) the method of Collective
Provision for Individual Needs; of which our system of elementary education, with its ramifications into free secondary and
technical education, may be regarded as the typical example—
this line of thought culminated in the Minority Report of the
Poor Law Commission 1909 and the campaign for the Prevention
of Destitution, which absorbed the main energies of the Society
for some years—: (iv) the method of Appropriative Taxation;
which acquired importance when it was realised how very large
was the number of industries which could not with convenience
be "socially managed".

(c) From 1911 onwards. This last period is marked by a
general reaction against the bureaucratic element in the Fabian
programme. Before the war it found expression in Syndicalism,
since 1914 it has been formulated as Guild Socialism. Syndicalism was an alien product, deriving its inspiration from French
writers like Sorel. "Syndicat" in France means nothing more
than "union", but as developed by the younger school of French
trade unionists Syndicalism was an uncompromising programme
of direct action. In England it was powerful in debate rather
than in deed. It vanquished the crude collectivism preached
by those who had not kept pace with the later developments
of Fabian thought, and its undisciplined vigour appealed to all
those who felt that the force of trade unionism was being stifled
by the burden of central control.

To this feeling Guild Socialism is a more studied response,
blending historical memories with a call to immediate action.
The Guild takes us back to the romance of the middle ages
and to the Arts and Crafts of a mediaevalist like William
Morris; and yet Guild Socialism is the antithesis of organisation by single crafts which we associate with the skilled unions
of the 19th century. Whilst prizing the spirit of mediaeval
craft-life, it sees beyond the single craft into the group of
activities, skilled or unskilled, which cluster round a particular
works or locality or product. It stops short, however, of the
Syndicalist demand that the workers in an industry shall exploit that industry for themselves. It retorts, as the Fabians

retorted before it, "The mines for the miners, the railways for the railway men—then why not the sewers for the sewage men?" Developing an alternative, it makes the community the owner of the means of production and the guild the lever in the interests of the community. Critics, indeed, are asking whether this sovereignty of the community is more than lip service. For we read: "Instead of the State 'recognising' the Trade Unions, the Trade Unions would 'recognise' the State"[1]. If this line of thought is pressed, in what does Guild Socialism differ from Syndicalism except in the fact that the State will have the pleasure and privilege of providing the money to buy out the present occupants of the capitalist strongholds?

But it is unfair to press an epigram too far; and doubtless Guild Socialists, as a body, will offer a less ambiguous allegiance to the State, where that State is reorganised on Socialist lines. At any rate it is no mean achievement to have produced a successful exaggeration, to have brought into line a wing of effort which by misconception or defect of leadership had fallen behind and to have focussed attention upon a contingency which the Government itself has introduced with qualifications into the region of practical politics. The Whitley Councils, which are being set up in accordance with the recommendations of the Committee on Relations between Employers and Employed[2], are intended to meet the demands of workers for a greater control than heretofore in the management of the workshop and the conditions of industrial employment. The Interim Report on Joint Standing Industrial Councils suggests among other matters to be dealt with by the Councils—"Means for securing to the work people a greater share in and responsibility for the determination and observance of the conditions under which their work is carried on"[3]. This offer, indeed, does not appear to be welcome to the Guild Socialists, who contend that it is a compromise with the existing system, and that much fuller guarantees are required that the Trade Unions will be recognised

[1] Cole and Mellor, *The Meaning of Industrial Freedom*, p. 23.
[2] *Final Report* (1918). Cd. 9153.
[3] *Interim Report* (1917). Cd. 8606, p. 5.

at every stage, national, local and workshop. But it is something that the offer has been made, and still more that its implications are being studied by all parties in terms congenial to Englishmen and free of the jargon of Russian Soviets or the New World Boss[1].

Down to 1914 the Independent Labour Party (I.L.P.) was the driving force in the Labour Party. It grew out of the New Unionism, which won its first victory in the London Dock Strike of 1889 under Tom Mann and John Burns. The first branch to be formed was the Bradford and District Labour Union, the outcome of a strike at the Manningham Silk Mills. Similar associations were formed at Manchester and Salford in 1892. The object of the new organisation was to create a separate Labour Party in Parliament; and for this purpose it was necessary to keep the Liberals out and to bring the Trade Unions in. Neither task was easy.

The Scotch members were less labour and more liberal than Bradford and Manchester, and liked their Labour candidate to be accepted by the Liberals. Keir Hardie, afterwards Chairman of the I.L.P. and an uncompromising advocate of independence, started life as a Liberal and won for the new organisation its first success, when he was elected for South West Ham on a Radical Labour ticket in 1892.

The question of independence was settled by the decision taken at Bradford in 1893: "All members of the I.L.P. to pledge themselves not to vote for a nominee of the Liberal, Liberal-Unionist or Conservative party, against their own nominee; if there is no Labour nominee the party to vote as the local branch decides".

This decision united the advocates of independence and permeation. It avoided the *non-possumus* attitude of the Social Democratic Federation, which then withdrew from the I.L.P. The Social Democratic Federation stood for a rigid Marxism and never had any serious influence on the Movement.

Independence having been secured, the I.L.P. proceeded to

[1] *National Guilds or Whitley Councils*, published by the National Guilds League, p. 2.

tackle the Trade Unions. Its plan was to permeate Trade Unionism with a political feeling, but this was not done in a day. From 1895 to 1903 the country was enjoying industrial prosperity, and in 1895 the I.L.P. lost ground in Parliament. On the other hand the active part played by the Party in the struggle for Municipal Tramways brought popular approval; for people who did not yet want Labour politics wanted Municipal trams.

In 1899 at Plymouth the Trade Union Congress passed a resolution instructing the Trade Union Parliamentary Committee to call a Conference of Representatives of Trade Union and Socialist organisations, in order to discuss ways and means with a view to increasing the number of Labour representatives in Parliament. The result of the Conference was the Labour Representation Committee (L.R.C.). The Trade Union world was now ready to come in. 1903–04 were years of industrial distress, and the Taff Vale judgment given in the House of Lords was a further inducement, for the Trade Unions realised the danger to which their funds were thus exposed. The way was thus prepared for the striking victories obtained at the polls in 1906.

Summarising the pre-war development of Socialism we may say: (1) that the Fabian Society formulated the theory of the Socialist revival; (2) that the Labour Party was its political expression; (3) that the Independent Labour Party supplied the stimulus to the formation of the Labour Party, rallying labour around a single political flag.

The war, as we have seen, affected the position of the Fabian Society. Similarly it affected that of the I.L.P. and Labour Party.

The I.L.P. became an anti-war organisation and, shedding some of its pro-war members, it enlisted many who had no previous connection either with Trade Unionism or Socialism. As the majority of organised labour supported the war, the I.L.P. suffered in prestige. Hence for the time being the leadership of the left wing of Labour has passed into other hands—to the Editorial Staff of the *Daily Herald* and to the trade union branch officials who worked up the shop-stewards movement. The importance of a Labour newspaper was demonstrated in the Railway Strike and Town Council Elections of 1919. For the first time the case for Labour was stated daily by labour men. For the first time Labour obtained a majority in the local government of London and other great towns.

The war also brought the Labour Party many stages nearer to the day when it would be responsible for the government of the country. At any period of the war the resolute opposition of organised labour would have paralysed our forces in the field; and during the later stages of the war Labour was represented in the War Cabinet and in departments of government in which it had a direct concern.

In 1918 a change, little noticed but of far reaching importance, was made in the constitution of the Labour Party. Individual membership was introduced.

Before 1918 the individual was only admitted as a member of an affiliated body. Such bodies were (1) trade unions, (2) socialist societies, (3) local labour representation committees (I.L.P. branches in particular), (4) co-operative societies. The Fabian Society was only influential in London, Liverpool and the Universities. Very few co-operative societies were affiliated. Therefore, unless an individual was a trade unionist (and this excluded nearly all women and all non-working men), the normal avenue to membership in the Labour Party was membership in the I.L.P. To this there was one exception. A few local labour groups—prominently the Woolwich Labour Representation Association—had departed from the pattern of the parent body and admitted individual members into the Labour Party direct. By the decision of 1918, the Labour Party in effect adopted a constitution modelled on that of the Woolwich L.R.A. It decided to set up in every constituency branches of the Labour Party, to which members individually may belong. This change has a two-fold significance: (1) The Labour Party has given official recognition to brain workers as well as to manual workers. (2) Individual allegiance is direct. It is owed at first hand to organised labour as a whole and not to a particular section of it. There will be no feudal hierarchy in the Labour Party of the future.

5. ENGLISH AND CONTINENTAL SOCIALISM COMPARED

A comparison of English with Continental Socialism[1] is instructive:

i. As in England, so abroad there has been a bifurcation of socialist thought, the one side being termed "Revolutionary" or Marxist, the other "Fabian" or "Possibilist" or "Reformist"—this last term being the most exact and comprehensive. The difference is not between the party of violence and the party of peace; it is a difference of tactics. The one school stands for a programme of doing many things simultaneously on one complete system. The other stands for a programme of doing each thing successively and piecemeal; one step paving the way for another. The latter is exceptionally congenial to English instincts.

ii. A further difference is noticeable between the progress of Socialism in democratic countries, such as England, Belgium and France and in autocratic countries such as Germany, Austria and Russia. In the former countries socialists have been able to exert an influence proportionate to their numbers. There was something to be got by agitating for piecemeal reform, it was possible to negotiate with and even to enter the Government. In non-democratic countries this was impossible. Here socialists had to content themselves with increasing their numerical strength, and for this purpose a hard and fast aggressive programme and uncompromising resistance to arbitrary Government offered the greater attraction.

Hence, in democratic countries the socialists tend to be fewer in numbers, less united and less uncompromising, but on the other hand more constructive and influential. In undemocratic countries they tend to be more numerous and imposing, but doctrinaire and limited in outlook.

iii. England is the home of Trade Unionism, and the course of Socialism since its revival in the '80's has been determined by this fact more than by anything else. The modern Labour movement began in England with economic association, which

---

[1] Cf. R. C. K. Ensor, *Modern Socialism*, Introduction, p. xxxiii.

equipped its members for collective bargaining. Then it passed over very cautiously to State Socialism, at the instance of an active minority. Even after winning more substantial instalments of State Socialism than any other country in Europe, it calls itself the Labour Party and not the Socialist or Social Democratic Party.

German development proceeded on reverse lines. The Labour movement there began with whole-hearted adherence to Marx, who mistrusted the Trade Union and Co-operative Movements, but the majority of the social democratic party in time rejected his tactics, and, faced with the strongest autocracy in Europe, built up their strength within the shelter of the Trade Unions and Co-operative Stores.

CHAPTER XXI

THE REMEDIES OF THE NINETEENTH CENTURY

1. THE SPIRIT OF THE CENTURY

EVERY century has its own spirit, and the spirit of the 19th century was industrial. The men of the 19th century, not less than we who look back on it, were impressed by the pace and magnitude of the industrial expansion. "March", "strides", "leaps and bounds" were the phrases on all lips. But nature, and especially human nature, does not progress by jumps. Civilisation is a very strong plant if it is carefully tended, but weak and futile if it is choked by parasites and weeds. Happily a century of peace gave the nation time to realise this and to steady the pace of material progress in the interest of social well-being. Performance often fell short of intention, and there were motes of narrowness and prejudice in the eyes of the most zealous reformers, but they were earnest and sensible men and they appealed to a people which had a tradition of freedom and an instinct for making the best of things. Therefore the measures conceived and advocated by enthusiasts were given a fair hearing and won general acceptance, even from old opponents, as soon as experience proved that they would work.

Official publicity, a free press, popular education, preventive and enabling legislation based on impartial investigation were the remedies which the 19th century deemed appropriate to its genius and to the social ills by which that genius was oppressed.

2. PUBLICITY

The first step towards social betterment was publicity.

In the unreformed House of Commons it was the tradition that the member of Parliament instructed his constituents concerning the intentions of the legislature and the legislature concerning the needs of his constituents. The reformed House of Commons determined to widen and strengthen this slender channel of communication. In 1833 and 1835 Committees of the House advised:

i. That a branch of the Board of Trade should arrange Returns relating to the industrial and commercial condition of England and include in these information upon general subjects such as education, the state of crime, saving banks, etc.

ii. That Parliamentary Papers should be rendered accessible to the public by purchase at the lowest price at which they could be furnished. Papers, said the Committee of 1835, had hitherto been too much confined to members, "but the advantage to the community by the diffusion of that information which can in the generality of cases be obtained only through the House of Commons, must be evident to every member"[1].

By 1837, the year in which Queen Victoria came to the throne, the public circulation of Parliamentary Papers was fully established.

A further step was taken in 1852 when another Committee recommended the distribution gratis of selected Parliamentary Papers among the Literary and Scientific Institutions and Mechanics Institutes throughout the United Kingdom. 272 petitions had been presented in favour of this course, and these emphasized the importance of the diffusion of accurate information in correcting misrepresentations and enabling the mass of the people to form for themselves a just opinion on subjects of legislation.

Of recent years, with the enormous increase in output, the free distribution of Parliamentary Papers has been curtailed, but the policy of publishing them at a low price has been encouraged. This is a most valuable asset to the post-war student of economics. For a total expenditure of 3s. 6d. it was possible to procure at the time of publication:

[Cd 9236] *Report of Committee on Trusts* (1919), containing in appendix an able study of Trade Organisations and Combinations in the United Kingdom by Mr John Hilton.

[Cd 9070] *Report of Departmental Committee on the Textile Trades after the War* (1918).

---

[1] *Commons' Committee on Printed Papers* (1835) *Report.*

[Cd 9071] *Report of Departmental Committee on the Iron and Steel Trades* (1918).

[Cd 9092] *Report of Departmental Committee on the Shipping and Shipbuilding Industries* (1918).

In the official encouragement of popular enlightenment we see the triumph of the Benthamite Radicals over the reactionary anti-Jacobin view that popular ignorance was a political safeguard and that the people had nothing to do with the laws except to obey them. When the House of Commons was debating the question of Education in 1833, John Arthur Roebuck expounded the Radical case in these terms:

If, as heretofore, the majority of mankind were content to be a slumbering mass—an inert utterly inactive body—then the policy, as a selfish policy, might possibly be defended. But this is no longer the case.....Within these last few years a new element has arisen, which now ought to enter into all political calculations. The multitude...are filled with a new spirit—their attention is intently directed towards the affairs of the State—they take an active part in their own social concerns,—and however unwilling persons may be to contemplate the fact, anyone who will calmly and carefully watch the signs of the times, will discover, and if he be really honest and wise, will at once allow that the hitherto subject many are about to become paramount in the State[1].

This view anticipates the celebrated anti-Radical dictum of Robert Lowe: "We must educate our masters".

3. A FREE PRESS

The complement to parliamentary publicity was a cheap and untrammelled press. For this the people had to fight. We have seen already how Cobbett opened the battle with his *Political Register* and *Twopenny Trash*, and how in 1817 Hone, the publisher, gained a verdict for the liberty of the Press[2]. The second stage was fought between 1830 and 1836. Castlereagh's hated Stamp Act was still in force, when Hetherington, Cleave, Watson and Carpenter, the publishers of Radical journals, re-

---

[1] Hansard, 3rd S. xx. 139–66.   [2] See above, pp. 24–6 and 77–8.

opened the battle. Hetherington, in October 1830, began the issues of *The Penny Papers for the People*, published by *The Poor Man's Guardian*. When this was pronounced a newspaper at law, Hetherington (July 9, 1831) defied authority, inscribing on the title page: "Published contrary to 'Law' to try the power of 'Might against Right'". Prosecutions followed, and Lovett organised a Victim Fund to assist the champions of the People's Press. Finally, after a jury in 1834 had decided that *The Poor Man's Guardian* was not an illegal newspaper, the Government replaced the 4*d*. stamp by a penny stamp (1836).

Thirteen years elapsed before the third stage of the fight began, but during this interval the diffusion of knowledge was greatly stimulated by the lectures, leaflets and journals which the Anti-Corn Law League, the factory reformers and the Chartists used in their campaigns.

In 1849 the "Taxes on Knowledge", as Leigh Hunt happily termed them, were three in number:

(i) The paper duty, which brought in three quarters of a million:

(ii) The tax on advertisements of 1*s*. 6*d*. per advertisement:

(iii) The penny stamp duty; and bound up with this the securities for good behaviour which each publisher had to give.

G. J. Holyoake played a notable part in the assault on these. The Government was winking at the infraction of the law, but was unwilling to part with the substantial revenue derived from the big dailies. Therefore in 1850 Holyoake caused Charles Dickens' *Household Narrative of Current Events* to be prosecuted as a test case. In 1851 he thwarted the scheme of the newspaper proprietors and paper manufacturers to put the repeal of the paper duty in front of the other measures, by inducing a meeting which they had summoned to resolve that it was not a trade question but a public principle. The Association for the Repeal of Taxes on Knowledge then got busy. It included middle class Radicals like Milner-Gibson, Cobden and Bright; working-men Radicals like Francis Place and the old school of Reformers; and "Knowledge" Chartists, like Watson, Collet and Moore. They gained their first victory in 1853. The budget of that year provided for a reduced advertisement tax, but by a snap division, as finally passed, it specified a tax of "£0. 0s. 0d." on advertisements. The second victory was won in 1855. The Government was hedging on the question of the Stamp Duty and Securities, when Sir Edward Bulwer Lytton carried the House by an eloquent appeal for the complete freedom of the press. The stamp duty was thereupon abolished, and the security system, which depended on it, in time (1869) died a natural death. The Repeal of the Duty on Paper involved a struggle with the House of Lords, which in 1860 threw out the Government's Bill of Repeal. The Commons drew up a series of resolutions stating their rights in the matter of taxation, and next year the Government effected its purpose by including the Repeal of the Paper Duty in the general budget, which passed the House of Lords without alteration[1].

4. POPULAR EDUCATION

In the first half of the century the Government's direct share in education was inconsiderable, but a spirit of education was alive in the working classes, and the Government, by publishing official news and establishing a free press, gave food for thought and discussion to a people which was clamouring for social knowledge. The working classes tried to teach themselves; and in this heavy task they received generous help, financial and educational, from philanthropists and reformers[2]. Dr Birkbeck, the founder of the Mechanics Institute in London (1824), which inspired imitations in every big town; Joseph Sturge, the organiser of Adult Day Schools in Birmingham; Lord Shaftesbury, the friend in turn of the poor lunatic, the factory hand, the "climbing boys", the ragged urchin and the slum dweller; Frederick Denison Maurice, the apostle of Christian Socialism, who inaugurated the London Working Men's College in 1854 and became its principal; Samuel Morley, the Nottingham hosier, the munificent builder of Schools and Chapels; James Stuart, the

---

[1] Cf. Sydney Buxton, *Finance and Politics*, i. 213.

[2] Cf. A. E. Dobbs, *Education and Social Movements* (1700–1850), published in 1919.

pioneer of University Extension; Hodgson Pratt, the advocate of international arbitration, through whose efforts 3000 British workmen visited the Paris Exhibition of 1867; Arnold Toynbee, a Tutor at Balliol and social lecturer, after whom is named Toynbee Hall, the first University Settlement in London; and the late Canon Barnett, its beloved warden—are shining examples of men who had mastered the lesson first expounded by Owen that education is the heart of the social problem.

Working class education was always more than a response to patronage. In the second quarter of the 19th century it was not uncommon for adult members of the working classes to collect libraries, to form naturalist clubs, and to meet in small groups for mutual instruction in the three R's and other subjects. While the Mechanics' Institutes with their scientific and vocational aims were the precursors of technical instruction, these smaller mutual improvement groups point forward to the study circles developed in later years by the Workers' Educational Association and other bodies. They suffered often for want of guidance; they were isolated units; and thus they were weak in those points in which the W.E.A. is strong. But enthusiasts stick at nothing. When the People's College at Sheffield lost its founder in 1848, the students reorganised it and managed it for more than 20 years.

However, in its widest sense popular education embraces more than formal instruction. In the Trades Clubs and the Trades Unions, in the Committee Room of the Co-operative Store and the Lodge of the Friendly Society, in the Chartist Churches, in the Halls of Social Science and at the feet of social missionaries the people of England struggled from darkness into light. Their schoolroom was a life lived in common, the medium of instruction was the informal clash of mind and mind, and the lessons of the unwritten syllabus were self-discipline, business fellowship and the pursuit of a clearly-planned objective.

The student of English Education in the 19th century will appraise at its full worth the contributions made to adult education and the elementary education of children by sectarian bodies—by the Church of England under the inspiration of Bell, and by the Nonconformist bodies under the inspiration of Lancaster[1]. The State's part at first was a very small one. All the eloquence of Brougham availed nothing in 1816, and the education bill which he introduced in 1820 foundered on religious jealousy and dislike of change. Not till 1833 did the House of Commons venture on a vote of twenty thousand pounds to education, and then it distributed the sum between existing voluntary organisations. The administration of the annual government grant was given in 1839 to a special committee of the Privy Council, appointed by Order in Council, and by this executive instrument the State acquired a modicum of control over education at a time when a general education bill had no chance of passing the Upper House. But by this date the State was becoming seriously involved in education by the circuitous route of factory legislation. Whitbread in 1807 had tried to introduce education through the Poor Law, but failed. Similarly by the Factory Act of 1833, when the restriction on the hours of factory work created what was considered to be a dangerous amount of spare time for children, the State ordained that the factory children should be educated and threw the responsibility on the employers in whose mills they worked. Hence the half-timer. In 1912, the author visited a survival of this early system, the Factory School of Messrs Don Buist & Co., Jute Manufacturers of Dundee.

At first the education given in the Factory Schools was a farce, and Sir James Graham endeavoured to make more adequate provisions in his Factory Bill of 1844. But the educational clauses excited such animosity between Churchmen and Nonconformists that they had to be dropped. "Religion", wrote Graham to Lord Brougham, in October 1841, "the keystone of education, is in this country the bar to its progress"[2].

Such in England was the medley of antecedents to the first general measure of national education, the Education Act of 1870.

---

[1] Cf. Dobbs, *op. cit.*, c. 4.
[2] C. S. Parker, *Life and Letters of Sir James Graham*, I. 339. Letter of October 24, 1841.

5. Parliamentary Papers

The Parliamentary Papers, or Blue Books as they are often termed, supply four classes of information:

i. The Reports and Evidence of Select Committees of the House of Lords and House of Commons.

In the early period the Lords Committees are sometimes the more instructive (e.g. their Committees on the Corn Laws (1814) and on the Wages of Persons employed in the Manufacture of Silk (1823)). Latterly, they have made such problems as health, housing and sweating their special province.

In nearly all the Committees of Lords and Commons alike (the early Committees on Combinations being an exception) the reader is struck by the fairness of the chairman and the out-spoken answers of the witnesses. Nowhere is impartiality more admirably shown than in Bright's Game Laws Committee (1845), when Lord George Bentinck, as chairman, insisted on a fair hearing for a case which at every turn hit his own order.

ii. The Reports and Evidence of Commissions appointed by royal authority extending from the famous investigations of the '30's and '40's—the Factory Commission, the Poor Law Commission, the Hand-loom Weavers' Commission, the Children's Employment Commission, the Midland Mining Commission, the Framework-Knitters' Commission (the two latter by individual Commissioners)—down to the Royal Commission on Labour (1891–94), over which the Duke of Devonshire presided.

The Labour Commission produced a monumental work. Other countries may be ahead of us in statistics and technical reports, but no other country could have introduced into an official enquiry the frankest interchange of social and economic opinion between questioners and witnesses drawn from every class of society and representing every school of thought.

iii. The Reports of Commissioners appointed in accordance with an Act of Parliament to supervise the introduction of an Act and to report on its operation. As examples we may cite the annual Reports of the Poor Law Commissioners (1835–48);

and the Reports of the Commissioner (Mr Tremenheere) on the Operation of the Mines Act and the State of the Population in the Mining Districts (1844–49), continued annually in a second series (1850–59).

iv. The Reports and Evidence of Departmental Committees. These have become more common of recent years. Examples are the *Report and Evidence of the Departmental Committee on the Truck Acts* (1908), and the *Report and Evidence of the Departmental Committee on Small Holdings* (1906). This type of enquiry may be considered as the precursor of the Reports recently issued by the Ministry of Reconstruction.

6. INVESTIGATION AND LEGISLATION

Full public enquiry preceded all the important social legislation of the 19th century. In this sense legislation was truly democratic, and it is interesting to note how closely the two were associated.

The first branch of this legislation is preventive.

Investigation	*Legislation*
Report of Royal Commission on the administration and operation of the Poor Laws (1834).	Poor Law Amendment Act, 1834.
Annual Reports of the Poor Law Commissioners (1835–48).	Minor amendments to Poor Law.
Commons Committee (Sadler's) on Bill relating to Labour of Children in Mills and Factories (1832). Report of Factory Commissioners (1833–34).	Factory Act of 1833 (establishing the Factory Inspectorate).
Report of Royal Commission on the Employment and Condition of Children and Young Persons. Second Report. Trades and Manufactures (1843).	Factory Acts of 1844, 1847, et seq.
Report of Commissioners on Employment of Children and Young Persons in Trades and Manufactures not already regulated by Law (1863–67).	Factory Extension Acts of 1864 and 1867. Workshops Act of 1867.
Report of Royal Commission on the Working of the Factory and Workshops Acts (1876).	Factories and Workshops Consolidation Act of 1878.

Royal Commission on the Employment and Condition of Children and Young Persons. First Report. Mines and Collieries (1842).	Mines' Act of 1842.
Lords Committee (1849) on Accidents in Coal Mines—following a Commons Committee on Catastrophes in Coal Mines (1835).	Act of 1850 establishing the mining inspectorate, and dealing in particular with prevention of accidents and explosions.
Commons Committee on Explosions in Coal Mines (1852), and Accidents in Coal Mines (1853).	Act of 1855 strengthening the Mining Inspectorate.
Reports of Commissioner on Operation of Mines Act (1844–59).	Mines Act of 1860.
Report of Commissioners on Conditions of Mines in Great Britain with reference to the Health and Safety of the Miners (1864).	Mines Act of 1872. (The Acts of 1860 and 1872 strengthened the Mining Inspectorate, compelled the publication of regulations at mines and instituted the Miners' Check-weighman, whose powers were enlarged by the Act of 1887.)
Employment of Chimney sweepers— Commons Committee 1817, Lords Committee 1818, Lords Committee 1834, Lords Committee 1840.	Act of 1840, prohibiting such employment.

The second branch of democratic legislation is concerned with the recognition of workers' rights and employers' responsibilities.

Investigation	*Legislation*
Commons Committee on Artisans' Machinery and Combination (1824).	Combination Act of 1824.
Commons Committee on Combinations of Workmen (1825).	Combination Act of 1825.
Report of Examiners on Intimidation relating to Sheffield (1867): and Report of Royal Commission on Trades Unions and other Associations (1867–9).	Trade Union Acts of 1871 and 1876. Combination Act (Conspiracy and Protection of Property) 1875.
Commons Committee on Employers' Liability (1876–77).	Employers' Liability Act, 1880. Workmen's Compensation Act, 1897.
Commons Committee on Laws respecting Friendly Societies (1825–27).	Friendly Societies Acts of 1829 and 1834.
Report of Royal Commission on Friendly Societies and Benefit Building Societies, etc. (1871–74).	Friendly Societies Act of 1875.
Commons Committee (Slaney's) on the Means of giving facility to Safe Investments for Savings of Middle and Working Classes (1852).	Industrial and Provident Societies Act of 1852. (The "Magna Charta" of co-operation.)

The third class of democratic legislation is concerned with health and housing. The connection between investigation and legislation becomes less close, when these matters fall within the province of the Local Government Board and of the local authorities.

Investigation	*Legislation*
Commons Committee on Health of Towns (1840).	1848. Public Health Act.
Royal Commission on State of Large Towns and Populous Districts (1844–45).	1871. Establishment of the Local Government Board (L.G.B.).
	1872 and 1875. Public Health Acts.
	1874. London County Lodging Houses (Sanitary Law Amendment) Act.
Various Committees on Housing, e.g., Commons Committee on Torrens Bills (1868), Commons Committee on the Artisans and Labourers dwellings Acts of 1875 and 1879 (1881)—leading up to the Report of the Royal Commission on the Housing of the Working Classes (1884)[1].	1868, 1879, 1882. Artisans etc. Dwellings (Torrens) Acts.
	1875, 1879, 1882. Artisans etc. Dwellings (Cross) Acts.
	1885. Housing of the Working Classes Act.
	Act establishing County Councils, 1888.

7. The Factory Acts

The word writ large over English factory legislation is "piecemeal".

Factory legislation began in 1802 with an act of elementary mercy for parish apprentices and ended in a great code embracing every type of factory and workshop and pushing across the domestic threshold.

The Act of 1802 was confined to apprentices in cotton and woollen factories; that of 1819 to cotton factories, that of 1833 to textile factories, excepting lace and partially excepting silk factories. The Act of 1864 embraced the dangerous trades and trades structurally similar to the textile trades—pottery making, lucifer match making, percussion-cap and cartridge making, paper staining and fustian cutting. The legislation of 1867 extended the list; and the Consolidating Act of 1878, abandoning the arbitrary distinction made in 1867 between factories and

---

[1] The then Prince of Wales, Cardinal Manning and Lord Salisbury were members of this Commission.

workshops, attempted the first general definition of a factory. The definition was unlovely: "Premises where any articles are made, altered, repaired, ornamented, finished or adapted for sale by means of manual labour exercised for gain, if mechanical power is used on the premises"—together with certain enumerated premises whether using power or not.

The piecemeal method had certain disadvantages:

i.   It was slow and in the meanwhile the workers suffered.

ii.   It was unequal and therefore there was a danger of driving evil from regulated factories to places which in the eyes of the law were not factories.

iii.   It necessitated multiplicity of laws. For example, when the ten hours day was won in 1847, further legislation was required between that date and 1853, in order to convert the maximum of ten hours per day per person into a normal ten hours day for the factory as a whole. Until this was done it was impossible for the Inspectors to prevent evasions (p. 179, n. 2, above).

The advantages, however, outweighed the disadvantages:

i.   The piecemeal method helped the legislature out of a philosophic dilemma. They were determined in principle not to interfere with freedom of contract between adult males, but it was no violation of this principle to protect minors. Therefore they began with children, proceeded next to young persons (13 to 18), and after the lead given by the Mines Act of 1842 included women. Having thus embraced the majority of workers in the factory, the legislature prescribed conditions of safety and sanitation, which applied to all concerned. It was said at the time that the men were fighting their own battles behind the women's petticoats. This, like the charge against the Anti-Corn Law League of desiring to lower wages, is one of those accusations which lead nowhere. The facts are that the factory reformers did not speak or work for the Ten Hours Movement in this spirit, that the Factory Acts benefited most those to whom they were intended to apply, and that the men obtained by Trade Union action hours shorter than the maximum laid down by the law.

ii.   The piecemeal method, through the instrument of the

Inspectorate, made the operation of the law sure. The laws being passed after preliminary investigation and consultation with the inspectors were relevant and reasonable. Therefore, when the original prejudice against interference had been overcome, the later extensions were attended with little friction. The Government officials, in the course of collecting information, were often able to persuade reasonably minded employers that the element of irregularity which they supposed inevitable in their particular industry could be removed. But for the reasonableness of the laws and the co-operation of reasonably minded employers a host of factory inspectors could not have enforced them.

8. THE MINES ACTS

Mining legislation, too, was piecemeal in the sense that step followed upon step, but from the first it was clear what a mine was and where mining took place. You could not do coal-mining at home. It is possible that a suspicion of factory labour being diverted to coal mines first drew public attention to the necessity for the regulating the latter. Mr Hickson, a Member of the Hand-loom Weavers' Commission, when on a tour in the North of England (1840), "took some pains to enquire into the fact which I have heard asserted in several quarters, that one effect of the Factory Regulation Bill had been to send many of the children formerly employed in factories to work in coal-pits"[1]. But although Parliament was prepared in 1842 to prohibit altogether the employment of women and children in mines, it was slow to authorise a general code of safety regulations and the enforcement of that code by inspectors. The Committee of 1835 went so far as to "deem it their duty to state their decided opinion that the interests of humanity demand consideration"[2]. The Committee of 1849, having received strong evidence that "even in an economical point of view a safe and healthy condition of a mine may be ultimately the most profitable to the

[1] W. E. Hickson, *Notes made on a tour through the Weaving Districts* (1840), p. 49.
[2] *Commons' Committee on Catastrophes in Coal Mines* (1835), *Report*, p. 5.

owner" [1], proposed Government inspection, but jealously limited the inspectors' powers. There was, they argued, no analogy between "the power to order a simple defence against dangerous machinery (sc. such as the factory inspectors possessed) and directions for the improvement of ventilation, or as to methods of working collieries, or prescribing the many other changes which may be desirable for their safety".

The Miners' National Association, which was revived out of earlier failures by Alexander MacDonald between 1858 and 1863, brought the struggle to a successful conclusion. We must remember that in Northumberland the yearly bond lasted till 1844 and that in Durham it survived till 1872. The men therefore were not free to organise strong local unions. They suffered severely from excessive fines. If a corve of coals contained more than a small percentage of split coals or grit, it was laid out, i.e. forfeited to the owners. The contents of the tub being gauged by measure, the hewer used to walk round the tub and rock it in order that the jolting might not lower the coals below the rim and thus cause forfeiture of the whole tub. In 1862, during a strike on the Durham coalfield in which these abuses figured prominently (hence called "The Rocking Strike"), the miners had a ditty:

> The rocking, so shocking, long, long we have bore,
> Farewell to the rocking, we will rock them no more[2].

The National Association therefore fought for a more efficient mining inspectorate, and in 1860 procured by Section 29 of the Mines Act of that year the right for the miners in a mine "at their own cost to station a person (being one of the persons for the time being employed) to take account of the weight, measure or gauge of coal". The coal-owners did their best to defeat the law by discharging the check-weigher or hampering his access to the weighing machine, but his position was strengthened in 1872 and still further in 1887. The legislature thus recognised the corporate claims of the workers and provided Miners Unions

---

[1] *Lords' Committee on Accidents in Coal Mines* (1849), *Report*, p. 5. Lord Wharncliffe was Chairman.

[2] Wilson, *History of the Durham Miners' Association*, p. 3.

with branch secretaries gratis. The course of legislation between 1842 and 1887 says little for the decency of the coal-owners; and also, because of its success, explains why the miners have been ahead of other organised trades in securing a legal limitation of hours (1908) and a legal minimum wage (1912).

9. THE TRUCK ACTS

The legislation against truck has a different history. The Act of 1831 prohibited truck in general terms: "Contracts for hiring of artificers must be made in current coin of the realm and must not contain any stipulation as to the manner in which wages shall be expended". The Act, however, in many trades broke down, first because there was no adequate machinery for its enforcement, and secondly because all workers were not wage-earning artificers. Therefore the eradication of truck is closely connected with the evolution of particular trades on capitalistic lines and the growth of Trade Unionism in those trades. Thus, in coal mining, we pass from section 6 of the Mines' Act of 1842 (prohibiting payment of wages at public houses) to the sections in the Mines' Acts of 1860, 1872 and 1887 which defined the powers of the check-weighman. In the hosiery trade the Truck Act of 1874 was concerned with the prohibition of frame rents. Section 1 enacted that: "In all contracts for wages the full and entire amount of all wages shall be actually and positively made payable in net, without any deduction or stoppage of any description whatsoever". The Truck Act of 1887 extended the scope of the Truck Acts by definition. The artificer in the old sense, as used in the Act of 1831, becomes the artificer as defined in the Employers and Workmen Act of 1875. Similarly, the Truck Act of 1887 defines home workers in the textile trades as workmen and dealers who buy their work as employers. Finally, the amending Truck Act of 1896 deals with fines and deductions and embraces shop assistants as well as workmen. Taken as a whole, the truck legislation from 1831–96 is an illuminating commentary on the growth of the wage system under capitalism.

10. No Remedy for the Hand-Loom Weavers

The three great enquiries into the condition of the hand-loom weavers were all without legislative fruit. The Emigration Committees of 1826 and 1826–27, which were largely concerned with the hand-loom weavers, produced a few crude recommendations for emigration, which a Manufacturers' Relief Committee offered to assist with a donation of £25,000. The outcome of the Committee of 1834–35 was Fielden's abortive Minimum Wage Bill. Finally, the Hand-loom Weavers' Commission of 1839–41 concluded a merciless survey of the situation with a eulogy of free food and a virulent denunciation of combinations:

> We believe that the general evils and general dangers of combinations cannot easily be exaggerated. We believe that if the manufacturer is to employ his capital, and the mechanic and chemist his ingenuity, only under the dictation of his short-sighted and rapacious workmen...we shall not retain the industry, the skill, or the capital on which our manufacturing superiority, and, with that superiority, our power and almost our existence as a nation depends[1].

11. Recognition of Trade Unions, and Employers' Liability

The Royal Commission of Enquiry into Trades Unions was appointed amid the excitement caused by the Sheffield "Rattening" outrages of 1867. Three barristers reported on the outrages[2] to the Commission, which issued in 1868 a Majority Report, and a Minority Dissent signed by Lord Lichfield, Thomas Hughes and Frederic Harrison. The Majority Report was cautious. They were prepared to recognise within strict limits an unwelcome growth, but their proposal to divide the funds of the Unions into two, Trade Funds and Benefit Funds, showed that they had no sympathy with the corporate life of Trade Unionism and the

---

[1] *Hand-loom Weavers' Commission, Report* (1841), p. 117.
[2] A specimen threat to a master saw manufacturer was worded thus: "November 4, if they handel-makers of yores doesn't send their money i shall come and feth strings if the devil stand i 't road".

means whereby that life could find effective expression. Fortunately the minority view prevailed and the legislation which followed was pursuant to it.

The Combination Act of 1875, says Professor Dicey, "is, on the face of it, a compromise between the desire of collectivists to promote combined bargaining and the conviction of individualists that every man ought, as long as he does not distinctly invade the rights of his neighbours, to enjoy complete contractual freedom"[1]. The Trade Unions were enfranchised in terms of the individual. They were rescued from the toils of the common law against conspiracy by the individualistic formula that things done by one or more persons in furtherance of a trade dispute shall not be indictable as a conspiracy, when such Acts committed by one person would not be punishable as a crime.

The Trade Disputes Act of 1906 reversed the Taff Vale Judgment and gave to Trade Union funds immunity from liability for civil wrongs. Moreover, it took certain acts, such as procuring breach of contract, out of the category of actionable civil wrongs, if done in furtherance of a trade dispute. Thus, from a legal standpoint[2], the status of the Trade Union became as exceptionally favourable as it once was exceptionally unfavourable.

In addition to securing the rights of Trade Unions in terms that were certainly generous Parliament increased by further legislation the duties of the employer. From 1837 to 1880 the judicial rule, or doctrine, of "common employment" told heavily against the worker. If a railway accident occurred through the negligence of the engine driver, every passenger damaged thereby could obtain compensation from the Railway Company, but a guard or a porter, since they were injured through the negligence of their fellow-servant, could obtain no compensation whatever. This rule was modified by the Employers' Liability Act of 1880 and deprived of application in the Workmen's Compensation

---

[1] *Law and Opinion*, p. 268.
[2] Cf. Dicey, *Law and Opinion*, Appendix, Note 1, p. 475. "Severity has given place to favouritism: the denial of equality has, by a natural reaction, led to the concession of, and promoted the demand for, privilege".

Acts of 1897 and later, which gradually introduced into the law the new principle that an employer must, subject to certain limitations, insure his workmen against the risks of their employment. The National Insurance Act of 1911 extended the principle of insurance against risks of employment to insurance against the risk (in a different sense of the word) of unemployment and sickness. This Act has carried one stage further the practice, which is as old as the Factory Schools of the 30's, of throwing responsibility on the employer, because he is the party that can be reached and made accountable.

CHAPTER XXII

THE GROWTH OF CORPORATE LIFE

1. The Heritage of the Past

LET us now take the century decade by decade and endeavour in conclusion to single out the contributions which each decade made to the growth of corporate life. Social movements have most individuality when they are in the early stage of enthusiastic propaganda, or when at a somewhat later stage their practical achievements make them a model for general imitation. In time they are incorporated in the life of the nation, which becomes so accustomed to their presence that it takes them for granted. From this two things follow. Old established movements must be refilled with energy from time to time if they are to mean to us what they meant to those who created them. Furthermore, by historical study we must learn to draw on the inspiration of the past. Nature endows the countryside with perennial freshness, but a people which lives in great cities must constantly be clearing away the blots and mistakes of the previous generation. To such a people the historical sense is a mighty ally. As we plan each new advance, we must bear in mind the steps by which the starting point has been reached. For we are the trustees of a great heritage, and if we are to enrich it for our children we must understand how it has come about that we fare better than our fathers.

2. The 20's and 30's

In the 20's men awoke from the gloom of war and repression. Purposes were fused in the white heat of idealism. There was to be a new heaven and a new earth. Their first thought was of an economic Utopia and the issue was an Owenite Community! In the 30's, still in a mood of idealism, they mingled with earthly things. The spirit of association ran riot in Political Unions, militant Trades Unionism and the nervous intensity of Chartism. The immediate results were disappointing, but it was a time of educational preparation. The working classes were beginning to challenge economic individualism in terms of itself; that is to say, they were learning the meaning of self-help by voluntary association. And yet the outlook was dark. To many thoughtful minds it seemed that the old standards of corporate existence were being overwhelmed by the human floods from Ireland and from the new industrial regions of Scotland, England and Wales. Francis Place knew how vastly superior the London of his old age was to the London of his youth, when the working men of London brutalised themselves in Gin Palaces, when the streets resounded with filthy songs, when fraudulent beggars exhibited their artificial sores, when at Charing Cross pillory women pelted the victim with horse dung, when, as he passed by the Fleet Prison, he was asked to step inside and be married by "a squalid profligate parson, clad in a tattered plaid nightgown, with a fiery face and ready to couple you for a dram of gin or roll of tobacco"[1]. To one who had watched in the Metropolis the dawn of a fairer civilisation the rapid and disorderly growth of industrial England was a thing of ill-omen. Does not this help to explain the fear which Place and the Radicals had of an excessive population? The same batch of MSS. contains a letter from Place, in which he says: "Any suggestion which does not tend to a reduction in numbers of the working people is useless, to say the least of it.... The remedy again is *good* teaching— which will in time make easy the evils of redundant population"[2].

3. THE 40's

The 40's were a period of exasperation, yet, withal, of fruitful sowing. The Reform Movement had stopped short at the enfranchisement of shopkeepers, and a second assault was called for. The Chartists made it; but the result of a nation's travail was—the Repeal of the Corn Laws. The National Convention of

---

[1] Place, British Museum, Add. MSS. 27,827, p. 15. [2] *Ibid.* p. 117.

Chartists dissolved to make way for a peddling co-operative store; and over the grave of large hopes the Amalgamated Society of Engineers affixed its business-like rules. But with these matters we have dealt fully.

4. THE 50'S

How shall we distinguish the 50's? One way of determining what the people is doing in a particular decade is to ascertain what the Government did in the next. In 1861, when Mr Gladstone was Chancellor of the Exchequer, the Act creating Post Office Savings Banks was passed, the State offering its security for the repayment of all monies deposited through the Post Office. About the same time on the Continent Co-operative Credit Banks and Communal Savings Banks were arising to supply the needs of countries which had advanced less far in large scale industrial organisation. The savings of the locality were invested in the locality with farmers, shopkeepers and small scale employers. The contrast indicates the trend of English development. In England the wage-earning and salary-receiving elements were larger. The demand for security exceeded the demand for local application. Therefore the Post Office, with its machinery of branch deposit and central investment, succeeded. Even the co-operative stores found that the best outlet for their overflowing capital was provided by the operation of large scale factories under the control of their Federal Wholesales.

In the 50's, therefore, we have to record the spread of thrift and saving among the middle and working class. This is reflected in the statistics of the Friendly Societies. Dr Baernreither, in his *English Associations of Working Men*, shows that the Friendly Societies movement, though it had its origin in the 18th century, made its greatest progress between 1840 and the time he was writing (1st edition, 1889). He shows its widespread ramification through the middle and working classes of England. He shows the many varieties of thrift—the ephemeral dividing society, the village, town and county clubs, the larger burial societies, the societies confined to a single industry, such as mining, and the societies established by individual employers or by the big railway companies. All these were surpassed by the great working men's Orders, which had their headquarters in Lancashire and Yorkshire. The biggest Order, the Independent Order of Oddfellows (Manchester Unity) had 46,000 members in 1837 and 617,000 members in 1886. The Ancient Order of Foresters (headquarters, Leeds) had 65,000 members in 1845 and 667,000 members in 1886. These two Societies took the lead in the compilation of insurance statistics and standardisation of Friendly Society finance. Similar progress was made by the Order of Druids, the Loyal Order of Shepherds (Ashton Unity), the Order of Rechabites (Salford Unity) and the Sons of Temperance.

The immediate purpose of the Friendly Societies was provision for burial, accident and sickness, but they achieved far more than this. They educated their members in self-government. They were a part of the corporate life of the workers. Friendly Societies and Trade Unions, says Dr Baernreither, "are only different sides of the same historical process....Both owe their existence to the same powerful reaction of the working classes against the deterioration of their material condition; both are among the most conspicuous examples of English self-help; they work side by side; they mutually supplement each other; they are twin children of the same spirit"[1]. Sir David Dale, in 1871, wrote the Trade Union leaders of the North of England a testimonial which would have amazed Nassau Senior and his colleagues on the Hand-loom Weavers' Commission: "I may say this, the leaders of the men's union in the North of England, who are also the leading operative members of the Board of Arbitration, are almost all teetotalers and that upon which they would chiefly dwell in their communications with the men would be the importance of abstaining from drink if they wished to hold their own in the competition... with capital, and those same men are advocates for weekly pays to the iron workers"[2].

---

[1] *English Associations of Working Men*, p. 158.
[2] *Truck Commission* (1871). Evidence, Q. 44,612.

5. THE 60's

To the 60's belong the Lancashire Cotton Famine of 1861–63 and the Trade Union Enquiry of 1867–69. We have discussed already the legislation issuing from that enquiry, but a few words must be said about the Cotton Famine. The distress came suddenly and lasted longer than was expected. It bore with special severity on the towns in which the cotton industry provided almost the total maintenance of the people. Thus Ashton, Bolton and Stockport fared worse than Warrington, Garstang and The Fylde. Bolton, however, which spun fine cotton, although almost wholly dependent upon the cotton industry, suffered much less than Rochdale, where a considerable percentage was engaged in the woollen manufacture, the reason being that the class of cotton goods produced by Rochdale required a larger proportion of the raw cotton which the American War cut off[1]. Thus in one way or another the Lancashire cotton trade was highly vulnerable to a sudden stoppage of supplies. But the specialisation which was a short-period weakness was also a long-period strength. The crisis was surmounted without challenge to Lancashire's textile pre-eminence or prolonged lowering of the operatives' standard of life. The masters showed less hysteria than in the days of 1842. They had confidence that they could weather the storm; and they set about opening new sources of cotton supply in Egypt and India, in order to escape from the dangerous dependence on a single market. The support from without was generous and sustained. A Mansion House Relief Fund produced over £500,000; of which nearly £200,000 came from the Dominions and foreign countries.

The Government made its first essay in relief works for unemployed, which were not a financial disaster only because they were not used mainly to relieve unemployment. About a third of the men taken on were workmen skilled in construction and such distressed cotton operatives as accepted work on them were engaged at labourers' rates of pay[2]. They, therefore, left the work as quickly as they could; and the Government was able to

[1] Cf. Dr John Watts, *Facts of the Cotton Famine* (1866), p. 253.
[2] Cf. Webb, *English Poor Law Policy*, p. 93.

congratulate itself that at a time of great industrial distress it had made up arrears of drainage and public works.

Those who earned the greatest credit were the operatives themselves. They were no longer living on the margin of subsistence and they were able to draw on savings, which they had placed in Co-operative Stores and Savings Banks. Molesworth writes:

At the time when the American war commenced, the example so successfully set in Rochdale had been followed in almost all the great manufacturing towns. They had provided the working classes who inhabited them with a safe investment for their savings, from which they received five per cent. regularly paid them besides profits; they had also taught them habits of frugality, temperance, patience, sobriety and self-reliance; and to this it was in no small degree due that when the cotton famine did come upon the working classes of the manufacturing districts, it found them prepared to bear with a firmness and resolution which extorted the admiration of the civilised world. During that famine the original society flourished in spite of the heavy drain caused by the withdrawal of their deposits by many of the members, who were compelled by want of work to fall back on these resources. They of course underwent some temporary inconvenience, and during these trying years there was a diminution in the amount of their business and their profits. But this was merely a temporary reverse; and as soon as the famine ceased, and indeed even before it had ceased, the societies resumed their onward course, doing more business, obtaining greater profits, and paying larger dividends than ever. During the severest distress, when there was a kind of run on them for money, there was never the slightest hesitation or delay in paying those who wished to withdraw their money in accordance with the rules of the societies. And this was the case not in Rochdale only, but in almost every part of the manufacturing districts in which Co-operative Societies had been founded on the Rochdale model[1].

The operatives, like the hand-loom weavers 20 years earlier, maintained their proud and independent spirit[2], and although

[1] W. N. Molesworth, *History of England* 1830–1874, III. 216.
Molesworth also notes the failure of two co-operative *productive* societies (cotton mills) at Rochdale:
"The cotton famine rendered the newly-erected factories almost useless and entirely profitless. It compelled a great number of the shareholders to part with their shares to persons who were not so fully imbued as themselves with the original spirit of cooperation, and who purchased them simply as a speculation" (*ibid*. p. 214).
[2] At the height of the famine, the winter of 1862–63, a visitor offered a starving family some relief tickets, but the poor woman began to cry and said "Eh! aw dar not touch 'em; my husban' would sauce me so! Aw dar not tak' em; aw should never yer th' last on it." (Dr John Watts, *The Facts of the Cotton Famine*, p. 135.)

Lancashire got its cotton from the Southern States, the cotton operatives enthusiastically supported the cause of anti-slavery throughout.

6. THE 70's

The 70's saw a broadening of the economic basis of Government. The Public Health Acts of 1872–75 owed their success to the revival of municipal self-government. A survey of the progress made in housing and public health during the century would compel us to break new ground; which is admirably plotted out in an article in the *Economic Journal* of December 1913[1]. Suffice it here to say that one town after another shows evidence of the mistakes committed before 1870 and of the improvements effected since. Of the early part of the century the writer says: "Everywhere the diseases of dirt still flourished, though the beginnings of sanitation brought about some little improvement. Smallpox was, of course, still the permanent scourge of the country.... Typhus and gaol fever were also of frequent occurrence....Cholera was an epidemic visitor". Of the middle period he writes: "The rate of growth of towns between 1851 and 1871 was not less rapid than in the preceding twenty years. How were these crowds housed? Everything was sacrificed to cheapness, and cheapness was attained, not merely by excluding all conveniences such as the laying on of water but by restricting the ground space". In 1872–75 a new chapter of town life begins. In Birmingham, with its heavy burden of the past, the new suburbs are healthy by contrast with the old centre. For the clearing of central slums is a vast expense; and meanwhile, "the comparative cheapness of the houses, their proximity to works and good yards, and to public houses and picture palaces, make them veritable traps for the easy going and a boon to the vicious". Leicester, with a small burden of the past, effected a notable reduction in its death rate, the result of "an energetic and enlightened administration in sanitary matters acting under favourable historical conditions".

[1] *Economic Journal*, No. 92: F. Tillyard, "English town development in the nineteenth century"—a paper read before Section F of the British Association (Birmingham, 1913).

7. THE 80's AND 90's

The Trade Union Commissioners in 1868 commended two methods for the avoidance of industrial strife, which had been brought to their attention. One was the method of profit-sharing, as practised at the Yorkshire Collieries of Henry Briggs, Son & Co. Ltd. The other was the method of arbitration and conciliation. A. J. Mundella explained to them the good work he had accomplished with his Board of Conciliation in the glove and hosiery trade. Rupert Kettle, a County Court Judge of Worcestershire, testified to similar success in the building trades of the Midlands.

These boards presumed a trade union. When the union demanded a collective bargain for the industry, the masters federated to meet the demand. The next step was the conversion of occasional bargaining into permanent bargaining procedure. The machinery was voluntary and styled, according to its evolution, a Board of Arbitration and Conciliation, a Wages Board, a Joint Committee, etc. Each industry has its own record—to those already mentioned may be added the Boot and Shoe Trade, the Iron and Steel Trade, and the Cotton Trade with its piece-lists and plan of adjustment formulated in the Brooklands Agreement of 1892.

In the 80's the miners drew level with the rest and carried forward the torch of corporate life. Study, as a sample, the coalfield of County Durham. In the 60's Durham was spoken of as the black spot of Unionism, but the environment was favourable to its growth. For in 1863 the missionary ardour of Thomas Burt created the Northumberland Miners' Mutual Association, and in 1869 Sir David Dale, the life-long friend of Unionism, set up a Wages Board in the highly organised North of England Iron and Steel Industry. It was not long, therefore, before the Durham miners rid themselves of the reproach. In 1870 the Durham Miners' Association was founded, and it was followed immediately by the Association of Durham Mine-owners. In 1872 representatives of the Miners and Coal-owners' Associations for the first time met each other. During the trying years of falling wages (1874–77) the leaders of the Durham Union, by the exercise of almost superhuman tact, averted a serious strike. In 1877 a sliding scale was tried, but it was unpopular. "The scale", says the Secretary of the Miners' Association, "ended just when a boom in trade set in, and many men believed that it had been the incubus which had in an evil manner weighted the trade and kept wages down"[1]. The men's leaders regretted the abandonment of the scale because, for a time, it meant a return to looser methods of bargaining. A "county ballot" generally voted a strike, whether the bargaining conditions were favourable or not. The leaders, therefore, favoured a return to more organised methods. In 1895 (three years after a long and bitter strike) a Joint Wages Board was set up, similar Boards having already been set up in Northumberland and the Federated Districts of Yorkshire, Lancashire and the Midlands. The Durham Board was at first termed a Conciliation Board, but in 1899 it was reorganised with Sir David Dale as Chairman and Lord Davey as Neutral Umpire. Durham, like Northumberland and South Wales, was hard hit by the coal export tax imposed at the end of the South African War; but the Board survived the wage reductions due to this and other causes, and operated with success down to the national coal strike of 1912.

8. Work and Play

Life is not all labour. If a man is to work well, he must also play. When a Parliamentary Committee was enquiring in 1840 into the health of towns, it questioned the witnesses upon the opportunities for amusement. What amusements had Manchester? "None athletic, except when a number of the more disorderly stole off to the borders of Cheshire or Yorkshire—to have a 'mill' as they called it"[2]. How different is Lancashire to-day! The operatives have their regular holidays at the seaside. For a week they descend on Southport and Blackpool, to devour ham and eggs at a pace which fills those of a less robust digestion with envy. They play cricket and watch cricket, they

[1] John Wilson, *History of the Durham Miners Association* (1907), p. 208.
[2] *Commons' Committee, Health of Large Towns* (1840), Q. 1315.

play football and watch football; but football is the leading sport.

Liverpool—at any rate before the War—was divided into two great camps, those who followed Liverpool and those who followed Everton. The author, as a school boy, followed Everton. This was a serious occupation. It meant that you despised your brother or nearest friend if he followed Liverpool. If their goalkeeper got water on the knee, you hastened in all sympathy to communicate the disaster. If your hero, for whom your Club had paid £1000, developed measles, you suspected foul play. Then there was the great day when the two Clubs met before a crowd of 40,000 strong. The monster demonstrations of the Chartists and their simultaneous torch-light processions must have been something like this. As you looked into the sea of faces in the gloom of a December afternoon, there was not a second when a match was *not* being struck. What moments of mass excitement! The wings break away, and the hopes and fears of 40,000 men break away with them. The centre forward steadies and shoots. The ball starts low and travels over the bar, dropping on to the rails. The roar of expectancy starts low, rises as the ball rises, and drops in disappointment. The next moment the tension is broken, and the vast crowd splits up into buzzing groups, each explaining exactly how it happened and what should be done with the luckless defaulter. A football match is infinitely more exciting than slaughtering Germans or threatening your neighbours with revolution.

Thomas Cooper, the veteran ex-Chartist, wrote at the end of his life: "In our old Chartist time, it is true, the Lancashire working men were in rags by thousands; and many of them often lacked food. But their intelligence was demonstrated wherever you went. You would see them in groups discussing the great doctrine of political justice...or they were in earnest dispute respecting the teachings of Socialism. *Now*, you will see no such groups in Lancashire. But you will hear well-dressed working men talking, as they walk with their hands in their pockets, of 'Co-ops' (Co-operative Stores), and their shares in them, or in building societies....And you will see others, like idiots, leading small greyhound dogs, covered with cloth, in a string; they are about to race, and they are betting money as they go!" etc. etc.[1]

So the old generation laments the new. And yet, must life always be so hard and cruel that it has no light moments? May we never feel certain that there is life in our veins, unless somewhere the human flesh is being pricked until blood runs out? Only a few years ago the old generation was talking just in Cooper's strain. England was becoming soft and luxurious and over-civilised. Then came the War, and this soft, luxurious, over-civilised youth of the 20th century proved itself the greatest fighting nation of all time, enduring strains unimagined by soldiers of old. They made good and disproved the prophets of decay—but the price?

[1] *Life of Thomas Cooper written by himself* (1873), p. 393.

INDEX I

INDEX II

ACTS OF PARLIAMENT

PARLIAMENTARY PAPERS

CAMBRIDGE: PRINTED BY W. LEWIS, M.A., AT THE UNIVERSITY PRESS

Charles Seale-Hayne Library
University of Plymouth
(01752) 588 588
LibraryandITenquiries@plymouth.ac.uk